C000277630

A Retake Please!

A Retake Please!

Night Mail to Western Approaches

PAT JACKSON

ROYAL NAVAL MUSEUM PUBLICATIONS AND
LIVERPOOL UNIVERSITY PRESS

First published in 1999 by
Liverpool University Press
Senate House
Abercromby Square
Liverpool L69 3BX

and Royal Naval Museum Publications

Copyright © 1999 Pat Jackson

The right of Pat Jackson to be identified as the author of this work has
been asserted by him in accordance with the Copyright, Designs and
Patents Act 1988.

A catalogue record for this book is available from the British Library

ISBN 0-85323-943-6 *cased*
ISBN 0-85323-953-3 *paper*

All rights reserved. No part of this publication may be reproduced,
transmitted, or stored in a retrieval system, in any form or by any
means, without permission in writing from the publishers.

Typeset by Wilmaset Ltd, Birkenhead, Wirral
Printed in Great Britain by
Redwood Books, Trowbridge, Wiltshire

Contents

Introduction

Fay Compton, so her son told me, said to him in his early teens: 'Tony, darling, I'm too poor to educate you properly, you'll just have to go on the stage'. Anthony Pelissier did, and amongst many other endeavours made a success of everything that he undertook. But he was an enviably talented man. Sadly this is not a biography about Anthony, though one is long overdue. No, no. Here we are dealing with much smaller fry. But, the smallest salmon parr on reaching the sea is liable to have strange experiences and meet many large fish in the oceans of his travels, some of them so large that they have influenced the recent history of our times. How then did I have the chance not only of meeting some of them but filming them? How could it be that I, the ex-messenger boy of John Grierson's G.P.O. Film Unit, could nine years later be face-to-face with the Commander in Chief (C. in C.) of the Western Approaches, Admiral Sir Percy Noble, outlining to him how I proposed to make the film he had requested on the Battle of the Atlantic? And, some years later, confronting L. B. Mayer, the founder of Metro Goldwyn Mayer, with the simple challenge: 'Use me or release me. Otherwise you are wasting your money and my time'?

In retracing my steps they will not lead me to the confessional. I shall not, as the great Jean Jacques Rousseau in his vast volume of confessions, gloat over every temptation and his failures. He spares us nothing except the movement of his bowels. The confessional is for The Brompton Oratory, and greatly though I may be in need of it, I shall spare you the list of my failures and wrongdoings. I am only concerned here with the struggle to find my little niche in the world, the struggle that is the common denominator of us all. As I walk back over my pebbly path, if you will come with me, even part of the way, I shall be delighted and very flattered.

I

Faltering steps

A momentous day that of March 1933—my seventeenth birth-day—for I was to have an interview with the great John Grierson, the founder of the British documentary film. He had won his spurs with his film *Drifters*, an account of the workings of the North Sea herring fleet. Its success enabled him to form the G.P.O. Film Unit. Many a famous director and cameraman were to make their first mistakes in that unit.

Happily, as I set out for my interview, I was unaware that every graduate from Oxbridge was queuing up to join the great man's unit. Ignorance was bliss for I had not even passed Common Entrance, let alone School Cert or London Matric. In academic terms I had nothing to offer. I could read and write and speak the King's English—hardly an advantage today—and that was about the extent of my marketable assets.

My only experience of the film industry had been a two-week stint as a loading boy for a Bell and Howell camera. A quota quickie was being made at Welwyn, starring Wally and Barry Lupino, and I owed this peep into film making to a dear friend, Henry Blyth. He had got his job by writing an angry letter to the Wolfe brothers, telling them how short-sighted they were not to answer letters from people with ideas and enthusiasm, anxious to join the industry. They were so impressed by his letter and by him, when they deigned to give him an interview, that they gave him a job there and then. They got a bargain for Henry was a brilliant man and a graduate of Wadham. He was good enough to recommend me when an assistant cameraman was suddenly needed. The Wolfe brothers may have thought that a similar bargain was on the way.

They didn't have time to find out as the job only lasted two weeks. The series came to an abrupt end.

Nevertheless, I managed to expose the first 1000-foot roll that I was to load for Jack Parker, the lighting cameraman (I had forgotten to remove the key of the magazine which kept open the light-proof slits which allowed the film to pass into the camera and back into the take-up half of the magazine). Not to remove the key before switching on the light of the dark room was the loading boy's worst crime, and I had committed it.

Almost in tears, I walked on to the floor and confessed my crime to Jack Parker, expecting to be sacked, instantly. He smiled, sent me back to the dark room and told me to do better this time. Such kindness at the age of sixteen is never forgotten. During those two weeks we rarely left the studio before nine at night, a thirteen-hour day, no overtime and a half-crown allowance for a taxi. I had earned four pounds.

*

I was not in the most confident frame of mind when I left home— Newlands, North Park, Eltham, SE9—and headed for the trams which would take me to New Eltham Station, up to Charing Cross and then a panicky walk to 39 Oxford Street, the H.Q. of the G.P.O. Film Unit. I decided not to mention my two weeks' career as a loading boy to Mr Grierson. No, better keep quiet about them.

I could hear the trams wailing in sympathy with my mood as their wheels bit and ground into the rails, rounding the sharp bend by the parish church, on their way to Greenwich. I paid my penny fare and walked up to the station for the train which would flip me past those seven stations, and I wished that they girdled the earth for a never ending journey instead of a measly half hour or so.

I was well aware, also, not only of my lacklustre credentials but that I was not part of the 'Old Boys' Network'. Its value must not be underestimated, even though often derided. As Evelyn Waugh so pithily remarked: 'It's perfectly all right to sneer at public schools so long as you make sure that you have been to one.'

For reasons beyond anyone's control, my formal education was almost non-existent, though it was planned to start in the conventional middle-class fashion, a south coast 'prep' school. Mine was to be Chesterton, Seaford, Sussex.

Two weeks before my first summer term, my favourite brother Kit, a year older and with whom I looked forward to sharing our school days, died within a week of becoming ill. When I was deposited at Chesterton I was still traumatised and my academic career started on the wrong foot. On my first night I was sick in the dormitory. It was a large dormitory. To wake up and be confronted by 13 scowling faces was not an encouraging start. There was worse to come: I sensed it on this Sunday morning of 4 May 1926.

We new boys, clutching our prayer books, were herded into a classroom, shown our desks and left to wonder what the fates held in store. We didn't have long to wait. The door burst open. A gowned master, sharp nosed as a ferret, strode towards the dais and large desk below the blackboard. He opened the lid of the desk and produced a prayer book and then confronted us and with a steely voice greeted us: 'Good morning boys. I presume that you all have your prayer books.'

'Yes, Sir.'

'Very good. You may or may not know that this is Rogation Sunday and you will please turn to page 286.' Fumbling fingers rustled through the thin rice paper pages as if thousands of newly printed bank notes were being counted. 'Have you all found it?'

'Yes, Sir.'

'The column on the right hand side of the page is the collect for today. You all see it?'

'Yes, Sir.'

'Very good. You will learn it and when you have, put up your hand. You will then recite it and you will not leave here until you have. Is that clear?'

'Yes, Sir.'

'Very well. You may start.' I looked at the collect, or rather it confronted me. I had never heard of a collect, far less read one. I not only failed to understand it but, far worse, knew immediately that I would never be able to learn it.

We were not a very churchy family. My parents were not atheists, far from it. They just could not take the bleating of our vicar and often Father said he felt more depressed and wicked when he came out than when he went in. Neither had either of them, it seemed, approved when they heard that certain bishops had blessed the cannons before the awful Battle of the Somme. They felt that this was 'off side' and expecting too much of God, who, they were asked to believe, had sent his son to preach love and brotherhood. In short, they were not too keen about the established church. Right or wrong their moral dilemma was of no help to me in my present one as I tried to get the first line to stick, but it simply would not and I had been several minutes at it already. And then a hand went up in front of me.

'Yes, Roberts?'

'Ready, Sir.'

'Very good.' Whereupon he stood up, that bright little beast, and recited it without halt or fault.

'Very good Roberts, you may go.'

'Thank you, Sir.' I can see him now with that smug smile as he turned to go, looking at us, knowing that we were left to fry. He was, so I was to learn, the son of General Roberts, not that that would have helped to endear him. And then another hand went up, and another. Still that first line had not stuck. We were not a very poetry-minded family either, given to learning things by heart. 'Hickory, dickory, dock', 'Jack and Jill' and 'Three Blind Mice' were more in our line. This, this thing was a different kettle of fish. This was sheer hell, or a message from it. I could see myself stuck here till kingdom come! Hands were popping up all over the place: almost queuing up they were to recite the wretched thing. As I feared, I was the last, alone with whoever he was. He looked down at me. 'Well, Jackson?'

'Not ready, yet, I'm afraid, Sir.'

'Dear me. I'll be back in half an hour. You ought to be ready by then.' I doubted it but I didn't tell him as he left. Panic was setting in fast, now. I looked out of the window, open at the top, and I could smell the sweet honey of new-mown grass. The birds were

4

singing away, happy as could be. How I envied them. I was like one of their unfortunates, trapped in a cage. What was I to do? I started to blub, buckets, and that didn't help because now I couldn't even read the thing through my tears and I hadn't got a hankie. My brother, Kit, never told me it would be like this. I'm not surprised. I wondered how quickly his hand had gone up. Quickly, I felt sure, because he had had brains and I obviously hadn't. I was the slowest boy in the class as the last minutes had just proved. What was to become of me?

'Are you ready yet, Jackson?'

'Not yet, Sir, I'm afraid.'

'Will you ever be?'

'I don't think so, Sir.'

'Dear me. You'd better go, but I'll have to give you a bad conduct mark and you don't want too many of them.'

'Yes, Sir, I mean, no Sir, and thank you Sir.'

I left with little dignity and have never been able to rely on my memory as a trusted friend since that Rogation Sunday, except for 'Oh that this too, too solid flesh would melt, thaw and resolve itself into a dew'. I have that soliloquy off pat because my Mother drilled most of Hamlet's outpourings into me, remembering Sir Johnstone Forbes Robertson's every intonation. She'd heard them often enough and they'd have given Gielgud a run for his money.

I was saved from holding the record number of bad conduct marks for a first termer by being whisked off to Switzerland, again. Two years previously we had all gone to Davos, it being discovered that my Father was suffering from T.B. So the whole tribe, Michael my older brother by seven years, Jocelyn my sister, three years older, and Christopher, a year older, and our very special Mildred Brown from Rotherfield, our Nan. Six months of bliss is what we had in a lovely villa in Davos Platz. Dad returned, apparently cured. But, two years later it was considered essential that he should escape the wintry London fogs. So, off we went again.

If I'd been a clever little stinker like that Roberts boy, clever, prim and proper, I would have said to my parents: 'I don't think I should come with you to Switzerland; I think I should stay here and get on with my studies, otherwise, you see, I shall fall so far behind that it will be very difficult for me to catch up, if I ever do'. Perhaps my parents should have said that. I certainly didn't. I jumped for joy. Come to think of it, perhaps Roberts might have, also. He was probably quite normal. The thought of Telemarks in powdery snow. Bliss.

Six months later, though, on my return to Chesterton, it was anything but bliss. The problem posed in my imaginary goody-goody reasoning for staying at school rather than romping in the Alps now became a hideous reality, and though my Telemarks and open Christies, for a ten-year-old, were well above average, that prowess wasn't much help in the classroom. They were certainly not the foundation upon which to prepare for a scholarship or even the basic requirement—Common Entrance.

Sooner or later, then, a public school of some sort had to be found. The classy jobs with that potentially valuable if not essential old boy network were by now both financially and academically a light year beyond our reach. Where then to send me? One of the 'Stately Homes of England' came to the rescue. No, no, not Stowe, by then too classy. Bryanston was the answer. In 1930 their drag net was well and truly out, trawling everywhere for whatever it could catch. Consequently I was considered acceptable and my brother Michael, 'in loco parentis', drove me down and deposited me there with the parting words: 'Have fun old boy'.

I did have fun. I was beginning to enjoy myself enormously in that summer term of 1930. I was proud to have become a tender-foot in the Cuckoo patrol and I'd always wanted to wear that hat and punch those three juicy bruises in it. The Cuckoo patrol taught me four invaluable knots which have been of the greatest possible use to me: the bowline which my patrol leader told me would be a great help hauling me out of a crevasse when I fell into one; the sheep-shank for shortening a piece of string without cutting it; the clove hitch so that your shoe-laces won't come undone; and the running half-hitch for mooring your yacht when you're trying to win the Americas Cup. All essential information for everyday living. I became and still am a bonny bonfire maker for the camp stew and can guarantee to get a fire going under any conditions. I earned my bonfire badge all right.

These memories had brought me to the first stop on my journey to John Grierson: Kidbrooke Park, then Blackheath, New Cross, London Bridge, Waterloo and then Charing Cross. Dear me, I'd be there in a flash . . . Mustn't panic. I escaped to Bryanston and the River Stour winding through the playing fields and below the endless driveway whose steep bank down to the river was thick with beeches and limes. Under the shade of their overhanging branches, birch bark canoes were idly paddled with the ease of the Cherokee and Sioux. I longed to be part of that glamorous regatta.

To qualify it was necessary to swim the widest part of the Stour, opposite the boat house. We had to be fully dressed: shorts, shirt, full-length and sleeved cricket sweater, socks and gym shoes. Whether my dog paddle would be up to it only time would tell. It was half way across that the buoyancy test was severely threatened. The soaked and cloying sweater was no help and in desperate need of a schnorkel I just managed to clamber up the opposite bank. The birch bark canoes were in my sights.

For leaving a vest on the changing room floor I received four of the very best from my house prefect. He reminded me of a warthog, this sixteen-year-old, and I resented him not because he looked like a warthog particularly but because I thought that the punishment he had the right to mete out excessive for so petty a crime. A week or so later he gave me another six of an even better best for blowing a downy feather across the dining table, in hall. My rainbow stripes from the previous lot had hardly lost their technicolour hues before these six were superimposed.

Let no one pretend that these playful wiggings from the prefects were anything but very painful. They hurt like Hades and it was with considerable difficulty that I refrained from squealing like a harpooned pig. I was now at Lewisham. New Cross next stop.

My House Master was Harold Greenleaves and I remember him with affection, and he was the House Master of Chopin. How odd that sounds but, at that time, all the houses in Bryanston were named after famous composers. My musical knowledge was unworthy of so

7

august a name. Our ignorance of music was not due to our parents denying us the chance of becoming infant prodigies; far from it, for Mother had a beautiful baby grand Broadwood of 1905 vintage. Nothing wrong with that, but perhaps the unlucky choice of piano teacher, a Miss Peppercorn who came twice a week. When, after a year of these visits, Dad returned from the City to hear my sister make the same mistake at the same bar of the same piece that she had been attacking for a year, it was the end of Miss Peppercorn and a non-starter for me. Just as well, perhaps, for she might well have slammed the door on that subject for ever more. Happily, I first became aware of the joys of music listening to the Broadwood being brilliantly played by some of our lodgers. Our home had now been turned into a boarding house. Dad's death and the cost of his long illness had left the family almost broke, and the 1929 crash completed the job of emptying the family coffers. Very soon I found myself growing up in a league of nations of foreign students, many very musical. I remember a young French girl. She must have been all of fourteen and her musical talents were phenomenal. She romped through Chopin's Etudes as easily as Chopsticks. She was already a beauty, with raven black hair flowing down her back and her sexual curiosity was as advanced as her use of the keyboard. My virginity was severely threatened, but, of course, in those far off days barbed wire had that taboo subject severely fenced off.

The train pulled into New Cross. Only three more stations.

Bryanston was experimenting with the Dalton system of education. So far as I recall the theory was that it would encourage self-discipline, and to create this desirable condition a master class in each subject was held every week and assignments of work were issued for the coming week—these to be completed as and when you liked, but completed they must be. Whether the system worked I have no means of knowing. I was not there long enough to discover. No, I was not expelled, but in the last week of that glorious summer term the school was attacked by a vicious virus. I was the last to succumb and the ensuing quinsy made even the swallowing of ice as agonising as another turn of the rack in the Tower's torture chamber.

The train was at London Bridge.

My one term at Bryanston ended my school days. The poison engendered by that quinsy created complications and I was an invalid for over two years. Churchill described the worst years of his early life as the 'Black Dog'. A period of despair and bitter misery. I could see no way out of the dilemma in which I found myself. I had no education and was trained for nothing, and even worse felt good for nothing. 'Black Dog' kept growling at my heels but, by the oddest of coincidences, help was on its way.

Sir Kingsley Wood was not only our local M.P., he was also Post Master General in Baldwin's Government. He had also, as luck would have it, been a great admirer of my Grandmother, on Dad's side. She had been a Gulland and the belle of Fife. Kingsley Wood, being the P.M.G., was automatically head of the G.P.O. Film Unit and therefore John Grierson's boss. My enterprising Mother wasted no time in writing to her M.P., not for an instant hesitating to mention that she was the daughter-in-law of his old flame Miss Gulland. Though I was not to be a part of the old boys' network, suddenly, the old girls' network appeared which had set me on my way to meet the Daddy of Documentary, jumping the queue thanks to the one and only contact that we could muster.

My train pulled into Charing Cross—journey's end. I was not brimful of confidence as I crossed over to St Martin's in the Field. I stood for a moment and watched a famous London character at work. The portrait painter who was known as REM. Not for nothing had he taken the initial R.E.M. for he fancied that he painted in the same manner as the great master. In fairness it has to be admitted his likenesses were magical. He was one of the sights of London, attaching his canvasses to the railings surrounding the yard of St Martin's. He was at work on a copy of Franz Hal's 'The Laughing Cavalier'. I looked over his shoulder, as he sat on his canvas stool, charging his brush with a dab of white from his palette, the edges of which were engrained with London's grime, encroaching on the colours. A highlight was dabbed on to the Cavalier's nose. His smile shone from the canvas, as confident as

9

ever. I envied that smile and the skill of REM which was evident in spite of the poor man's reduced circumstances.

Still a quarter of an hour before my appointment. Up the Charing Cross Road, window shopping and held by a collection of Boudin's schooners in Le Havre, displayed in Zwemmer's window. They cost £400 to £500 a canvas—an unimaginable sum of money for a picture. How many would Zwemmer sell in a week, I wondered, in these distressed times. The Dominion Cinema, turn left into Oxford Street and 39 can't be far away on the south side. Yes, there it was with a newly painted sign in gold lettering on a shining mahogany board—G.P.O. Film Unit. A lift to the third floor, through the swing doors and a friendly young girl looked up and asked if she could help. 'I have an appointment to see Mr Grierson.'

He didn't keep me waiting long. He was a small dynamo of a man—one sensed that immediately. His eyes were violet and piercing but not in an unfriendly way. The knot in his tie was huge, yellow and of a homespun sort of material. He gestured for me to take a seat. 'Jackson, I have a letter from the P.M.G. asking me whether I could give you a job. I don't know what he had in mind. Do you?'

'No Sir.'

'Have you any qualifications? Higher Certificate? London Matriculation?

'None at all, Sir, I'm afraid. Not even Common Entrance.'

'Where were you at school?'

'Bryanston.'

'Ah, the Dalton System. How did you find it?'

'I wasn't there long enough to find out, I'm afraid, Sir.'

'Why? Were you expelled?'

'No Sir. I caught a virus in my first term. It laid me low and I was never able to go back.'

'Are you all right now?'

'Yes, thank you, Sir. Fit as a fiddle.'

'What have you read, Jackson?'

'I've just finished a book by General Groves on the use of anti-aircraft artillery.'

'Why on earth did you want to read that? I meant literature.'

'Oh . . . Oh yes, of course. Well . . . *Oliver Twist*, that sort of thing.'

This grilling went on for a minute or two longer when it became obvious to Mr Grierson that he was dealing with a chick, prematurely hatched. Mercifully, he put me out of my misery. 'Jackson, I'm inclined to carry out the P.M.G.'s request. You can be our messenger boy at 17/6 a week. You can start now, or would you like to think about it?'

'I'll start now, Sir, and thank you very much.'

'Good lad. Come with me.' He took me up a flight of stairs, through swing glass panelled doors and into a bare store room with three doors in the opposite wall. A burly, smiling hunk of a man was there. 'Ah, Watt, this is Jackson, our new messenger boy. Show him the ropes will you.'

2

Dog's body

I was face-to-face with Harry Watt, later to make his name with *Target for Tonight* and *Overlanders*.

'Hullo Jackson, I'm Harry.'

'How do you do, Sir.'

'We drop all that, here. Just call me Harry. What's yours?'

'Pat, Sir—I mean, Harry.'

'Very democratic, the film bizz, very informal, though we do refer to Mr Grierson as the Chief. Tomorrow, get out of your suit, because you'll be expected to do all sorts of odd jobs apart from running messages: flannel bags and an old hacking jacket's the ticket.'

Then, out of the centre door on the right, appeared a composed looking youth, about my age. He was blinking. 'Chick, this is Pat, our new messenger boy.'

'Hullo Pat, I'll see you properly in a tick; when you've been in the dark room . . . it takes a second or two to focus, properly.' Chick Fowle was to become a great cameraman, who was to shoot many of Humphrey Jennings's films: *Spare Time*, *Listen to Britain*, and many others. He showed me the enlargements he had been doing. Beautiful prints of Ceylon, as it was in those days. Wonderful studies of Buddhist temples and close-ups of Sinhalese dancers in their fantastic head-dress and ceremonial garb. Basil Wright, he told me, had just returned with thousands of feet of film which was to become the famous *Song of Ceylon*.

Chick kindly asked me to join him for lunch. It cost us sixpence, a ham roll and cup of tea in a small cafe in Rathbone Street which was almost directly opposite 39 Oxford Street—most convenient. Chick had been with the unit about six months and was a true

Londoner. He too had started as 'the messenger boy' and was thoughtful enough to be encouraging about that lowly station. 'You'll soon be doing a bit of everything, apart from running messages', he said.

'Such as?'

'Enlargements, running the "dailies".'

'Running the dailies. What on earth are they?'

'The rushes—not the Moses kind—are the prints of the previous day's filming which have been developed overnight at the labs.'

'How am I supposed to run with them?'

'Run, project them in the little theatre, little cinema on the fourth floor.'

'A projectionist, you mean, as in our local cinema?'

'That's it.'

'But that's a highly skilled job.'

'Nothing to it. You learn how to thread the film on the projector in no time, light the arc and off you go.'

'You make it sound simple enough.'

'Everything is—take it bit by bit, and then there's the enlargements, you'll soon be on to them. Loading, in the loading bag for the Newman Sinclair.'

There seemed no end to the simple little odd jobs that a 'messenger boy' might be expected to do. We paid for our lunches and sauntered down Rathbone Street towards 39 Oxford Street. 'You going to be a cameraman or what?', Chick asked.

'I dunno, Chick; early days. At the moment I'd like to make sure that I can keep afloat.' He smiled and it was a slow gathering smile, with depth to it.

'You'll catch on.'

'What do you want to be?'

'Oh, a cameraman. Magic carpet; take me everywhere. Just imagine John Taylor; he's only a year or so older than us and he was with Robert Flaherty on *Man of Aran*, developed all his rushes, on a portable lab, and now three months with Basil Wright shooting this Ceylon film. Bloody marvellous. Mostly on a Newman Sinclair, too.'

We crossed Oxford Street and soon were back on the fifth floor of 39. Chick showed me some of the 'blow-ups' he'd been doing from John Taylor's stills of Ceylon. And then the 'vaults'. I would be expected to look after the vaults. In other words, librarian, for the 'vaults' was a cavernous room with racks either side, filled with 1000-foot cans of film. 'This lot, here, is Basil Wright's Ceylon stuff, about 30 000 feet. He'll start doing a rough cut soon, so you'll need to know what's in each can. You can forget about this row, that's the Chief's boob. P.L.A. . . . Proper cock-up.'

'You mean Mr Grierson?'

'Yes, the Chief, we call him.'

'And he made a cock-up?'

'And how.' And then a voice called from the floor below. 'JACKSON!!' I hurried to the swing doors and called down: 'Here I am'. A girl's voice answered: 'Rushes for Humphries, right away'. The ever helpful Chick sauntered out of the vaults and explained. 'Humphries are the labs and they'll develop a new batch of Jonah Jones's stuff, just back from the Scillies with Donald Taylor.'

'Where is Humphries?', I interrupted.

'Pass the cafe where we had lunch, keep going into Charlotte Street and fourth left is Chitty Street. Almost opposite is a bloody awful building. Can't miss it. Take the rushes to the top floor.'

'O.K., thanks.' I rushed downstairs on my first mission. The nice receptionist girl gave me three small 200-foot cans with a delivery slip which I must get signed from Humphries' despatch department, and off I went, with winged feet. When I returned I was immediately sent off to D'Arblay Street, off Wardour Street, to take a letter to a Mr Auton, our accountant. Wardour Street, the epicentre of the film world, couldn't have been less impressive—tatty and run down, hardly representative of this glamorous world of cinema which I had just joined.

Entering 39 Oxford Street for the fourth time, I took the lift to the fifth floor, through the swing doors, into this deserted room with its three doors for vaults and dark room. I wondered what to do next. I couldn't just stand there. Perhaps I should sweep the floor; at least it would show that I was keen, but I could find no broom or dustpan. There was not even a chair to sit on. I wandered over to the window and looked down at the traffic below. Too much of this hanging about could be deadly. Perhaps I'd been too hasty in accepting the first job that came along. My increasing anxiety was, happily, of short duration, for Harry came to my rescue, bursting through the swing doors. 'Jackson, you might as well learn to join. Come on, I'll show you.'

He took me to a cutting room on the top floor and sat me down at a bench. I was between two metal discs which revolved. The one on the left held a roll of film about half the width of the one I'd exposed at Welwyn, and it was full of paper clips, like a girl's hair in curlers. It seemed to be solid with paper clips.

'This is a rough cut, a few hundred feet of a film I'm making— bloody boring too.'

'Are you sure, Mr Watt?', I replied, trying to be at my most tactful.

'Perfectly, it's on the Mount Pleasant Sorting Office: nothing but mail bags being loaded and mail vans rushing about. Give me good old cowboys and Indians, any day. Now all you have to do is this.'

I watched as Harry scraped away a narrow strip of the film's emulsion, painted it with acetone which smelt of sweet shops and pear drops, and fitted it on to the shiny side of its neighbour, attached by a paper clip fixed to a sheet of blotting paper.

'There is a joining machine but Donald Taylor's pinched it in the downstairs cutting room.'

'What film's he making, Mr Watt?'

'Do try and drop the Mister; Harry is quite good enough. He's making a film on the Scilly Isles, nothing but daffodils being crated.'

'What have they to do with the Post Office?'

'Not much except that the orders from Covent Garden are made by telephone.' He had once more shown me how to make a join and then told me to take over. I took his place and he sat on the chair beside me. I scraped the narrow strip of emulsion with a safety razor blade, painted it with pear drop solution, turned it over and married it to the shiny side of its partner, hoping that they would never part. I made sure that the gaps between the sprocket holes were identical. If not my join would jump the sprockets of the projector, as Harry explained, like an express train jumping the points and resulting in a horrid pile up. He inspected my first join and I felt that my whole future depended on his passing it. He ran his finger along the rim of join to make sure that there was no barb and that sprocket separation perfectly matched. 'That's O.K. You've got it. Carry on.'

He settled down in the chair alongside and started on another small roll, equally loaded with paper clips. My first join: passed. I was thrilled. I felt that I was learning a craft, apprenticed as though to a great master, like Raphael, and that I would follow in his footsteps. I was so grateful, already, to this helpful, friendly man. He must have been about Mike's age, seven or eight years older than me. He had a wonderful smile and seemed everyone's friend. He asked me how I'd got this introduction to Grierson because I was very lucky. Everyone was trying to join his unit. I told him.

'Ah, nepotism, eh?', he said, with a broad grin. Sadly, the word was new to me. I didn't try to cover my ignorance and naively asked: 'What's that?'

'Nepotism? Unfair use of influence through social or close re-lations.'

'Oh my God, how awful.'

'I shouldn't worry. It's not as though you've landed the top job, is it? I only got here because I'd worked with Robert Flaherty on *Man of Aran*.' He started to explain that most of the unit consisted of people of high academic honours, for it was Grierson's belief that only the highly trained mind would be capable of handling this tricky medium of such potentially communicative power. The academic training was essential to analyse a subject, get at the essential facts, organise them into some sort of narrative form and know how to illustrate those facts by the proper use of the camera. Only a well trained mind would be capable of coming to grips with so demanding a medium, and not only a well trained mind but a

well read, well informed mind. This dissertation of what was ex-
pected of anyone working for this elite outfit went on and on.
Stuart Legg who was making a film on a cable ship—a double first.
Basil Wright who had just come back from Ceylon—a double first.
Humphrey Jennings—a double first. Arthur Elton who was making
Aero Engine—a double first; and then there was little me ... not a
snowball's chance in hell! In desperation I asked: 'Are you a double
first, Mr Watt? ... Harry?'

'ME? Not bloody likely. I only got a sort of pass degree at
Edinburgh—nothing like good enough for Grierson, but he gave
me a chance, I think, not only because of Flaherty but because I'd
knocked around a bit. I'd sailed the Atlantic in a windjammer and,
after having made that herring fleet epic, *Drifters*, Grierson respects
anyone who takes on the sea. No fear, I'm no academic, no intellectual. You'll meet plenty here, before you're much older.'

Half an hour older and my first small reel of joins was done. I
waited a few moments until Harry had finished his larger roll. He
rewound it and joined the front of his on to the end of mine. He
called out to Chick who appeared from the dark room. 'Chick,
run this for me, will you, and you might as well show Pat how to
lace up the projector.' We went down two floors, along a corridor and I found myself in a pokey room which housed two
projectors, standing on a concrete dais. Chick decided to use the
right-hand machine, opened the loading spool and quickly threa-
ded the film through the gate and over various sprocketed rollers
and finally into the take-up magazine. He struck up the arc, poked
his head round the swing door of the small theatre and asked:
'Ready Harry?'

'Fire away.'

Chick started up the machine, as he opened the shutter, and a
beam shot through the small optic panel and on to the screen of the
small theatre. 'Want to look?', he asked, nodding for me to look
through the panel beside the other projector. I climbed up and
peered through. This was my first glimpse of a rough cut, of a film
coming into being. Harry was right. It was boring. It was to be
Harry's first film for the G.P.O. Film Unit *6.30 Collection*. Soon the

film ran through the machine, perhaps four or five minutes of it, and the swing door opened and Harry's tousled head appeared. 'As I said, bloody boring. How do you pump life into a mail bag?'

Chick had by now whipped out the reel from the take-up magazine and was rewinding it. This took a few moments and with a deft reverse movement he had the reel off the plate and was handing it over to Harry, who seemed none too pleased to take possession of it. We went back up to the top floor. Chick disappeared into the dark room. Harry went back into his cutting room and I was left stranded in that bleak upstairs room.

I looked out of the window and down at the passing traffic, the hordes of people all seeming to know where they were going and what they were about. I envied them. I couldn't see at all where I was going: how I could possibly fit into this august assembly of brilliant brains. I felt at a very low ebb, very demoralised.

The dark room door opened and Chick appeared. 'Want to see a bit of Ceylon?'

'Love to.'

'Lovely line in Buddhas coming up.'

He closed the door behind me, put on the red light, a negative under the enlarger, a large sheet of print paper into the holder below the enlarger (the paper, I was told, was not sensitive to red light), and then he switched on the enlarger. A negative Buddha was projected down on to the positive print paper. 'He's an awkward bugger this one. I've had three goes at him, already. This dark part of him needs a lot of cooking to get the detail, but that overcooks these lighter bits. So I've got to hold them back by fanning over them, trying to get a balance. Hit or miss really.' He was using both hands to fan over the lighter areas, like a conjuror about to produce a rabbit, and in a way he was a conjuror. A loud alarm clock was ticking away, and now it rang. He switched off the light, and put the sheet into a bath and peered down, expectantly. 'Maybe somewhere near this time.' Slowly, Buddha appeared. It was a magnificent picture of this sitting Buddha, carved out of the cliff face and sitting there so serene and calm as if to say: 'Take it easy, now. Things will work out.'

'That's about it. He's cooked.' He took the print out of the developer, washed it under a running tap and dropped it into a fixative of Hypo. After a moment or two he turned on the incandescent light and looked at it with a critical and already very professional eye. 'Yes, that'll do. Try this one.'

He put another slide into the enlarger. It was of one of the faithful who had brought his offerings of fruit and placed it on the dish below the enormous statue's hand. Chick looked at the negative image, studied the light variation and adjusted his alarm clock accordingly. 'Not too contrasted, this. Not much fanning.'

He switched on the enlarger and then Harry called: 'Jackson?'

'Don't open the door, you'll bugger my print.'

'I'm in here, Mr Watt, and I can't open the door because Chick's developing. So sorry.'

'O.K. Now when you've collected the rushes from Humphries, first thing, I'd like you to join my reel. I've left it on the rewinder.'

'Yes, of course, Mr Watt.'

'Oh and don't forget, flannel bags and an old jacket. I'm off.' I heard him stamp out of the place.

'What time do I collect the rushes, Chick?'

'Oh, 8.30ish.'

He had now put the print into the developer. A wonderfully sculptured face appeared, his hands held in front of him, folded like Durer's famous study, and his eyes closed as he fervently prayed to his Buddha. A stirring image.

'Not bad.' It was perfect and I realised that Chick was not one to waste words. He washed it and fixed it. My first day was coming to an end. Chick pushed the button and a small lift appeared and took us down and I was out amongst the milling crowd whom I had so envied half an hour ago, but now, I was beginning to feel something almost akin to hope. I had met two wonderful guys and they had already taught me something. My first day was over. I was on my way. Certainly I was the lowest form of animal life in the film industry, but starting at the bottom has its compensations: there is only one way to go and I would earn 17/6 a week, a tanner more than my age.

*

Though I find it hard, these days, to remember what I was doing last week, I can recall, vividly, what I was doing over sixty years ago in my early days at the G.P.O. Film Unit. During my first year I did not cover myself with glory. When asked to project Arthur Elton's new show copy of *Aero Engine*, I set it on fire in the projector. I was not given the sack. When asked to work the switchboard I promptly cut off everyone, including Grierson, who snorted out of his office: 'Jackson, you've cut me off.'

'I'm so sorry, Sir.' I'd said something like that after burning *Aero Engine*.

'Get me reconnected at once.'

'I wish I could, Sir, but I don't know how.'

'What are you doing on it?'

'The telephonist suddenly felt ill, left in a hurry and asked me to take over. The only trouble is that I don't know how to work it, not just like that, on the spur of the moment.' Grierson looked at it and was clearly as puzzled as I, and retreating into his office said: 'Find someone who can, and quick about it.'

Though it was a tradition of the place that everyone pitched in, it does not follow that you know how to work a switchboard in an emergency. It was now buzzing alarmingly and I looked at those grey switches and had no idea which one to touch. On top, in the middle of the thing, was an awful hooded orifice which winked at you after a successful connection. It certainly wasn't going to wink at me. I was looking at a time bomb with the fuse about to burn out. Then, in walked Chick Fowle, nonchalantly smoking a cigarette. He took a disdainful look at the buzzing monstrosity, flicked up and flicked down one or two of the switches, got a couple of winks for his efforts and peace was restored. Though I disconnected the Chief, I was not given the sack, so I would like to dedicate these memoirs to all those wonderful people in that remarkable unit who helped a very raw egg become a little more hard boiled.

I'd had the good fortune to have joined a unique fraternity in which all contributed their enthusiasm and endless hours of work with no suggestion of overtime—the very idea! We were learning and seeing something new developing. We didn't realise it but we were the first students of the first film school in Britain, thanks, probably, to the great Robert Flaherty whose magical *Nanook of the North* inspired Grierson to make his *Drifters*. Cashing in on its success and aided by his dynamic personality, he persuaded Sir Stephen Tallents to transfer the funds allocated to the dying Empire Marketing Board and form the G.P.O. Film Unit—a masterly stroke of public relations.

At the end of 1933 we moved into larger premises, 21 Soho Square and a small studio in Blackheath at the end of Bennett Park Road, conveniently just opposite the station. We also acquired a very important new toy, Visatone Sound System, housed in a large Post Office van. We put it to use immediately by adding a sound track to a two reeler, a twenty-minute short *Granton Trawler* shot and edited by Edgar Anstey. The crew were rugged Scots, and Harry Watt, the only Scot in the unit, apart from Grierson, was assigned to supervise the recording of natural sounds to illustrate the activities of trawler and crew. So it was that I found myself sitting on the floor of the small stage of the studio. I was flipping and flapping bits of linoleum and told by Harry to flap like hell when the fish were to be emptied from the trawl on to the deck. Harry retired into the sound van and the section of the film was ready for projection. We watched the screen and made ready for our flapping, Chick Fowle, Jonah Jones, Freddie Gamage, our three trainee cameramen and a new chap, Martin, trainee sound. Five skilful flappers, at the ready. In came the trawl, up over the stern, and spewed its catch over the deck. Never was there such a use of linoleum employed so effectively, as we thought. Harry came from the sound van: 'Not bad, but much louder at the start. Try it again.'

Martin suggested that it might help if we had bigger bits of linoleum as ours were all similar in size. Harry thought that this made sense, so we went to work hacking off larger bits from an old sheet of lino that had covered the studio floor. Armed with more powerful flippers, we wetted them hoping for a more convincing flap—we were not documentary film makers for nothing. Up came the trawl and we gave it the works and waited for the verdict. Harry returned, all smiles. 'Very good, that'll do. Now for the next section.'

This required mumbling, grunting, and the odd Scot semi-expletives as a long line was winched aboard which had cod, hake, skate and heaven knows what, but as the only Scot was Harry and he'd be in the sound van, sitting in judgement, we were aware of our limitations. We had a run at it and as a huge hake was hauled over the side a voice was heard to say: 'Oh, well caught, sir'. Harry came back and smilingly suggested to me that I was not on a cricket field but a tough Granton trawler. My 'voice-over' career clearly had no future. I apologised for my excess of zeal and promised that I would not get carried away on the next rehearsal. This time I contented myself with a shuffling of feet and a guttural boozy cough which I was rather proud of but which went unnoticed. We got the track done, though it took us into the early hours. We slept on the studio floor and the film was ready for its trade show, due in a couple of days. We hoped that sooner or later one of our films would be shown 'theatrically' in a cinema before a paying audience, and then we would have broken into the 'big time'. For the most part, all we could hope for was the non-theatrical circuit, showings in village halls and Women's Institute meetings. All very educational, very earnest and unexciting. Harry Watt had other ideas. Our films must be good enough, entertaining enough to be shown on the major circuits of the land. He was soon to be given his chance. *Night Mail* was to launch his career and set the documentary movement on a new and exciting path. It was also to cut the movement into two rival camps. The old established commentary expositional and the new story documentary. The use of drama, dialogue and the search for the non-professional actor, representative of his or her region of the country: the backbone of the country and its true representative. A fascinating and exciting approach to film making was about to be explored, and *Night Mail* was its prototype.

3

Night Mail

Its working title was *The Travelling Post Office* and Basil Wright was assigned to write a script on the subject. I read some of his early notes. I recall vividly his suggestions for the now famous Beattock sequence, immortalised by Auden's verse:

> This is the Night Mail
> crossing the border
> bringing the cheque and postal order.
> Pulling up Beattock a steady climb
> the gradient's against her but she's on time.

Basil's equivalent, scribbled in one of those large Post Office note-books, read roughly as follows:

Over close shots of the locomotive's funnel belching smoke as it struggles up the Beattock gradient, the puffs get slower and greyer and maybe we could lay over a voice saying; 'I think I can, I think I can'.

Whether he ever finished that script I don't know. Certainly I never saw it. Neither, I suspect, did Harry Watt and I was with him on every shot in the making of *Night Mail*. However, during the birth pangs of this recognised classic, when the search was on for an idea, a conception of how to tackle the subject, John Grierson came down to the pub at the end of Bennett Park Road where seniors and juniors would gather to discuss the day's work and generally put the world to right. We juniors would make our half pints last as long as possible, listening to the great minds at work, and there *were* some great minds at work: Humphrey Jennings not the least of them. Grierson had been talking about documentary and possible lines of approach to tackle this 'Travelling Post Office' subject, our most ambitious and complex one to date.

He summed up and I can almost quote him verbatim, even though I heard his words over 60 years ago.

Can we imagine a society without letters? Of course we can't. But does anyone appreciate the postman? Of course not. We take him for granted like the milkman, the engine driver, coal miner, the lot of them. We take them all for granted, yet we are all dependent on them, just as we are all interdependent one to another. It has nothing to do with class or education. The simple fact is that we are all in each other's debt. We must acknowledge it and pay it with respect and gratitude one to another. This is what we must get over. This is what documentary is all about.

The compelling simplicity of such thinking was at the heart of Grierson's mission. To inform: to open eyes to new perspectives, new ways of thinking about social problems. He was an extension of the Andrew Carnegie tradition and he applied it to the use of cinema. A well informed people was the first essential of a sound democracy. If the commercial circuits were not interested in his product, very well, he would do without them and find other means of dissemination. He wasn't fussy how, so long as what he thought to be important information reached the people. He organised an army of portable projectors and technicians to tour the village halls and any public meeting prepared to come and sample a free film show.

He could not, of course, foresee that with the advent of television and the over-exposure of the world's problems and horrors, we would become punch drunk and insensitive to information, wearied beyond redemption by problems so immense that we feel powerless to help, demoralised and sickened by the horrors that we inflict on each other and our one and only globe, kicked around like a hooligan's football.

Harry Watt, though agreeing with Grierson's aims, thought that there might be quicker and more effective means of achieving them. Though not double first material, he was a born journalist with a nose for a story, a vignette, a little happening which he could transpose to the screen, and he had the warmth and humanity to do it.

I was thrilled to become his first assistant on *Night Mail* and soon found myself carrying the tripod as Jonah Jones carried the Newman Sinclair and Harry the reflector board. We were some miles north of Hemel Hempstead, measuring our steps from sleeper to sleeper as we trudged down the main 'down fast' line to Crewe. The L.M.S. railway company had provided us with a 'ganger' for our safety. He carried a red flag, had a whistle permanently between his teeth which he blew with monotonous regularity. The whistle would then drop suspended from a cord necklace and he would solemnly intone: 'Up fast. Stand clear', or 'Down fast. Stand clear'. These ups and downs came with infuriating regularity, making our progress not hazardous but tedious as we were driven into the sidewalk.

We came across a gang of plate layers, and like prospectors we thought we had struck it rich. We had come to shoot more or less anything: signals moving, passing trains, shifting points, the permanent way bouncing up and down, reacting to a train passing . . . Stock shots that might come in handy, though heaven knew when. Harry went up to the gang and explained what we were about, that we were making this film about the Travelling Post Office, and would they mind being in it. The usual badinage about becoming film stars with their mugs, ensued. But Harry was a natural catalyst and was always at ease and put at ease whoever he met, no matter what the circumstances or the company—an essential asset for the budding film director. We now filmed an off moment in the plate layer's routine. A shared quart bottle of beer, a few comments from one to another—I noted their remarks for revoicing later— and close shots of these weather-beaten faces, a life's work imprinted on each. This, I could already sense, was the thrill of documentary, putting the people of Britain on the screen, recorded for all time.

Next morning when we saw the rushes at Blackheath we were very happy with the day's work. Harry asked me to break them down and make a first assembly of the shots, a rough cut in other words—my first attempt at editing, being a 'cutter'. I was thrilled. The sequence was perhaps 90 feet long, about a minute. I took it over to the movieola and was almost trembling with excitement. My first cut sequence. Something was wrong. I had joined them in the sequence that Harry shot them but they wouldn't come together. I ran and reran it. It didn't work. I had to show it to Harry eventually and his language was not conversational. He simmered down after a bit. 'I've done it . . . The unforgiveable . . . I've crossed the line.'

'I thought you had to be at sea to do that.'

'Not the equator, idiot, the eye line.'

'Oh I see.' He saw that I hadn't.

'Cav warned me about it, even drew it for me. I thought I'd got it into my nut, but I bloody well haven't.' He then drew for me the same sort of diagram that Cavalcanti, who had recently joined from French cinema, had drawn for him. He explained his mistake by drawing a line between two characters A and B. There is not a director alive or dead who, at some time or other, has not made this mistake and will make it again unless careful. A and B are talking to each other, perfectly natural that now and then they should occasionally look at each other. One will look 'Camera Right' and the other 'Camera Left'. Joined together the looks will cross and give the impression that they are looking at each other. Sounds simple enough but the platelayers were all looking right and seemed to be looking away from each other, so back we went and reshot the sequence. We were lucky to find the same gang two miles further down the line.

In such faltering steps we started on the more exciting sequences of the film. The first was to be in the operations van. This contained the equipment to despatch the leather-pouched mail bags and receive them as the train continues its journey at sixty to seventy miles an hour. Quite an exciting process, visually. There was no way we could hope to shoot these scenes with synchronous sound, impossible to have put our massive sound van on to a truck of the T.P.O. (Travelling Post Office), and there was no portable sound equipment in those far-off days. As there was considerable dialogue involved in the apparatus sequence we would have to trust to luck and put the voices on afterward—'post-synching', as it is called.

Armed with banks of batteries, Chick Fowle was able to get sufficient light in the apparatus van for us to start. The sequence we were to shoot was the middle climax, in fact the only climax, and therefore wrongly placed in the construction of the film. A trainee was being instructed how to bind the mail bags into a strong leather pouch. This was then attached to a metal arm which he had to lower at the correct moment. The pouch hanging from it would then be swept into a net set up on the ground. A net from the side of the train would then be lowered to reverse the process and collect the pouches hanging from gibbet-like posts at the side of the track. These processes take place as the train travels at sixty or seventy miles an hour. All very cinematic, we hoped. The sequence would be built with the trainee standing by the opening of the van, waiting for the critical moment to lower the metal arm to which is attached the mail pouch. He is getting nervy. He looks towards his instructor and shouts, anxiously: 'Now?' His instructor shakes his head and shouts back: 'No, no. You want two bridges and 25 beats.' The first bridge passes and soon after the second. Harry comes into close shot as the trainee starts to count beats of the wheels.

He cuts to the trainee's fingers beating on the man's chest. Cuts to the instructor. Back to the trainee's fingers: 21, 22, 23, 24, 25. 'Now', shouts the instructor. Down goes the arm. The ground net sweeps it away. The train's net is lowered; ahead are the hanging pouches. Shooting through the mesh of the waiting net, we see the pouches gathered and swept on to the floor of the van. It all worked splendidly. The visuals were safely in the can. The men came down to the studio, we recorded their voices and they fitted the picture very well. Nobody would know that their voices had been laid on afterwards. But, there was a problem. How to get rail beats to fit the counting and the finger movements of the trainee. We tried all the tracks we had recorded of wheel beats: none fitted. Unless they did, the sequence would be ruined. The film was being edited as we went along for we could not always shoot on consecutive days. We were in the hands of the L.M.S. and their facilities. So there would be three or four days to edit the material already shot. I was editing the apparatus sequences and was in despair how to find a matching track for the counting process. It was the Jackson toy cupboard that provided the solution.

My brother Michael had been keen on model railways. He had had a Bassett Lowke steam engine. It took a gauge one track. There was still quite a good length of this track left in the attic and a bogie, also gauge one. I took them to the studio the next day and Ed Pawley, our sound engineer, recorded my pushing the bogie over the join in the track. I worked on getting a perfect series of 'te tum te tum; te tum te tum: te tum te tums'. The next day I was able to cut the sound track so that the 'te tum te tums' exactly fitted the finger movements of the trainee. With the roar of the train laid over, nobody would ever know. Nobody ever did.

We next moved up to Crewe, the main junction of the Midlands, where mail came in from all parts of the country. Trolley loads had to be collected and loaded on to the T.P.O. to be dropped off throughout the night as the train went north towards Scotland. Frank Brice, our electrician, had a massive job laying cables under the tracks to supply power from the generator to arc lights, for this sequence had to be filmed at night. We were several days shooting this central sequence. We shot synchronous sound in the station bar as the Scots sorters relieved the English. Harry made up some dialogue for them, just a line or two—'There's no water for the Jocks' tea'—and then as the English meet the Scots one says: 'I hope you enjoy your tea', and the Jock retorts: 'I know what that means. No water.'

When the day's shooting was over, I was given the rushes and boarded the T.P.O. southbound so that I could get them into Humphries. I slept on the mail bags. Then I would wait at Humphries and continue my nap until I could take the rushes back to the unit. These were shown in the local cinema to check that no retakes were required. It was not a long sequence but it took time, probably a week, and at the end of it I became quite expert at reading the sound of the track and knowing where we were.

Double running 'te te tum, te te tum' meant we were approaching Watford. I've forgotten most of them now but the sorters could tell within a mile exactly where they were on the run between Euston and Crewe. I was having the time of my life playing around with these wonderful steam engines. It was a glorious adventure.

By now the sets were ready for us on the tiny stage of our studio. Two sides of a sorting van had been built by the Jacob brothers. Two wonderful master carpenters—just the two of them, and they built all the sets for future productions, never calling on extra help. They were wonderful craftsmen. Bunny Onions with his Vinten was the lighting cameraman and these sequences were shot 'in sync'. No problems and no further mistakes in 'crossing the eye-line'. All that remained were the shots of the 'Night Mail' climbing Beattock and descending to its destination in Glasgow. Harry would shoot off the cuff for there was no script for this part of the film except a generalisation of what was needed.

Harry, Jonah Jones and I positioned ourselves on the summit of Beattock and waited for the 'Night Mail' to appear. It was cold, I remember, and we played 'rugger' with my battered old trilby to keep warm, and then she appeared miles below us. Two puffing funnels were shooting white smoke up the valley for there was a pusher to help the climb. As already mentioned, these shots were eventually to carry the opening lines of Auden's verse: 'This is the Night Mail crossing the border, bringing the cheque and the postal order'. The following day we boarded the footplate of the *Royal Scot* to get shots of the driver, the fireman and the passing country for the rest of Auden's verse—'Past cotton grass and moorland boulder, shovelling white steam over her shoulder'.

We climbed aboard her at Carlisle and as she pulled out of the station and gathered speed along the track I was consigned to the coal tender with a reflector board. Jonah wanted me to try and get some light on to the footplate. I climbed up on to the top of the coals to get the maximum effect from the reflector. I soon found that it was no easy matter to hold a five by three foot board travelling at forty miles an hour. I very nearly took off. I regained a foothold and tried again.

We were travelling eastwards and the sun was in the east so the wind resistance was almost too much for me. Then we headed north which meant that the reflector was feathered slightly against the wind. I could see that I was getting some light on to the footplate. I was, of course, focusing on the fireman and driver, not on the way ahead. The reflector was torn out of my hands. I'd forgotten that there were such things as bridges and was delighted to find that I still had my scalp intact—a closer shave than I would have liked. Jonah now had to make do without his reflector. But he got some wonderful shots. The Epstein face of the driver, wiping his face with cotton waste. It was to carry the lines: 'The climb is done, down towards Glasgow she descends'.

When we'd done all the shooting the fireman let me feed the furnace and I soon realised that there was more to it than just shovelling coal. There was an art in maintaining a level bed of evenly burning coals for the boiler to be given a reliable head of steam. It was not to be learnt in one easy lesson, nor were the muscles built to sustain a hungry furnace with a few sessions in the gym. It was a revelation to realise what the job involved. I recalled Grierson's speech in the Railway Arms; he could well have added: 'Do we appreciate the fireman and engine driver?'

To be able to say that you have stoked the *Royal Scot* was quite something. I was not quite nineteen and realised how lucky I was to have these experiences and see at first hand how the other man lived with all the hardships involved; to meet these wonderful characters who were the backbone of England. I was very privileged, I realise now, but obviously not sufficiently then.

But, alas, the shooting of *Night Mail* was coming to an end and the final editing took place. My sections, the apparatus van and the sorting office were simple enough. It was R. Q. McNaughton who had the tough part, the second half, for the film seemed to peter out. The action stuff, the gutsy part, was in the first half. The wrong shape and we were heading for an anti-climax. It was then that Basil Wright had the inspired idea of calling upon Auden to write some verse for the second half, where the weakness lay.

Auden started to write reams of verse in the nether regions of

21 Soho Square. Shamefacedly, Harry is on record as saying that he threw a lot of his stuff away, thinking it was quite unsuitable and telling Auden to go back and have another go. Auden had another go with results that are now famous and which contributed so greatly to the success of the film. It was Basil also who thought that he might give a young composer, Benjamin Britten, a trial. Benjamin faced no easy task. Finances would not permit him more than five instruments.

Until we could give him exact measurements of the sequences which were to carry music, Benjamin hung around the studio, and saw each running as we were finalising the editing. During this time, Benjamin would come home to play tennis on our somewhat imperfect lawn. He was lethal and not only a fine player but up-staged us all by appearing with one of those Bunny Austin rackets which looked like an Alaskan snow shoe—outrigger struts from handle to racket frame. Most offputting. Worth a point, every game. Had he not been so gifted musically he would have swept everyone off the Centre Court.

The great day arrived when the final cut was accepted. Sequence lengths were measured to the frame and transposed into minutes and seconds. Benjamin could now finalise his score and Auden had his verses ready. Final recording was prepared. First, the simple narrative commentary. Basil thought that my voice would be suit-able. Well, well. Never more surprised in my life, I faced the 'mike' and my dulcet tones are immortalised in a few simple statements concerning the workings of the T.P.O. It is a horrifying experience to hear your voice for the first time as others hear you. I sounded like some Oxford pimp on the prowl, and never having been to Oxford, I should know.

Benjamin Britten's five instrumentalists, chosen by him, of course, recorded his score and he conducted as each section of the film was projected. For this noble work he received a handsome fee of £13.10. He was delighted, for he, quite rightly, felt he had put his foot, not into it, but into a new world that might lead to greater things. He was quite right, for a year or so later he was given the score for a Hollywood epic starring Anne Harding and Basil

Rathbone, a bone chilling thriller. I have forgotten the name of it but he must have been paid more than £13.10. We were all thrilled that our humble efforts had helped him on his way into the suspect world of commercial cinema. Anathema, of course, to us purist documentalists. How snooty; how high brow; how elitist we were. Cat's whiskers, or is it pyjamas, we thought we were. Compensating like mad, of course, because we thought none of us would make it into the big pond of the 'Big Time'. Snoot was the obvious defence mechanism. Stuart Legge's voice was chosen and had no trouble in matching the rhythm of the verse to Britten's music.

It began to look, at long last, like the G.P.O. Film Unit's first serious attempt at making a film had produced a finished product. The powers that were, either through Basil Wright or Grierson, I do not know, meant that *Night Mail* was to be shown for the first time at 'The Arts Theatre', Cambridge. It would be the first film to be shown there; a double launch, as it were. The college was 'down' and so it was easy to put us up. I cannot remember in which college I found myself for I was to see the first showing with Basil and Harry the following morning. All I remember was the effect it had on me, my first glimpse of a seat of learning since my one term at Bryanston. It knocked me sideways.

Next morning, I was sitting between Harry and Basil as we waited for *Night Mail* to be shown. The lights dimmed, the tabs parted and up came the titles. One card of credits with very few names on it. Grierson didn't much like credits—over-emphasised the ego and truncated the sense of service, and I would not argue with that. He was right, in many ways.

We were off. Very soon, something new and unexpected happened, new anyway to the documentary film makers of that time. There was a laugh, a deep and glorious belly laugh. It shook the theatre, or seemed to, and it certainly shook us. I remember whispering to Basil: 'My God, they're actually enjoying it'. At this moment the documentary movement split into two schools, and for the following reason. The dramatisation of the apparatus van sequence and the little light human touches which were all Harry's showed the way forward towards a more compelling form of presentation. In short, the story approach, the use of drama, dialogue and characterisation instead of the straightforward commentary expositional exposé of a subject.

Harry had never been in any doubt which way he wanted to travel; after all, he was a disciple of the great Robert Flaherty. In the years ahead it was those who followed Harry's approach to film making who were to produce the feature-length story documentaries which were to be shown on the commercial circuits with profit to all concerned. It was to be a year or two yet for this to become evident. But, it was *Night Mail* that blazed the trail for us.

Nobody knows who wrote the final script, if there ever were one. Certainly, I never saw Harry refer to it. He just went out and shot the film, sequence by sequence, by guess and by God, hoping for the best. If Basil Wright, who had initially researched the subject and had fully developed those action sequences into shooting script form as he could easily have done, for he and I had seen first-hand the process at work—if he had fully appreciated the visual ingredients, he would have discovered the value of a dramatic presentation and sensed the power of suspense, and he would have used these weapons in his later work. He never did. He remained imprisoned in the expositional mould, as did the original disciples of Grierson, faithful to the belief that a service which attempted to provide objective information was a big enough crusade. To this school was attached the aphorism 'Creative interpretation of reality'. Flawed from the start for reality is subjective, and can there ever be objective reporting? Stop press news, perhaps, such as England declares at 307. But, let interpretation enter the scene and objectivity takes a bow and exits. Interpretation means a point of view, therefore a bias. 'To thine own self be true and it must follow as the night the day thou canst not then be false to any man.' I wonder? What is true for me may be false to you. The truth for Hitler and Stalin was death for millions. How is the truth to be interpreted in Northern Ireland, yet it was the truth, as we thought, that we tried to put on the screen. Knowingly or unknowingly, even in those far off days, we held immense disseminating power, and what about those who presently hold it?

They are the problem of our age, for like it or not we are affected by the manner in which they wield it. We scarcely realise what is happening to us and to our children. The degree to which we are being manipulated and disturbed, our compassion long since exhausted by seeing endless coffin-carrying in Northern Ireland, famines and millions dying before us. A rhinoceros skin of callousness is required against these shaming and mortifying visuals channelled daily into our homes. You may say you don't have to watch it. Get rid of your T.V. How facile, and you and I know that that is not the solution. You and I know that we cannot protect our children. If they do not watch the 'box' at home they will watch it elsewhere. We cannot protect them from this visual attack on their childhood sensibilities and innocence. The discs of satellite television disfigure more and more homes as porn is pumped into them from depraved sources and we expect our children to be normal, to uphold the same values that once were considered essential to sustain a healthy society. Children are starting to kill each other. What is causing it? We know very well and we do nothing about it. We must be mad. But what can we do? We might as well try and stop the Gadarene swine. No doubt we shall soon be joining them.

Poor old *Night Mail*, your contribution was harmless enough, and so, at that time, was the media. You have crossed the border many a time since we were on your footplate. As for the media, that has double-crossed all of us.

4

Bernard Shaw exposed

George Bernard Shaw, rumour had it, was to visit us that afternoon to give a talk for the B.B.C. film we were making, *The Voice of Britain*. The G.P.O. controlled the land lines of the B.B.C.

True enough, in the early afternoon, a Rolls Royce drove down Bennett Park Road. The only form of red carpet to greet the great man was 'the Chief', John Grierson, who shepherded him through the studio to the stage. Having seen him arrive, this august presence, I hopped it to the sound van with Martin, who was now Ed Pawley's assistant and responsible for loading and unloading the sound camera and its magazines.

We could hear what was going on as Grierson played the host. He was not used to being upstaged but, of course, on this occasion he had no rank to pull. But he had to make an attempt to converse with the great man. He went into a lengthy description of how, for the first time in the history of film, we had recorded and shot synchronous sound by means of land line, the coaxial cable and so on and so forth. Shaw obviously listened politely enough and seemed suitably unimpressed as, in his glorious Irish accent, he replied: 'Very interesting, Mr Grierson, but now perhaps it might be as well if you were to tell me what it is that you would like me to talk about. I imagine you wish me to make a few comments on this B.B.C. that you are filming.' Grierson replied that that would be splendid, to which Shaw replied: 'Very well, then perhaps you will permit me to get on with it.' Grierson assured him that everything was ready and that he could start immediately. 'And you obviously want me to climb on to the rostrum and sit behind the microphone and start talking when you have half stunned me with your clapper board.'

'Exactly so, Mr Shaw.' We heard shuffling of feet, the chair being moved and being sat upon.

'You can clap me now, I'm ready.' Nobody dared to ask the great man for a few words so that Ed Pawley could get a level. Oh no. In went the board. Clap and he was off.

'I have been asked to say a few words about the microphone and I am not entirely sure whether I like it or not, whether it is a friend I can trust or someone to be very suspicious of and certainly to treat with respect. If you do not make it your friend it will be your mortal enemy, for it can catch you off guard and before you know it you have said something, which can mightily offend . . .'

He went on and on in the most wonderful humorous and satirical vein. Minutes went by and we were fearful that the ten minutes of film in both magazines would soon come to an end. He reached his peroration which went something like this: 'And so I warn you: treat the microphone with the greatest respect, otherwise it will not respect you, for I must tell you that I am now becoming aware not only what your announcers have had for dinner but what they have had to drink.'

We still had a few feet left. He had timed it perfectly and his talk, in every meaning of the word, was priceless. But that was it. No question of whether it was satisfactory for sound or camera. He was off and escorted with silent solemnity and final grateful thanks as the Chief and Stuart Legge saw him into his Rolls Royce. This was as near to Royalty as I ever hope to get, and we all felt that we had been privileged to have had him amongst us. Grierson and Legge were rightly overjoyed, for this material would be of enormous importance in the future, not only for the film the unit was presently producing. It was a scoop, for Bernard Shaw did not scatter his services here, there and everywhere. But to have his 'off the cuff' talk was a great asset. I went backstage, into the nether regions of the place, to discover Martin, coming out of the dark room. He was as white as the proverbial sheet. Looking bad and shocked. 'You O.K.?'

'No . . . I've exposed the Shaw rushes.'

'Oh . . . My God. Shaw. How?'

'What difference does it make? They're exposed. Is the Chief still here? I must tell him and oh dear . . .' He wasn't near tears; he was just shocked.

'The first person we tell is Ed. He'll tell you what to do.'

Ed Pawley received the news with momentary shock, of course, and then took charge in the most wonderful way. How long was the red light switched on, before the lid was put back? Perhaps three or four seconds. No more. Pawley told Martin on no account tell the Chief and resign until tomorrow when we would know the worst. Sound film was not as fast as picture film and it was just possible that the light had not penetrated dangerously and irretrievably into the Visatone Track. Even if it had, it depended how seriously. The sprocket holes in the film would have spread a line, like sleepers on a railway, which would create a low frequency. They would make a 'blurb blurb blurb', like a motor-bike ticking over, all through Shaw's speech. But such a low frequency could be filtered without seriously impairing the higher frequencies of Bernard Shaw's voice. Pawley arranged with Humphries to get a special rush print through and arrangements were made to bring it down to the studio. Pawley ran the track and, sure enough, a low-keyed motorbike covered Shaw's voice. Pawley tinkered with his box of tricks, put in a low frequency filter and erased the motorbike. Shaw's voice came through loud and clear and nobody knew anything about Martin's little crisis.

When the B.B.C. film was finished there was room for only a few sentences of Shaw's wonderful talk—a few seconds, no more. The rest of it must be lying in some vault. Somebody should be assigned to trace it for there is vintage Shaw somewhere. Many great men followed G.B.S. into that little Blackheath studio. H. G. Wells, and I can hear his high pitched squeaky voice saying, in the few sentences alloted to him: 'Unless Russia can discover a further liberation of the mind, her experiment will be spent, a wasted effort'. He recorded that in 1936. Low, the great creator of Colonel Blimp, referring to his opinion of politicians with his dismissive line: 'We give the waxworks, life'. And included in the film snippets of outside broadcasts, Queen Mary, hardly able to disguise all traces of a German accent on one of the few occasions when the people were ever to hear their Queen speak: 'I name this ship *The Queen Mary*. May God bless her and all who sail in her.' The B.B.C.'s film *The Voice of Britain* was twice as long as *Night Mail* and must have cost twice as much. It came and went, almost never to be heard of again. It was cold and shapeless.

5

Harry Watt challenged by the Savings Bank

Harry Watt, meanwhile, after his success with *Night Mail* (though Grierson, for reasons that I have touched on, did not give him the credit for having directed the film), had to be content with a shared credit with Basil Wright. He was bitter about that, and rightly so. However, he soon got over it and was now assigned to make a film about the Post Office Savings Bank. One had been made already by Arthur Elton, a year or so before. I had worked on it as Davidson's loading boy. The film was a crashing bore, a disaster. I don't know whether it was ever shown. If so, it was soon put into the vaults alongside Grierson's P.L.A.

So, Harry had not only to redeem the unit's reputation so far as this section of the civil service was concerned, but advance his own theories of how to go about this rather precious documentary film thing. He was getting sick and tired of too much intellectualising: too much of this dialectic materialism that everyone was on about, to coin a contemporary phrase. Left wing O.K. Everyone who thinks at all is bound, at some stage of their lives, usually early on, to be radical, very radical. But, you don't want to meet *Das Kapital* in the loo. It's not that sort of book, is it? There was a good deal of impress, impress: intellectual fireworks flying about. If that was the way to get on, O.K. for some, but not for Harry. Now, he was burdened with a film on the Savings Bank. If only to camouflage a boring subject he was determined to get the message across in story form. But to be anchored to the premise that it is wise if not virtuous to invest at three per cent so that when you are ready for the grave your capital will have grown sufficiently to give you a decent funeral requires inspired winching to get that off the sea bed. Find the right shape, though, and you can make anything work. Metal can be shaped to float. The sea! The sea had brought him to Flaherty and then to Grierson. He would launch his Savings Bank film on the ocean, somehow, somewhere. Perhaps a fishing village. He made for Cornwall. He reached Penzance and was not happy that he had found the ideal location. He was fast running out of coast-line. Newlyn wasn't the answer. He was now approaching Land's End and then he'd be rounding the corner and heading north-east.

Setting out from Newlyn his spirits were at a low ebb, only to be raised a few miles down the road when, rounding the corner, he saw the bewitching little fishing harbour of Mousehole. One look was enough. He was hooked. He'd earned a refresher at the local, The Ship Inn.

An hour or so later he knew, not only that he'd found his location, but his leading man, who was the local Postmaster, a William Blewett. They were getting merrier and merrier and Harry delighted in the company of Bill. His Post Office was a spitting distance from this most welcoming pub. He had a mesmeric gift of the gab, a glorious Cornish accent, twinkling blue eyes, a grin as broad as 'Popeye' and the charismatic charm of the Celt.

Harry booked in at The Lobster Pot which in the far off days of 1936 was within range of the limited expense account of one of the G.P.O. Film Unit's directors. Bill had so stimulated Harry that the vague story outline that had been forming soon took on flesh and bone. But he was not prepared to bank his all on the untried Postmaster of Mousehole. Who was to know whether the quality of the man would remain unimpaired before the camera, microphone, lamps and all the paraphernalia of a full unit surrounding him? If he could remain cool and be the same man as in The Ship Inn, the star role was his and he would carry the weight of the film on his shoulders.

Jonah Jones, our real 'Gor Blimey' true cockney cameraman, came down and was armed with tripod and the ever reliable Newman Sinclair and 500 feet of film. Bill was taken out of his little corner Post Office, whilst Hetty—later to appear in *The Foreman went to France* for Ealing—understudied as temporary Postmistress. A wonderful woman, a True Blue Londoner. She kissed her 'hubby' goodbye as though he were about to face the firing squad, which in a way he was: he probably felt that he was, and that was the point of the operation. He was marched down to the small sandy beach which appeared in the harbour when the tide was out, as did a few rocks. Bill sat himself on one and Jonah set up his tripod and camera. Hardy held the reflector board and Bill held the slate on which was written 'Test of Bill Blewett'. He was told to lay it aside after the camera had run a few seconds and then say whatever he liked. Jonah looked into the sky. The sun would be clear for several minutes and he nodded to Harry. The camera turned. Bill could hear it whirring and, totally at ease, he lowered the clapper board, and looked straight into camera as though talking to Harry in The Ship Inn, and spieled away. He invented some absurd story about seeing the P.M.G., Kingsley Wood, having a walk on the rocks dangling a prawning net. Utter balderdash, but put over with such conviction, Harry said, that if they had been recording, people would have believed him. It was masterly because it was confident; author-itative. It was as though, suddenly, he had found his true metier.

I was to find this when six years later I was casting *Western Ap-proaches*. It is a rare and extraordinary experience to find star material, a nugget, shaped and formed by the background that created both the nugget and the natural star, not one manufactured synthetically by the drama schools whose candidates are already tainted by the ego trip which, in spite of their talent, will slowly distort them. If successful they are imprisoned in the bondage of fame and then the haunting fear of its loss.

Harry had found his leading man. Indeed he had, for Bill Blewett was to make many films for Harry, even after he went 'commer-cial'—went to Ealing, to Mick Balcon. He took Bill Blewett with him and made *Nine Men*, in which Bill played a leading role.

Very soon *The Savings of Bill Blewett* was in production and Mousehole was invaded by the G.P.O. Film Unit with its gen-erators, arc lights, sound van, Bunny Onions and his blimped Vinten, and how the village responded. Everyone helped in the making of what they naturally considered was their film. They made it. They played in it, enacted the simple story of a wrecked boat and how money was scrimped and saved to buy another. No great story, perhaps, but acted with sincerity so that one's heart went out to a community, its characters and their problems. This was powerful communication: no sterile exercise of visual and commentary to explain what was happening. Documentary was liberated.

Once again, I was Harry's assistant and those two months at Mousehole were the finest working holiday of my life. To participate in such a communal endeavour, to see how the villagers took hold of the story, made it their own, contributed their dialect and their way of saying things and being content to be their own unique and natural selves was a thrilling experience. The unit was lodged and scattered throughout the village, each landlady trying to outdo the other to produce the best Cornish pasties and the best reputation amongst the unit. Consequently we were spoilt rotten and fattened up like French geese for our 'foie gras'. It was the high life.

We had a sequence to film aboard a drifter because in the story Bill had to do all sorts of jobs, having lost his boat when it slipped its moorings. We went aboard her at Newlyn and in foul weather made for Longships Lighthouse, off Land's End. We were bouncing around, pitching and rolling, corkscrew fashion: 'Quite like old times for you, Harry, I suppose'. Harry nodded and was promptly sick over the side. Though he loved the sea, like the great Nelson, he was not the best of sailors. We passed the Longships Lighthouse heading for the Scillies. Towards evening, the weather eased and it became fine. The sea abated and a mile or so of nets were shot and we drifted with them. Our drifter was based in Hull and her skipper was a jovial, rubicund figure, Sam Spilling, an ideal Father Christmas for Selfridge's toy fair. He invited us for a game of poker in the wheel house. The table was an upturned empty crate for mackerel, covered with fish scales. He switched on his ship-to-shore radio and we listened to Henry Hall, playing *Night and Day* and all the hits of the middle thirties. This is the life, I thought, looking west through the wheel house as the sun was setting in glorious fashion. No nineteen-year-old could have been having a better time than I was.

Dinner was a trip to the cookhouse, astern. We were handed a fresh mackerel, cooked in batter, which we ate in our fingers, throwing the scraps up to the gulls. These were experiences to be cherished for a lifetime and I was being paid. Not much, perhaps, but to be paid for a training can't be bad.

Another job Bill Blewett found himself was on a long liner, a small craft converted from the dying pilchard fleet. Sanctions had been imposed by Anthony Eden on Italy, which was the chief customer of Cornwall's pilchards. Not surprisingly Mussolini had few friends in Cornwall. Harry hired the boat for a day which made a nasty hole in his budget. The ship had been temporarily laid up and so bait for half a mile of line had to be bought and wages paid to the crew of three. However, it was a necessary sequence and it had to be filmed. Bill, of course, was one of the crew working the small petrol winch which would haul in our baited line. Hooks were set every fifteen feet, and as there was some 500 yards of line there were several hooks to bait. Then it had to be carefully wound into its huge basket. It is a highly skilled job to shoot a line—hence the expression, no doubt. A watchful eye from the wheel house is needed, ready to throw the craft into reverse, for if the line should tangle it becomes a lethal web of hooks flying across the deck.

We went well beyond the Longships and shot the line without trouble and then anchored for several hours to give the bait a chance. An oily swell, riding to anchor, undid Nelson's understudy again and he took it with nonchalance—all part of the day's work.

With an hour or so left of good daylight, we started to haul: Jonah Jones, ready with his Newman Sinclair to capture on film these monsters of the deep that we had caught on our line. Dead slow ahead and the winch, foot by foot, hauled in the line. Any moment now. Yes, something silvery. It was a bare hook. Saucy monkey, pinched the bait and got away with it. Even on the round pond it would be thrilling to pull in a baited line. But out here, with the Atlantic on our doorstep, heaven knows what we were about to pull up. Three unbaited hooks followed in quick succession. This was like having a wet flannel flung in our faces. Then a baited hook, several of them and then a pathetic whiting—I'd caught bigger ones off Seaford Head when a toddler. This was not the stuff of drifters. Had Harry surrendered his all for nothing?

Our five hundred yards produced about 12 decent sized conger eels. Bill, we noticed, treated them with the utmost respect. 'Take your hand off like slicing butter', he muttered. No wonder he took his cap off, wrapping it round the head of each conger eel as he tried to unhook it. But from Harry's point of view, this was a disaster, for nobody was going to get rich on this miserable haul, let alone save a penny or two, and that's what, if you remember, he was supposed to be doing, poor chap.

'We'll have to have another go tomorrow, Pat, so you'd better preserve these congers', Harry told me when we got back to Mousehole. We were a bit downhearted.

'O.K. Harry.'

Off I went to see my new-found friend, and what a friend he was. Bill Hoskin, the carpenter. I explained my problem. He saw no problem. Within an hour he had knocked up a crate large enough to house King Kong. There was space between the slats to allow the free flow of water, lobster pot-style. We just managed to carry the thing, proud as punch we were, down to the harbour. Half the village was there. It had got around, as good and bad always does in tight communities, that our catch had been as near blank as made no difference. We were jeered and cheered all the way to the end of the jetty, the entrance to the harbour. There was still plenty of life in our 12 congers. They were handled into the crate as though they were 'man-eaters'. Having been weighted, the crate was lowered, to the same jeers and cheers, and with a splendid splash disappeared for the night.

The following morning was fine and we were 12 congers to the good. The sky was a cameraman's dream; white bushy cumuli. With an Aero 1, Jonah Jones would be in seventh heaven, up there with them.

Down to the harbour we went. My friend Hoskin was there, with more than half the village. The tide was high. Our long liner's motor was ticking over, the baited line in its basket, except for the last thirty yards. These were reserved for our congers. The mooring rope to our crate was untied from an old bronze ring in the ancient harbour wall which, we were told, went back to Roman times—an interesting fact that we failed to appreciate at that moment. Many lent a willing hand to pull up the crate. Easy whilst still in the water. On the surface a very dead weight. We had to wait for the water to drain. As it lightened we pulled it on to the jetty. Hoskin prised open the lid. Our conger eels were as stiff as ramrods. Instead of blowing his top and firing me on the spot, Harry roared with laughter and thanked Hoskin for all the trouble that he'd taken.

Off to sea we went and this time had better luck. Several hefty skate which would be worth a bob or two. Bill would have been able to save a few shillings from his share of the catch.

Inevitably the last shot was safely in the can and the never-to-be-forgotten Mousehole experience came to an end. I cut the film for Harry and, looking back, I realise that I did not have my name on the credits, either as assistant or editor. Golden days when one didn't even think about such things.

6

'In loco parentis'

Then it was that John Grierson stepped into the breach, once more, on my behalf. I am permanently indebted to him not only because he gave me a start but for the patience and tolerance he showed as I slowly struggled out of the crysalis and tried to spread my wings a little bit. As I have said, he believed education could be the cure for everything. For this reason, he sent his young brother-in-law, John Taylor, who had photographed *Song of Ceylon*, to Glasgow University to do a course in something or other. Even if he didn't get a degree he would learn how to concentrate through enforced essay writing.

During a visit to the unit at Mousehole, Grierson saw my French homework on the table of the digs I was sharing with Harry and his wife Lulu. I was doing a correspondence course with Wolsey Hall, trying to make up for the loss of my school years. Grierson, so Harry told me, was impressed that I was making some sort of effort and magnanimously suggested that when the film was finished I should take three months off on my pay of thirty shillings a week, go to France and get a better command of the language. Not only was this a wonderful gesture but he spread the word that contributions would be most gratefully received by his ex-messenger boy, he being the first to stump up five pounds, a lot of money in 1936. Many senior members followed his kind example. It was, as I said, a very special unit.

Conveniently, an aged great-aunt, another Gulland who lived in Kidbrooke Park, died and left her grand nephews and nieces £200 each. On this and the unit's contributions I lived like a lord for over three months in Grenoble. Mercifully the pound was uniquely strong against the franc, something to do with Leon Blum and the Front Populaire. As a result, for £2.10.0 a week I was able to pay my pension and university and 'High Life' cigarettes, aptly named. I bought a 'bike' for a pound which took me to and from my lodgings with a wonderful Buscarlet family of Avenue D'Eybens on the Route Napoléon, to the University.

Trying to play the role of a student had its humiliations. Grammatical terminology was Greek to me. Indirect objects, subordinate clauses meant nothing. I had to go to a French governess to learn English grammatical terminology before I could attack their French equivalents. Happily, I found a genius, a Madame L'huillier. She was as broad as she was tall; her favourite seasoning was garlic and she was liberal with it. She sprouted moles almost everywhere and I adored her. She was an inspired teacher. A few months with her and the years of lost schooling would have been made good in no time. She could have taught me anything and I could have passed anything—Common Entrance, poof!

My lodgings were spacious and grand. Madame Buscarlet, a stunningly handsome lady, fed us like fighting cocks and did her best to see that we didn't turn her establishment into a brothel. For the earnest student of French, there were too many English and when one of them was Ginger Corbett, nephew of the historian, E. Fisher, Master of New College, French irregulars went west, for Ginger was wonderful company, straight out of Pickwick with Micawber spectacles and a wry smile forever around his upper lip. Impossible to be downcast in his company. Neither of us much fancied our chances of getting our 'Certificat d'Etudes Françaises'. We tried to make a fair balance between work and play, and then the snow fell and the balance tilted towards play. There was a little place in the nearby mountains, Alpe d'Huez. The skiing was very good, one of the lodgers said, and she knew the farmer there who had a large barn, and he was prepared to let the students sleep in the hay loft, above the cows. His was the only farm there, apparently. So, off we went. Everything was as she described and on fine nights we skied in the moonlight. No ski tows, of course. We herring-boned our way up the slopes until we bought seal skins and were able to climb higher for longer runs. I spent my 21st in that cow shed. In spite of all the fun and games—and there were plenty of them—I did learn to work and got my 'Certificat' with a distinction. Madame L'huillier did her best to persuade me that perhaps I wasn't such a fool, after all.

7

Rungs of the ladder

I returned to the unit in the spring of 1937. Harry Watt was on location in northern Scotland with Chick Fowle, who was photographing Harry's finest film, *North Sea*, dramatising the reliance of the trawler fleet on the Post Office radio weather station at Wick in the most northerly point of Caithness. Bill Blewett, from Mousehole, was with him, a member of the trawler's crew, and being a non-professional actor would encourage the rest to be confident in being just themselves: no acting would be required, and in this regard Bill was to be a tower of strength to Harry and *North Sea* was to be a great step forward in story documentary. The rough conditions in which the trawler put to sea were extremely severe, vividly portraying the dangers trawlermen face. 'We take them all for granted. Yet we are all in each other's debt.'

Meanwhile, our small studio was a bedlam of hammering and sawing. The Jacob brothers, our master carpenters, were building what looked like a huge mushroom sock darner. This inverted mushroom was to be a rocker for the trawler's cabin which would be built on the flat top of the sock darner, mushroom at the base, of course. Wooden levers would protrude from it so that we could rock the set in front of the camera set up independently beside the rocking cabin. Had the camera not been independently set up there would have been no illusion of the trawler being tossed about in heavy seas.

Whilst Harry was hard at it with *North Sea*, I was allowed, on my return from Grenoble, to make my first faltering steps as a director. I was to complete a film that Harry had started but had had to lay aside for the more important subject of *North Sea*. However, as money had been spent on a film attempting to show how the Accountant General's Department worked, it had to be finished. It proceeded under the inspiring working title of *A.G.D.* It was completed and went out under the title of *Big Money*. Harry is credited with having made it. Not important, for I had the satisfaction of having written my first dialogue scenes and directed them for this rather dreary subject. They received the intended laughs when first shown, and years later, Paul Rotha mentioning Harry Watt's work referred to these scenes as the best of Harry Watt, so perhaps I had begun to repay the debt I owed Harry for his many kindnesses and wonderful support he gave me when I was a very tenderfoot. I am always grateful to him and will always remember him with deep affection. With those dialogue scenes under my belt I felt that I was now a serious threat to Cecil B. de Mille.

I was now asked to develop a story on the London Postal School. I didn't know that such a place existed and this was the fascination of working in documentary. What a dry word for a school of cinema manned by enthusiastic people trying to discover new territories, meeting so many interesting people making their living in ways and by skills we knew nothing of. So much to learn from them as we sought the drama of their everyday lives. This was our goal.

And so I went to the London Postal School. Some facts from its P.R. hand-outs, sixty years old: 'Before the Great War the Post Office had no system of training its employees. The new recruits were expected to pick up their jobs by watching others at work. This was the cause of much delay and interference with efficient staff perpetually interrupted by helping the beginner out of his difficulties. In 1935 the London Postal School was created. The recruits included about 75% ex-servicemen.'

I followed the course as though I were a candidate, hoping to pass the exams to become a postman. I soon found that it was not to be a walkover for anyone; certainly not for the ex-servicemen who were hoping for a secure job, perhaps their last chance.

There were 12 one-hour lectures, each packed with information on which copious notes had to be taken. For the middle-aged men the going became harder and harder. Their memories were not what they were. Success or failure depended on memory. Their final test was daunting. A pack of cards, a hundred or so with London addresses had to be sorted into their correct pigeon hole, and the margin of error was not generous.

I have an almost verbatim account of these lectures and they were made vivid by a wonderful cockney, Bill Highman, an ex-postman. His enthusiasm and vitality and his belief in the postal service was infectious. He almost had me trying in earnest, so exciting did he make the job sound. He was a gifted communicator and his desire to help these men to their last chance of security for themselves and their families was both moving and inspiring. I couldn't wait to put him on the screen. He had charisma and immense charm. Every day, as I listened to his lectures I realised how much these men were expected to learn and retain if they were to have any hope.

The London Pack became the dreaded obstacle to success: the Becher's Brook, which became higher and higher as the days went by. The knowledge that their future depended on being able to sort that pack correctly did not help. This was where the drama lay, and the suspense. That London Pack was to be the cause of sleepless nights.

Those cards would not go into the right pigeon holes. If a man has nine mistakes too many he has failed, and that is that. There is no question of giving him back those nine and mixing them up again and giving him another chance. Certain standards have been laid down and the supervisors must not depart from them. The official reasoning was that if a candidate under test made in 30 minutes 39 mistakes, in an hour he'd have made 78. In an eight hour shift 646. With 100 men working on one collection, the potential mistakes would be 64 000. Half might have to connect with the Night Mail. That meant 30 000 might be delayed and 10 per cent of these might lead to complaints: 3000 complaints that Head Office would have to try and placate. Service efficiency would be threatened. To avoid this situation the arduous sorting test was set. It was tough, very tough, and everyone knew that it was.

Hence the following that I noted in Bill Highman's sixth lecture, 'Printed Paper'. He entered the lecture hall, his usual bright and breezy self. 'Well, gents, how are you getting on with that London Pack?' Groans all round.

'What? You find them harder than the live letters in your sorting office?' (The trainees at the end of the school day go to their destined sorting office for night work and primary sorting. The Post Office puts them immediately into service even though only trainees who might not pass the test.) Bill jockeys them along.

'Do you think you earn that £2.10.0? Yes, I think you do. Are you more tired in the evening, Mr Johnson, now, than you were in your previous job?'

'Yes, I am, Mr Highman, even though I'm sitting down.'

'What were you doing before?'

'I was on road construction, working pneumatic drills, shook the daylights out of me but not as tiring as trying to get them cards in their right 'oles. I dunno. They will NOT stick.'

'They will. Don't you worry too much about them. Just keep sorting them and something inside you will tell you where to put them. It knows even if you think you don't.'

'Hope you're right, Mr Highman.'

'I am because I know. I've been through it, too. At the end of the week they'll fly in like homing pigeons, you see.'

I was moved by Bill's sympathy and understanding. He was a wonderful man, deeply sincere and committed to helping these men. I returned eagerly each day to his lectures. He was teaching me the art of communication, and rereading these lectures after all this time I am astounded by the amount of information that the men were expected to absorb in three weeks. When it came to their vital test, the strain proved too much for many and they were unable to do themselves justice.

*

My three weeks were up and I went back to Bennett Park Road to sort out my notes and write a report and a suggested outline for a film on the Postal School. I was asked to develop this into a script. This I did and the film would have run for about half an hour: a little longer than *Night Mail*. It was fully developed and dialogued.

There were a few lines of commentary to explain that every year 50 000 men returned to civilian life from the armed forces. The National Association for the Employment of Ex-servicemen did its best, but many were left to face unemployment. The Post Office annually absorbed 4000 of them so competition for this last chance of permanent and pensionable employment was very keen.

I followed four men through the course, observed the effect of the increasing strain on them and their families as the final test drew near: that dreaded test of the London Pack. Get it wrong and your family will suffer. I have lifted a few scenes from the script that I wrote 56 years ago, for they indicate all too clearly what was expected of these candidates.

SCENE 12

The men are sitting at their sorting bay. Their instructor, BILL HIGHMAN, *is walking about casually, throwing odd remarks to the men.*

HIGHMAN: Just take ten at a time, Gents, it's easier that way. You'll learn them all right. Just stick at them and they'll stick to you. And if you don't know London, now's your chance to learn.

MACAULAY, an ex-serviceman and established as having been unemployed. The job will mean more to him than the others. It is his last chance, perhaps, of a permanent pensionable job.

MACAULAY: I didn't know a postman was in for this packet.

He turns to his neighbour, Bert, who is gazing down at his cards constantly referring to the back of them for the answer.

Packet . . . you've said it.

He turns to his neighbour.

Ever heard of any of these places, Cock?

NEIGHBOUR: No. Been abroad 14 years. Could tell you something about Shanghai all right.

BERT: Bet you could, an' all (*turns over more cards*). Thank Gawd they put the answers on the back. Who the 'ell's ever heard of Busby Mews . . .

Fade out

Fade in

SCENE 13

The interior of BERT JOHNSON*'s house. He is sitting at table, having his high tea. His wife, by the hearth, filling the tea pot from the kettle, on the hob. She tries to lift his spirits.*

WIFE: You'll soon get into it Bert, I'm sure you will.

BERT: Do you know where Arnos Grove is?

WIFE: No.

BERT: Or Fetter Lane, or Broad Street or Roman Bath Street?

WIFE: Can't say I do.

BERT: Why the hell should you, but I gotter and about 500 more in London alone. After that we start on the whole blinkin' country . . . Gotter know it like me own back garden . . . Three weeks, that's all we got.

WIFE (*coming to table*): Like going to school again.

BERT: Worse . . . Far worse; could learn in them days.

Fade out

SCENE 22

MACAULAY*'s home. He is sitting at his table in his shirt sleeves. He is studying a list of names in front of him. His wife sits opposite, knitting a pair of baby's socks. He repeats some names and their districts under his breath and then hands the list to his wife.*

MACAULAY: All right, luv, hear me now, will you?

WIFE (*puts down knitting*): What, any of these?

MACAULAY: Yes, some of the muddling ones in the London lot.

WIFE: Kensington?

MACAULAY: W.8.

WIFE: Kennington?

MACAULAY (*hesitates, looking to the ceiling*): Wait a minute . . . S.E.11, isn't it?

WIFE (*smiling encouragingly*): Yes, well done. Grosvenor Square?

MACAULAY: W.1.

WIFE: No, Joe, that's wrong, it's in . . . (*As she looks down the list of*

answers a child starts to cry off scene and she leaves. Mac reaches forward for the check list and with a sigh starts again.)
Cut to

SCENE 23

Interior of BERT JOHNSON'*s house. Camera focuses on a mass of crockery which litters the floor. It pans to Bert who is sitting at the kitchen dresser which he has converted into a temporary sorting bay. He is sorting up the cards, quickly and confidently. He comes to one he is not so certain about.*

BERT: (*talking to himself*): Jermyn Street. (*Bangs down the card for inspiration.*) All Piccadilly W.1 except Jermyn Street and Duke Street which are S.W.1.

He bangs the card and picks up the next.

BERT: Edgware Road. W.2. All turnings off are W.2. Except . . . *He hears the latch key and his wife returning. He hears her voice off scene.*

WIFE: Oh dear . . .

BERT: Don't worry. Don't worry. Clear it all up in a tick. Hang on a minute . . . All turnings off Edgware road are W.2 except Fawcett, Harrowby and Stourcliffe Streets which are W.1.

He turns to his wife, pleased as punch.

BERT: What about that?

WIFE (*has to smile*): Worth the mess, I s'pose.

BERT: That old dresser really is coming into its own. About time too.

As the film develops, the tension gets to Bert and Macaulay. Both fail the test and it is painful to see their confidence draining away as they hold that fatal London Pack. The more they hesitate the worse things become. One bleeds for them.

Bill tries to persuade the supervisor to give them another chance; give them a dummy run to remove the tension from the older men. He is convinced that they know their work. They have deserved another chance . . . Their future depends on it. For several agonising moments the supervisor is undecided. But his liking and respect for

Highman and his dedicated work persuades him. He agrees and now Highman sets the scene for the two failed candidates. There is considerable suspense as the two pick up that pack and start to sort it. Very different this time. The occasional hesitation but the puckered brows are no longer so evident. The tension is lifted from them and they are able to do themselves justice, and then the dreaded count.

The supervisor appears. The faulty cards start to pile up beside each candidate. They are allowed 18 for a pass. Here were the ingredients for an intense climax of the most honest kind. Nothing to be faked. Nothing to be contrived. This was day-to-day drama, going on under our noses, but none of us knew anything about it: that a Postal School which provided us with one of the finest postal services in the world even existed. Grierson again: 'Do we appreciate the postman? Of course not.' No, sir, because we haven't been given a chance. Now I'd put that right.

Our two candidates are within the margin of permitted errors. They have passed and I for one was thrilled. Everyone liked the script and appreciated the research that had gone into it. But the film was never made. No reason was given. Perhaps my sympathies were too heavily on the side of the ex-service trainee and the Post Office top brass felt that they were portrayed as heartless employers, exploiting the under-privileged which, of course, they were. I let the facts speak for themselves, and if they produced a record unfavourable to those in power, it was easy for them to make sure that nobody heard it. It was a blow, for I so wanted to put Bill Highman on the screen. He was star material and one of the finest men I have ever met. He taught me a great deal. Use of voice, for one thing, and how to handle people, another. He and Harry Watt were splendid models to copy. And so, my first real script, in which I had great confidence, was still-born. One of the knocks to which this profession is heir.

(A side note. I could not remember the address of the Postal School. I phoned H.Q. London. P.R. talked to someone who had been in that department of the Post Office since 1971. He had never heard of the London Postal School. He told me new recruits are trained in their local sorting offices, just as Bill Highman was back in the 1920s. Time marches on? 17.12.94.)

Licking my wounds at the wasted time spent on the Postal School, the sea conveniently decided to break through on the Norfolk coast at a place called Horsey. I was sent off to film the incident. Whether there was a film to be made of it was questionable, but mine was not to reason why! Off I went with one of the unit's three permanent cameramen, Freddie Gamage, one of the grandest blokes, like Chick Fowle. We were still very raw but were on safe ground filming the sea breaking through the sea wall of sand dunes and sand-bagging the gap, and postmen rowing across flooded fields with farm equipment poking through the floor water. But invention on my part was sadly lacking. I should have been much more imaginative, thought up all sorts of little incidents to have brought the subject fully alive. But one does not become a fully fledged reporter overnight any more than a switchboard operator. Growing pains produce inevitable mistakes and it was by means of them that we were enabled to learn, all too slowly, perhaps.

Then came another ember for me to pick out of the fire. Harry Watt had started a film whose working title was not much more gripping than the 'A.G.D.' of *Big Money*. This one was *Health in Industry* and Humphrey Jennings had shot the opening sequence with the camera roaming over the famous London landmark, the Waterloo shot tower which had produced ammunition against Napoleon in the great Battle of Waterloo. Surely that should have preserved it for us all, but no, it had to go for some impermanent something or other.

Health in Industry, later known as *Men in Danger*, was shown at the New York World Fair, had a wonderful score by Brian Easdale, later to provide one for *The Red Shoes*. The film dealt with the four most dangerous industrial diseases: silicosis, which would take us down the coal mines; mule spinner's cancer, the cotton mills of Yorkshire and Lancashire; anthrax, the disinfecting plant for all imported skins and fleeces, particularly from Persia; and finally, asbestosis, the building sites and processing plants. Asbestosis, a name to be conjured with today, particularly by some unhappy

Lloyd's names, and yet in 1938 it was recognised as a most dangerous material and an industrial hazard so that when one hears today that recent users of this dangerous material were ignorant of its dangers, they are lying. Even before 1938 there were stringent Home Office guidelines that those handling asbestos must be provided with masks and their workplace installed with powerful suction air ducts. If any plant failed the Home Office inspectorate, heavy fines could be imposed. But, presumably, the old adage was still applied—'Where there's muck, there's brass'. Not surprisingly, but nonetheless sadly, many members of the unfortunate Lloyd's syndicates involved in underwriting the dangers of using this substance are now facing terrifying losses for the mishandling of asbestos.

Having touched on the medical dangers of various industries, we then dealt with the physical dangers: workshop accidents—how machines were fitted with guards and protective bars and barriers. In order to emphasise how important these guards were against revolving cog wheels, driving belts, pressing machines and the like, it was necessary to stage an accident to drive home the point. But how? Chick Fowle and I found ourselves in the Great Western Railway works at Swindon. We might have been there for a remake of *Metropolis*, for here were housed mammoth lathes, gouging out inch-thick slices of steel as they carved the great driving wheels of future locomotives. But no idea of how to stage an accident came to us, and yet with these monolithic monsters of machinery, surely it must have been the ideal setting. But they were not toys and, before one knew it, in trying to fake an accident one could create a real one. So, this was my first test as to whether I could use the medium properly and imaginatively to create the required illusion without danger to anyone. This problem haunted me for days. Eisenstein was to solve it for me.

Somehow or other John Grierson was able to get copies of some of the great works of Pudovkin and other Russian masters. These wonderful shows happened perhaps once a month in the Soho Square Theatre—not only Russian but American. I was puzzling how to stage 'my accident', and no nearer to solving it.

Grierson that night was showing *Potemkin*, Eisenstein's master-piece. The famous sequence of the Cossack's massacre on the Odessa steps was a revelation—the supreme example of montage. It taught me how to try and approach this accident that I had to stage. A series of close shots which on their own meant nothing but when joined together, like a resolved jigsaw puzzle, presented a coherent picture, a physical happening, or rather an impression of it. A kaleidoscope gives a series of ever-changing patterns of abstraction. Abstract because none bears any relation to another. Montage, on the other hand, is the very reverse. Each fragment of visual is a logical progression from its predecessor. Consequently, with this and Odessa steps in mind, Chick and I found ourselves in a massive engineering works somewhere. It was a hot-house of turning lathes, overhead driving shafts and driving belts down to the gearing of the turning lathes. I saw a machinist lean over his lathe to change its speed by shifting the driving belt on to a larger flange of the driving wheel. Suppose the button of his shirt cuff had come off and he hadn't noticed. His cuff would float about. It could catch under the belt and tangle around the driving wheel. His shirt would be pulled in and his arm with it, and finally himself. A nasty thought, but broken down into the Odessa steps it would be possible to shoot. It might take a dozen or so snippets of close-up shots, but the impression might be achieved of a very nasty accident. I suggested this to Chick and he thought that we could make it work.

We approached the machinist and told him our problem and how we thought that he could help us resolve it. Would he be willing? He was delighted. He removed the button from his shirt so that his cuff hung loosely. Then we started a series of our close montage shots.

1   His arm moves over to gear shift.
2   Driving belt whirling around flange of gear wheel.
3   His foot moves on to a spot of oil and slips.
4   Shirt cuff. Very close shot. Catches under belt.
5   Agonised face of machinist flashing past camera.

6 Both feet lifted off ground.
7 Torn shirt sleeve whirled around driving shaft above.
8 Alarm bell ringing.
9 Power switch turned off.
10 Silence as all machines stop.
11 Machinist slumped over lathe.

By the time all those shots had been strung together and Jack Lee, the elder brother of Laurie, had recorded for me his most blood-curdling scream, Chick and I had concocted a very nasty accident indeed. Thank you, Mr Eisenstein, for helping me to use montage in an emergency. My belated thanks, now I come to think about it, to dear old Jack Lee. His 'blood-curdler' could not have been bettered by Olivier. I doubt whether his lordship could have done as well.

Then to the cotton mills of Huddersfield for mule spinner's cancer. Middle-aged and bare-footed women minding the looms. Shoes of any kind were dangerous as the floors were slippery from the minute globules of oil thrown from the looms. The temperature was fetid and the sweat shone on the women's faces as they paced up and down feeding the looms, spinning new thread from fully charged cones on to the retreating thread of the emptied one. Deft fingers spun the thread into a join, skills handed down from generation to generation. These wonderful women, their faces tranquil in the acceptance that this was their lot and they had better make the best of it.

Having dealt with health and accident hazards, we touched on mental hazards: the psychological problems induced by boredom and the endless repetition of mindless movements required by the conveyor belts of industry, a problem so brilliantly satirised by Charlie Chaplin in *Modern Times*.

Peak Freans, the biscuit people in south-east London, hoped to alleviate boredom in their factory by encouraging singing to piped music. Unilever at Port Sunlight provided splendid recreational facilities, as did Boots, and there was some reason for us visiting John Players' cigarette factory in Nottingham. I've forgotten what it was but I do remember seeing a million or so cigarettes being made as the manager showed us round the plant. As we were leaving I took out my packet of Players and offered him one. He took it and I lit it for him. Not even a box of matches did he offer us, frightened that we might think he was bribing us, perhaps.

Finally we heard that the deepest pit in the Yorkshire coal field, Manvers Main Colliery in Doncaster, had started a school for fourteen-year-old boys who wished to follow their elders and become miners. The idea was to give them practical experience of where the dangers lay and how to avoid them. We heard, too, that a mining inspector, a Mister Johns, lectured them in a classroom hewn out of the rock along the main gallery or road in the mine. The thought of a classroom being a mile underground with fourteen-year-olds, straight out of school, was too good to miss. We had to film it. So Chick Fowle, Frank Brice, our one and only chief electrician and I set off for Yorkshire in Chick's large Armstrong. We all three squeezed in front. We had to, for Chick needed two 2k lamps and Frank as much cable as the car would take, for who knew where the nearest power point might be.

We arrived at Manvers Main Colliery. The manager gave us all possible help. Down we went with all our clobber. Sure enough, there was the classroom with a blackboard and 14 attentive little faces, smudged already with coal dust from their class in the demonstration gallery. What children they were: too young to be submerged into such a setting, with no option but to spend their working life in the dark. Yet their eager faces betrayed no fear or doubt. Chick made some wonderful studies of their photogenic faces. Given a scrub and brush up, a red cassock, white surplice and ruff they could have swapped places with the choristers of King's for its annual carol service. But, their future was to be in the dark, below ground where stamina and fortitude must replace perfect pitch.

As we could not take sound equipment down the pit, we filmed the training in the demonstration gallery—danger of moving trucks and so on—and laid the sound on afterwards. Mr Johns' lecture caused problems. We took close shots of the attentive faces of the boys; long shots from the back of the classroom, with the boys' backs to camera in the foreground, and that was that. Mr Johns then came to London for a couple of nights and came down to Blackheath where the Jacob brothers had knocked up a copy of the classroom. Inspector Johns gave his lecture most convincingly, cross-cut with these intent faces of the youngsters, the future generation of miners, which gave me a very human sequence on which to end the film. I shall never forget the faces of those lads, and Chick Fowle photographed them brilliantly.

I am not proud of *Men in Danger*, but as a rescue job it had one or two moments: a few sparks, perhaps, from that damp squib that I'd inherited.

*

Spring 1939. I have been assigned to make a film on the Post Office's cable ship, the *Monarch*. She was moored in the Thames, off the jetty at Charlton, a few miles below Greenwich. Moored alongside her was a Thames barge. The *Monarch* was taking on telephone cable whose diameter was perhaps two to two-and-a-half inches. Miles of the stuff had been carefully wound into the barge, which was now slowly disgorging its boa-constricting cargo, foot by hard-earned foot, into the belly of the cable ship. This process was done with the same care as the long line, with its baited hooks.

The cable snaked its way up through the huge wheel set into the bows of the *Monarch*, before being fed through winches along the deck, to make sure that no kinks could be fed down into the circular hold. There, there were twenty to thirty men, each responsible for handling his small section of cable as it was fed through from the upper deck. Each foot must be tucked up against its neighbour, the preceding coil. Just as the grooves in an old 78 gramophone record started from the outer rim and wound their way into the centre, so did the coils of this marine cable. There would be many layers to be laid on top of each other.

The concentration given by these men to this process was intense. Their future safety depended on the precision with which it was carried out. Every man knew that when the unwinding began, perhaps in a heavy sea, if the cable developed a kink, the kink could soon become a tangle and the men in the hold would be in mortal danger, caught in the constricting coils. They knew that the product by which they made their living, if not treated with the utmost respect, could kill them. No man took his eyes off that cable as it weaved its way down. He took his section and moulded it quickly into its alloted space, jammed tight against its neighbour.

Freddie Gamage photographed this sequence beautifully. The faces of those men! Each had its story to tell, and here was the fascination of this kind of filming, getting under the skin of a nation and into its flesh and blood. Commercial cinema can never do this. The same repertory of stars and supporting players and the same crowd artists. The people of a country, where are they? Nowhere. Not any more, now that drama documentary is dead.

We saw the rushes of the cable loading the next day with Alberto Cavalcanti. There was something creepily fascinating in seeing this monstrous serpent uncoiling from the barge and slithering into the bowels of the ship, not much bigger than a millionaire's large motor yacht. Cavalcanti said: 'Who would have thought a few miles of cable being loaded aboard could be so visual?' Gamage and I took heart from this. But, just as Horsey Mail had warned me, he and I were once more on a newsreel job. We would be unable to give any shape to the subject, only grab what we could and hope that something might come of it. No chance of being able to shape it into a dramatic form, building to a climax, unless one happened to occur naturally, which was most unlikely. These men were far too experienced to allow an accident to occur in the hold. We would merely refilm, as it were, the reverse process of what we had already done. Not a very cheerful prospect.

A week or so later, the *Monarch* was ready to leave. Fred Gamboy, as I called him, Jack Lee and myself boarded her to film the laying of her cable between the Isle of Islay and the mainland off the west coast of Scotland. This meant half a tour round the island. Leaving the Thames estuary, turn right at Margate, right again off Dungeness and keep going, more or less, to Land's End, right again and keep straight on, up the Irish Channel. Not exactly a taxi ride to Selfridges, and a sea cruise of that sort ought to have been a privilege, a rare treat, but we weren't on holiday, nor out to make a travelogue. Pretty shots of the Naval College at Greenwich wouldn't help us one bit. Fine for the tourist office but this trip was supposed to be for the Post Office.

We up anchored and slowly made our way down the Thames. Sure enough, the Naval College looked beautiful, and there, above, was the Greenwich Observatory. We resisted the temptation to start shooting for the sake of shooting. Here lay the problem; we had no story to tell, only a process to film, and as the process had no natural narrative shape, we were in trouble. In my bones I had sensed this. I knew that the only tension that lay ahead was when we came to unwind that cable. I knew, too, that I couldn't create a crisis, a climax by a kink in the cable. If it became tangled even for a second or two, heaven knows what disaster might happen. Obviously it would unwind as easily as cotton off the reel. There was no sound equipment: no chance of dialogue scenes; of getting to know the men, their background and their problems so that the audience might begin to feel part of the ship's company. Before long, we three suffered an awful feeling of guilt that inactivity breeds. Very soon we used up all the visual ingredients of shipboard life, and from a film man's point of view they were thin on the ground.

There is no question but that the life on the ocean wave has, does and will continue to bring forth characters of sterling quality. But it soon became apparent that unless one is a member of the crew with whatever responsibilities put on you, be you captain or ordinary seaman, life aboard was a deadly dull business unless part of the routine of four hours on and eight off. So, we three odd-bods were hard put to occupy ourselves, wondering what to film until that cable unwound itself.

We were not, after all, on a square rigger, with billowing sails, men running up the ratlines, reefing and unreefing, whilst below green foaming waves broke amidships and filled the scuppers. No such luck, and no Captain Bligh to keel haul a mutinous dog; no Fletcher Christian to stir the troublesome mutineers. No, only a distant smudge of a coastline that might have been Brighton by now, or who knows—Southampton? We shot the bows cleaving through very calm waters, we shot from the crow's nest (might come in handy). We shot the stern, the wake, the log whirling, the gulls permanently stationed as they hovered above, the steward emptying his slops, the officer of the watch pacing, the captain (we had to have him) pacing the bridge—we even had a boatswain's seat suspended from the cable winch, overhanging the bows, so that we saw the *Monarch* head on. Short of starting to shoot sideways, there was nothing left until that cable started to unwind, and we hadn't even rounded Land's End. This was newsreel shooting at its worst, for there was no news. This sort of snap shooting can never amount to anything, and so it proved. The unwinding of the cable went very smoothly. No kinks, no pile up, no problems of any kind. The end of the cable was pulled ashore and slotted into an aperture in a small concrete cable hut above the sea line, and that was that. The damp squib was made secure and we beat our retreat in a long boat, rowing back to the *Monarch*.

I had repeated what my master, John Grierson, had done years before in his Port of London Authority attempt. We had both produced several cans of unuseable film, and for the same reason— no shape.

8

The G.P.O. becomes the
Crown Film Unit

'I have to tell you now that we have received no such communication from Herr Hitler and consequently, from 11.00 am this morning, this nation is at war with Germany. You can imagine how I must be feeling after all my strivings for peace . . .' To hell with his feelings. How dared he lumber us with them! What arrogance and insensitivity. Who gave a damn how he felt when every family in the land knew that it was threatened, that it must face pain and tragedy for years to come, until peace returned to a world that could never be the same again.

Martin Boyd, the Australian novelist, was staying with us at Newlands. Neither of us had a gas mask so we walked down Eltham High Street to the Civil Defence Unit. We were each given a ridiculous cardboard box which might have contained anything. A looped length of string enabled them to be carried from the shoulder and we made for home. Entering the 'in and out' driveway, my sister Joss opened the front door and from the top step greeted us with her finest example of British sang froid. 'I'm afraid we're at war.' And then the air raid warning sounded, a banshee wail if ever there was. Would London be flattened in the next hour or so? I climbed the front steps and wondered how many times I'd done so since Joss and I returned from a visit to an uncle to find the blind and curtains drawn and to be told of Kit's death. None of us had ever got over it and never would. Maybe in the near future, an hour or so, I would be reunited with him.

We went inside to the drawing room and listened to the B.B.C., which was giving half-hourly bulletins. The R.A.F. had sent out a raid on the Kiel Canal, almost immediately after war was declared—a bellicose gesture if nothing else. Hibberd, the chief announcer and news reader, was his cool Edwardian England self, oozing King's English with every vowel and relishing them, and then the 'All clear' went, half an hour after that first siren sounded. How many thousand times were we to hear it? We were all stunned and sat around the radio, as though expecting some miracle announcement that would put an end to this nightmare. We realised that we were being idiotic and switched it off.

'I have in my hand a piece of paper which means peace in our time.' How we had lapped that up. The nation went mad with joy and now it was at war. There had been an air raid. London had not been flattened. We were still alive.

I looked out of the window on to the back garden. It looked painfully beautiful in contrast to a world that had suddenly become ugly. Our garden, so full of happy memories. The beautiful ash tree at the bottom of the lawn, whose largest branch still carried our childhood swing and whose trunk bore our initials, carved when we were children. They had become blurred but were still distinguishable. Painful nostalgia was interrupted by Hughes, our dear old butler, a survivor of the First World War's Gallipoli campaign. He announced that lunch was served. In we trooped to the dining room. We still had three lodgers. A fat old colonel, something to do with munitions at Woolwich arsenal, and the purser and his wife from 'the Shop' (the Military Academy), also at Woolwich, a Mr and Mrs Grigg. Hardly a happy group, almost lost in this large Victorian room with its lengthy dining table. Heaven knows what we all ate. I don't remember that anyone suffered from a loss of appetite and, in the normal way, coffee was served in the drawing room. The first three hours of the Second World War were over.

*

And now what? Was there a rush to the colours from the ex-messenger boy of the G.P.O. Film Unit? There was not. I was far from being imbued with nationalistic fervour to take the King's shilling. Far from it. I wanted the entire cabinet of the government courtmartialled. I was seething. From the time that Ramsay

MacDonald and Baldwin had formed the National Government, its foreign policy had been one of appeasement. Appeasement of Japan after the invasion of Manchuria and the betrayal of the League of Nations and the speeches of the then Foreign Secretary Sir John Simon are proof of this betrayal and are there for all to see. They are shameful and make one blush for Britain. And what truth was there that Montague Norman, the Governor of the Bank of England, had contributed to the funds of the Nazi Party, looked on as the first line of defence against the menace of communism?

The only education that I had had was gleaned from Grierson's Film Unit, and nobody knows better than I that a little knowledge is a dangerous thing. But, I had listened to men who were not fools, whose minds had been tested and proved in the highest seats of learning that this country has to offer, and they had earned the highest academic honours. They had proved that they could think and analyse a problem. The unit may not have prepared me for academic honours but it had taught me to open my eyes and see beyond the headlines. 'Don't immediately trust what you read. Question everything', Basil Wright said to me in my salad days. Yes Sir, and I had tried to do that. Victor Gollancz's Left Book Club had me questioning and pondering and doubting practically everything, and the Hoare–Laval pact which almost told Mussolini to help himself to Abyssinia was the final confirmation that total mistrust was justified.

Gollancz's publications *Inquest on Peace* and *The Private Manufacture of Armaments* are the lamentations of the twentieth century. Nothing has changed. The same filthy trade which allowed British-made barbed wire to be sold to Germany in the First World War through agents in Switzerland to crucify our men on the Somme still goes on. Except that now children are being killed and maimed throughout the world by British-exported land mines. If Guy Fawkes had been around in 1939 I might have given him more than an ear, or if the Nurenberg War Crimes Trial had been preceded by an inquiry into the motives behind the British Government's policy of appeasement since the Sino–Japanese war in 1931, some very awkward questions would have been asked. Had their mistakes been made in all innocence? Now the chicks had come home to roost. The bill for their blunders had to be paid, but not, of course, by members of government—they will be the last to feel any pinch—but by the innocent sheep who were no longer safely to graze. Was it to be the Somme and Paschendael over again for them as it had been for their fathers and uncles? They, at least, died in the belief that they were in a war to end war. Their sacrifice, they were told, was justified: noble! They have been betrayed.

Back to Blackheath, and for a time we were flotsam and jetsam. Clearly, there was no cause for us to make films about the Post Office. Grierson was no longer with us. He had gone to Canada to open the Canadian Film Board. Harry Watt and Cavalcanti were now in charge. We were still a government film unit but not yet accountable to any department. Soon the Ministry of Information came into being and we were automatically attached to it, and they hadn't the slightest idea what on earth to do with us. So Cavalcanti and Watt decided that we would record, so far as we were able, the day-to-day observations of England reacting to war: the filling of sandbags in the London parks; the new air raid wardens collecting their tin helmets, helping police direct traffic; the arrival of the balloon barrage; sandbagging and reinforcing hospital wards; children being evacuated and settling down in the country; girls in uniform looking longingly at glamorous evening dresses in shop windows. A snippet here and little happening there—this became *The First Days*, now a valuable visual diary of those early weeks of war.

We tried to get to France to cover the doings of the B.E.F., but the War Office would have none of us, even though they had not yet formed their own film unit. There had been a raid on the Forth Bridge and Harry Watt made a film on the barrage balloons moving up to protect it. This was called Squadron 992. Now we were called the Crown Film Unit.

One afternoon in late September I was walking up Bennett Park Road to assemble material that we had shot the previous day. I became aware of an ominous droning sound with an unpleasant throb to it. We hadn't heard that combination of sounds before,

and then the moaning whine of the air raid warning drowned it. I
went into the middle of the road for a clearer view and looked up
into the cloudless sky. A shoal of minnows, in tight formation,
little pin pricks of silver as the sun shimmered on them, was approaching from the south east, 20 to 30 thousand feet up, perhaps,
and then smaller minnows started to dart in amongst the shoal. The
droning, with its pulsating throb, was getting louder as one of the
smaller minnows dropped away, and as it fell flames burst from it,
and then a small white seed, which opened into a thistledown,
gently descending.

The throbbing and droning grew louder, counterpointed by the
'rat a tat tat' of machine guns. They were directly overhead now
and they looked beautiful, just as the R 101 had looked beautiful as
it floated over Newlands, on its last, ill-fated flight, before crashing
in Beauvais. Our three cameramen were in London. Stuart Mac-
Allister from the Edinburgh Academy, who was to edit most of
Humphrey Jennings' films as well as the famous *London Can Take It*,
was at the studio. There was a Bell and Howell camera also, with
film. Together we dug it out and once more I found myself loading
a thousand-foot magazine, something that I had not done since
those two fraught weeks at Welwyn, but once learnt never forgotten, I hoped, and so it was. We had no trouble loading the
camera—very similar to loading a projector. There was no battery
so I would have to hand crank as in Paramount's News, 'The Eyes
and Ears of the World'. Neither Mac nor I had driving licences, so
Gordon Hales said he'd act as our chauffeur. Gordon had studied
optics and had recently joined us. He was to edit Charlie Chaplin's
last film.

We drove across Blackheath and into Greenwich Park. We set
up the camera close to the Observatory and looked down on
London. To the left, St Paul's, serene as ever. Canaletto could have
been painting it, so calm and peaceful was everything. To the right
it was a different story. A massive range of mountains had suddenly
heaved its way through the earth's crust in London's dockland.
Dense smoke as of a gushing oil-well was climbing higher and
higher, and soon the base became suffused with red as the intensity

of flame increased by the minute. The clanging of fire engine bells was just audible. I cranked the camera handle at the same speed as the organ grinders of my childhood. There was nothing more we could do here. We had recorded this appalling scene which had taken the Luftwaffe perhaps less than half an hour to create. We returned to the studio to await nightfall.

When it came, we put on our tin helmets for the first time and felt ridiculous. Gordon drove us down to Charlton. There was a jetty there. From it I had filmed the *Monarch* loading cable, and if we could get to the end of it we would have a wonderful camera position.

As we drove down towards the river, heat waves came up to greet us. Cranes were red hot, some turning white and starting to buckle like boxers receiving too much punishment. The jetty was treacherous with wet weed as the tide receded. We took our time to get the camera fixed, making sure that the tripod's legs, with their metal toes, were biting into the surface below the weed. The end of the jetty had put us well into the stream. We waited a bit, wondering where to point the camera. It didn't seem to matter. Wherever we pointed it was flaming hell.

Strangely enough, we were quite oblivious to the bombs which were coming down. We were too worried about the camera to think about them. They sounded like expensive rockets, the star turns that always brought Guy Fawkes night to an end but, of course, they were going in the opposite direction.

'We don't have to worry about the stop, Mac; wide open obviously', I remember saying, and there was enough light from the fires to check that I was wide open and on infinity. 'Might as well start downstream. Tell me if you think I'm cranking about the right speed.'

'Aye, that'll do fine. Keep at that.' So, I kept at that and remembered the organ grinder who always came into North Park. He wore his campaign medals, Pip, Squeak and Wilfred, and he'd lost a leg. I must have been cranking about ten seconds when a factory, bang centre screen, caught fire. It didn't only catch fire, it sent a ball of fire which seemed to hover like a balloon above the roof of the place. Night retreated as the intensity of flame became whiter and whiter. It was now as light as day. The film would be hopelessly over-exposed but I couldn't do anything about that. All I could do was to keep turning. I had heard about the famous Silvertown Explosion in the First World War, on Thameside, and thought that the same sort of thing might be happening. We watched, spellbound. Slowly, the intensity of light diminished and when night returned I stopped cranking.

'That was some shot', Mac said in his glorious laconic way, and I can still hear his lovely accent which the years cannot extinguish. He was to put the master stroke into many of Humphrey's films. We panned and looked upstream. Everything was on fire. We turned a few feet, but Guy Fawkes had left, and so did we.

We were back on Blackheath, and I asked Gordon Hales to take us back to Greenwich Park as I thought that it would be interesting to take a comparative shot from the same set-up of the afternoon. We parked the car and walked across the heath to discover that the park gates were closed. I'd forgotten that. Too bad. We went back to the car. Searchlights were stabbing the sky and the ack-ack was cracking away as a bomber was caught in convergent beams.

'I'm sorry, Pat; I've lost the keys', said Gordon as though announcing that tea was ready.

'You can't have.'

'Sadly, I have.' Gordon was a dear chap, and was of a professorial turn of mind, phrase and bearing.

'But you only had them a minute ago.'

'That does not guarantee that I have them now.' There was logic in his reply so I did not persist. We helped him turn his pockets out once more. He was right. No keys. The second fire of London was blazing away. The ack-ack was blazing away. The searchlights were doing their best, and it was, in spite of all that, a dark night. There was no moon. Trust the Germans to have thought of that. No moon on their side. On our side there was nothing for it but for the three of us to go on our hands and knees and scrabble about on Blackheath, our fingers raking the turf.

There was nothing else we could do. So we did it. Creepy

crawlies. Down we went, searching for an ignition key on the first night of the Blitz on London. The humour of the situation was not evident at that time, as we crawled round the car in ever widening circles.

'Are you chaps all right?' It was nice of whoever it was to ask because, in the same circumstances, I think that I'd have run a mile.

'We're O.K., thanks. Just lost the car key, that's all.' Blow me, if the chap didn't get down on his hands and knees and start forking his fingers into the heath. He went so far as to strike a match and was promptly told to 'Put out that light!' by a less cooperative passer-by. As London was alight, a match, even a Swan Vestas, was not likely to aid the enemy to any remarkable extent. But he was a patriot, no doubt about that.

We found the key. Mac found it: thirty yards or so from the car. What combing! What a triumph on such a night! We thanked our new-found friend for his kind help and returned to the studio.

We learnt later, when we saw the rushes the next day, that it was the sugar vats of the Tate and Lyle warehouse that had caught fire. It was considerate of them to have waited for our arrival, for there is no doubt they did give us a most spectacular performance. Never to be repeated, I do hope. Harry Watt, I have to admit, promptly pinched it and tacked it on to the start of the film he was making on Dover. What it had to do with Dover, I have never been able to work out. It was spectacular enough, he must have thought, to earn its place anywhere. All in a good cause, of course.

*

'The test of a great fighter is whether he can get up after he's been knocked down. London does this, every day.' So said the American journalist Quentin Reynolds in a commentary he wrote for a film which was the result of our round-the-clock filming during the early days of the London Blitz. Quite by chance it became an important film thanks to Quentin Reynolds, whose reading public in the States was enormous and whose contacts with the White House of greater importance. It was one of those lucky coincidences that Harry Watt met him in the French Pub of Soho, if I remember correctly, and was immediately struck by Quentin's voice, which was of the bassest of basses with an enticing drawl. Being Harry, he made himself known and the two struck up an immediate accord. Quentin was interested to learn about the Crown Film Unit and that it had considerable footage, some quite dramatic, of the Blitz. Several rounds later it was arranged that Quentin would see this material, and if he liked it he would not only write a commentary but speak it.

This was, perhaps, Harry's greatest achievement: far more important on the successful progress of the war than his *Target for Tonight*. He had gained direct access to the eyes and ears of the President. Quentin was shortly to leave for the States and promised Harry that if we could get the film finished in time, he would take a copy with him and show it to President Roosevelt, who was pro-British and fighting hard against the isolationism of the States and struggling, on Churchill's behalf, to get the Lend-Lease scheme through Congress.

Thanks to Stewart MacAllister, who worked night and day, grabbing a few hours of sleep on the studio couch, *London Can Take It* was put together in just over a week. It was Mac's finest hour, following close on Harry's. Quentin took the film with him and showed it to President Roosevelt, who made sure that certain members of Congress were also there. It certainly could not have done our cause any harm.

*

During the last three months of 1940 I was assigned to make a film on the workings of the emergency hospital system. It was not going to set the Thames on fire.

Health in War, as the film was called, was a chore, but it had to be done. I gave it the semblance of a story line so there was some shape to it which saved it from being just a boring lecture. There was a beautifully photographed sequence by Chick of children evacuated in the country and helping to bring in the harvest to the accompaniment of Roger Quilter's Children's Suite.

We had a beautiful day in the Palladian home of the Drake family, Shardeloes, just outside Amersham, in Buckinghamshire. As we entered the long sweeping driveway which takes the eye to the mansion, we stopped, captivated by a scene of striking beauty. Thirty or forty horses of every hue were grazing on the cricket field which was surrounded by stately oaks, with the white mansion of Shardeloes in the distant background; a landscape worthy of Samuel Palmer. The horses were from Bertram Mills' circus and they were magnificent. Shardeloes had been turned into an emergency maternity hospital. There is a saying that once one has visited Amersham and stayed there for a day, the witch will make sure that you return and will never let you go. I learned of this ancient curse or whatever it is when I returned to Amersham, twenty years later, and have been living there ever since. I am determined that the witch will not have her way; I have no intention of leaving her my bones.

Health in War was a three-reeler. The authorities seemed to like it and I soon found myself once more on a medical subject. I was to film an operation to be performed by the great plastic surgeon, Sir Harold Ghillies, whose early work was performed during the First World War in hastily-built wooden-hutted wards in Sidcup, near Eltham.

It was a privilege to meet the great man. He explained the operation he was to perform. He was going to give a young girl of ten a chin. The poor child had been born deformed with no jaw bone. She had been fed through a tube in her mouth and a hole had had to be made through her teeth. She could not open her mouth with no jaw bone. We visited the child before the operation.

Her state was pitiable. Her new jaw bone had already been made from Sir Harold's designs, and this he was to fit into the girl's face. We filmed the entire process, whose details are beyond my power to describe. Two events during that operation remain clearly in my memory. Sir Harold was operating in an emergency hospital, Park Prewett, near Basingstoke. Much of the equipment had just come in from America under Lend-Lease.

During the delicate proceedings—everyone was in green, I

remember, as were the sterilised towels and sheets covering the patient—a wasp took it into its head to pay us a visit and managed to get into the theatre. Sir Harold, in the deadly hush surrounding him, broken only by his requests for instruments to the theatre sister, became aware of the intruder. For a while he took no notice of it. When, however, the wasp, attracted to the powerful overhead light and then the smell of something tasty, hovered over the lesion, Sir Harold put down his scalpel and said: 'Get rid of it'. Easier said than done, unless someone had been lucky enough to swot the thing on arrival. Anxious to obey the master's instructions, a quadrille out of *Alice in Wonderland*, choreographed by Sir Frederick Ashton, now took place. The theatre crew took up whatever came to hand, sterilised towels in the main, and like an undisciplined corps de ballet tip-toed after the invader, flicking here, there and everywhere. Flicks were flying thick and fast, masks and head caps all awry. Chick and I were tempted to join the dance but wiser counsels prevailed and we kept watch over our gear instead. 'If you can't swot it, anaesthetise it', suggested Sir Harold. The anaesthetist then joined the corps. Whether he had a spray of some sort I don't recall, only that the ether levels in the air went up and I wondered how long it would be before we were all in the same state as the patient. Happily, a lucky flick or a sniff too much and the wasp went under before we did. Sir Harold then completed the operation.

A few weeks later we filmed the child, and a pretty girl she turned out to be, happily sucking a sweet. It was decided that more of Sir Harold's work should be recorded, and though he asked for the same film crew, sadly Chick and I were now assigned to other projects.

9

A Passenger of the Ancient and Tattered Airmen

I was to prepare a film on the A.T.A. (Air Transport Auxiliary) while Chick was working for Humphrey on *Words for Battle*. The A.T.A. was known as the Ancient and Tattered Airmen, a christening given by ex-pilots of the Royal Flying Corps, many of whom were flying for the A.T.A. They were a remarkable bunch of men and women, as I was soon to discover.

In the spring of 1941, I found myself four miles west of Maidenhead, turning into a leafy country lane which was to take me to White Waltham aerodrome from which the main base of the A.T.A. operated. Here I was to meet the C.O., a D'Erlanger. He was resplendent in a specially designed uniform, cut like the R.A.F.'s, but the material was dark blue with wings of gold thread. It was not an agreeable meeting because he took an instant dislike to me and seemed to have no wish that a film should be made of his outfit. However, there wasn't much he could do to stop me. I had come on behalf of the Crown Film Unit, which had received instructions from the Ministry of Information which had received a request from the Ministry of Aircraft Production that a film on the A.T.A. would boost the morale of these civilian pilots whose work was exceedingly arduous and unknown to the public.

My initial briefing had told me that these men and women collected fighters and bombers from factories and maintenance units and then flew them to the operational aerodromes, thus saving R.A.F. pilots this chore when they were all overstretched on operational duties. Clearly, the work of the A.T.A. was of great importance. It was also very hazardous because they had to fly by viewpoint navigation only: no radio in case they interfered with the wavelengths of the R.A.F. In fine weather over a small country like Britain, duck soup. Follow the main line railway system and it will take you most of the way. Turn off left or right from the nearest big town or city and the aerodrome to be found will soon turn up. All very well in fine weather: not so funny when the cloud level is down to two hundred feet. The humblest hills become as lethal as the Himalayas. Poor Amy Johnson, forced lower and lower until visibility was so bad her only chance was to climb up and over the clouds. Easy to get up but not to get down. In trying she crashed into the Thames estuary. So, these men and women were the unrecognised heroes and heroines in a crucial stage of the war. This much I had gleaned before setting foot in White Waltham.

So, though the C.O. D'Erlanger was not, perhaps, my greatest fan, he could not stop me from coming to his aerodrome. Limpet fashion, I hung around the place, talking to everyone, soaking up the atmosphere, sizing up the characters and personalities of ground staff and pilots. Sooner or later someone took pity on me and invited me into the mess. Before too long I was accepted.

Not many days later I was being taken as a passenger on their short and long hauls, staying overnight in the homes of pilots' friends and continuing with them on the next day's flights. In a week or so I had covered the length and breadth of the U.K. and landed at most of the collecting points and a good few operational aerodromes.

The reliable Avro Anson was the taxi aircraft, piloted by a jolly chap, Ellis, who dropped the pilots off, one by one or two by two, according to the number of planes to be collected from any one factory or maintenance unit. Then Ellis, like a faithful old sheep dog, would round them up in the evening and fly them back to White Waltham.

One day, Jimmy Mollison appeared and climbed aboard the Anson to be flown to Castle Bromwich to collect a Spitfire. He was a jolly chap, too, and I enjoyed his company, though his aftershave or whatever was powerful. The Anson ponged for quite a few days. But let no one think that or get the wrong impression. If anyone so much as hinted at such a thing J.M. would have him outside and counted out in no time. Very handy indeed was Jimmy Mollison, with his mitts.

There is no doubt that even in those far-off days, the lure of the camera was powerful. Inevitably, everyone became aware that I was there to make a film, and I give the camera the credit for my being accepted and allowed into the mess. And what a wonderful collection of people I was privileged to meet. Keith Jopp, from the Royal Flying Corp (R.F.C.), had his head trepanned, left hand and one eye gone, or of very little use: souvenirs of a meeting with the Richthoven circus over the Somme, in 1916. But, he was flying Spitfires and Hurricanes from factories and maintenance units to the operational squadrons throughout Britain. I remember him telling me that he landed at Northolt, a fighter aerodrome of Spitfires, in the height of the Battle of Britain. The squadron that day had suffered heavily and morale had suffered accordingly. Poor old Keith Jopp said that he had no idea what to say to them when invited into the mess. He knew that they were feeling very low, for his own memories of the Western Front told him that. Seeing that he had 'Pip, Squeak and Wilfred' up, someone asked him about the First World War and he started to tell them a little about his experiences in the R.F.C. They listened as though he were reading to them out of the *Boy's Own Paper* or *Chums*. In some strange way it seemed to give them some sort of comforting reassurance. 'I can't think why', he said. 'Maybe because, even though I'd been a bit bashed about, I had survived and there was a chance that they would.'

During this exploratory time I was not only on the hunt for ideas of how to shape the story so that all the ingredients of the ferry pilot's job and its dangers would be fairly represented, but even more important, I wanted to find the people capable of playing in the film. Maybe I would strike lucky, as Harry Watt had been in Mousehole. There was no alternative but to hang around the place, keeping my eyes and ears open, for voices were as important as looks. Somehow or other I must find a spot for old Keith Jopp, simply to honour the memory of the R.F.C. The bar was the most likely place to find my cast. Here I could slowly get to know the pilots, hear their stories and their voices. Important to know whether they had timbre and were not monotonous, ending sentences always on the same note. It is quite extraordinary how rarely one finds people who have a natural sense of how to get the maximum range of tone and expression. In the main, people seem content with three or four notes and make do with them. So, with these provisos, like an Eskimo over his blow hole I waited, watched and listened. Who held his audience when telling a story at the bar? Could I hear him even when some distance away? Did he look you in the eye? Or were his darting to right and left, fixed somewhere in infinity over your shoulder? If a potential member of your cast doesn't look you in the eye, he or she is unlikely to enjoy having a camera pointing at them. The attraction of this kind of film making was that until the camera started to turn, like it or not, you were a one-man band. That is the way we worked at Crown. Given an assignment, off you went to research it, develop a story line and finally a master scene script. A juggling act, hunting for facts, searching for a story line and scouting for the natural talent to bring the film to life. A daunting challenge, but we were free, unencumbered by endless story conferences, accountants' considerations about box office returns, getting the right star to play or the film won't get off the ground, and all the barbed wire that prevents 'take off'. We were given creative freedom that we were never to experience again.

About my fourth or fifth day at White Waltham, I was outside, talking to a jolly fellow, a test pilot called Frank Weir. We had been watching a Wellington land, and now the pilot was approaching. He had a broad grin on his face as he recognised Frank and hailed him in a most welcoming manner. Frank introduced us and we went into the bar. Within a few minutes I knew that if I could find an acceptable story I had found my leading man. Here was my Bill Blewett in the shape of Bradbrook—Brad, to all the world. He had an amusing face, hair that stood on end, a merry twinkle in the eye and he was fun. He spoke well, had an outgoing personality and I took to him at once. He told me that he was on his way to the Vickers plant at Brooklands, in Surrey. Would I like to come? I accepted at once. The Wellington had been refuelled as he had brought it from the north somewhere for minor repairs to be carried out at the Vickers plant.

Off we went. I climbed aboard, struck by the smell of all sorts of varnishes in the aircraft—rather like a studio floor, I thought. I sat in the co-pilot's seat alongside Brad and he now told me that he must go through his catechism or the equivalent of the Lord's prayer before take-off. I remember it well: 'Hot Tempered Member of Parliament, Flaps, Gills'. H for Hydraulics; T for Trim; M for Mixture; P for Pitch (pitch of the propeller blades: fine for take-off and coarse for more thrust once airborne); F for Flaps; G for Gills around the engine, to be opened or closed to control temperature. Once this ritual was over, and the ailerons and elevators checked that they were in working order, the engines would be started. With chocks still in place and elevators in the up position to keep the tail down, the engines would be revved up to clear the jets, and we were ready for take-off.

It was a fine day. The wind was from the south-east which meant that we would have to cross the east-to-west runway, making our take-off run across meadowland. It was bumpy at the start, but as we gathered speed the bumps gradually lessened as suction slowly took us into the air. We rose over three Spitfires which were parked in the dispersal area. We were soon over Windsor Castle and I was thoroughly enjoying this airborne view of these famous tourist attractions. It wasn't long before I recognised the Byfleet banking of the famous Brooklands race track where Mike and I had seen one of the Bentley boys, Clive Dunfee, kill himself, going too fast round the bend, losing control and skidding over the top. An unhappy memory, and things didn't look too happy below as we circled over Brooklands. Smoke was pouring out of the main workshop and bomb craters peppered the runway, making it impossible to land. Brad indicated that we'd have to hop it back to White Waltham. We learnt that the Luftwaffe had paid this visit shortly after we'd taken off.

A few weeks later, I was back in earnest with a completed script and the Crown Film Unit. Chick Fowle was the cameraman, Ken

Cameron with his new R.C.A. recording van and Frank Brice the unit's electrician, always a tower of strength who had been with us on *Night Mail* and from the earliest days of the G.P.O. Film Unit. He was a true blue Cockney, a real Londoner.

I had done a careful test of Bradbrook just to confirm my hunch that he was the man to carry the film. There was no doubt that I had struck lucky. Phillip Wills, who was to become Britain's champion glider pilot, performed valiantly. Two very attractive girls suddenly appeared from their base at Hatfield: Audrey Sale-Barker who had skied for Great Britain, and Joan Hughes, five foot nothing, raven hair, pretty as a picture and before the war was over would be flying Lancasters, Stirlings and Halifaxes; a truly remarkable feat, and I imagine totally unrecognised for I never heard that she got so much as a mention. Both wonderful girls who brought a touch of glamour.

Perhaps the finest performance went to Alex Henshaw, the chief Spitfire test pilot who, at Brad's request, flew a Spitfire from Castle Bromwich and put on a superb display for us over White Waltham. Chick had the devil's own job in being able to pan the camera up sufficiently as Henshaw went into his vertical spiral climb. When Alex phoned the next day to find out whether we had all we needed, I explained the problem and he said that he would come and give us another display when we had the necessary tripod. With a free head Chick could go beyond the perpendicular, if necessary. Alex came down again and his performance was even more breathtaking. It gave a great visual highlight to the film and I have never ceased to be grateful to him for helping us out in such a generous manner.

As shooting progressed, we always had a stand-by Anson ready for us and my new-found friend Ellis would summon up his faithful Anson taxi, and Chick and I would bundle into it when a particularly dramatic formation of clouds settled over White Waltham. Up we'd go and Ellis would weave a wondrous way through the cumuli and as near to the floating elephants of barrage balloons as he dared. Chick got some wonderful effects, and when Dalrymple and Humphrey Jennings saw the rushes, I was somewhat aggrieved to learn that Humphrey had pinched the shots for title backgrounds for the film he was making *Words for Battle* spoken by Olivier. I felt justified in being very angry with Humphrey for I could not now use my own material for the film I was making. I was angry with Dalrymple, too, for having permitted this. He suggested that I raised my sights a little. I tried but have never totally forgiven Humphrey, which shows how petty I can be. Of course, it was all in a good cause and I should have been big enough to realise that, but one is bound to be possessive if there is to be pride in one's work. I still get a pang when I see shots taken from our films and tucked into T.V. productions of today. This may be all very right and proper, but not when sequences are lifted and put into other people's work. That is plagiarism.

We were now coming to the end of shooting: just as well because Bradbrook was due to leave A.T.A. to join the Atlantic ferry service to fly Liberators and other four-engined bombers in from the States. We had one major sequence still to shoot. It was an important one, leading to the climax of the film where the Witley bomber he is ferrying is spotted by a Messerschmidt 110. At the time, the only available Witley bomber was at a small aerodrome in Leicestershire called Ratcliffe. We were to film there the following day. Ken Cameron and his sound crew would drive up first thing and be ready for Chick and me, who were going to be flown there by Brad who had a twin-engined long-nosed Blenheim to ferry to Ratcliffe. It seemed an ideal arrangement. The only trouble was that the following day the weather closed in and Brad couldn't get Met clearance to take off. We waited. An hour passed. Still no clearance. Another hour passed. Mist still heavy on the ground. It was now 11.00 am. Brad was looking anxious. We were cutting things very fine. We should all have driven up by car. Had he landed us in the cart? It began to look like it and he grew more and more worried, well aware of the serious situation if we were unable to complete our shooting by the end of the day. It was now midday and three hours' shooting had been lost. At 12.30, or thereabouts, we received clearance. We hurriedly piled into the Blenheim, parked just outside on the tarmac. Two other ferry pilots came with us. Chick took up the nose position so that he could shoot through the perspex nose, and I sat just below Brad. I could see through the nose and out to my right, not that that mattered at all.

I saw Brad go through his 'Hot Tempered Member of Parliament, Flaps, Gills' catechism, heard the engines come to life, being revved to clear the jets, then chocks away and we were off in a south-easterly direction, as for Brooklands. I knew that the first hundred yards would be bumpy across the field, as they were in the Wellington, and that very soon they would decrease as we neared the moment of take-off. They should be getting less bumpy now. They weren't. A few seconds passed. We were still very bumpy indeed. No suspicion of their diminishing. Bumpety bump bump. I looked up at Brad. We didn't seem to be gaining speed as we should. I looked through the nose. Four Spitfires in the dispersal area were a good full blooded tee shot away—about 250 yards. Bumpety bump. Brad, come on. Get her off. A three iron shot away. Soon it'll only be a chip. For God's sake, Brad. NOW. I looked up at him. He was drained. He pulled the machine off the ground. We just cleared the Spits and hung on our props. Hung on them for several seconds. I thought we were going in. But that Blenheim clung to the air and we made no height for several more seconds. Mercifully we were clear of trees and over ploughed fields. Slowly, we gained height, but it had been an uncomfortably close shave. Where ignorance was bliss. Had I 'known my stuff' I would have realised that for once, Brad had slipped up on his cockpit drill, on the 'P for Pitch'. He'd taken off in coarse pitch, as though trying to drive off in top gear.

We arrived at Ratcliffe, shot the final sequence and the film was safely in the can. Brad had done me proud. He put in a splendid performance and had been of the greatest help as well as being a wonderful friend. He had added lovely touches of dialogue and his charming personality had contributed enormously, not only during the making of the film but in the result. He was a great friend. He arranged for me to share his digs in a beautiful Georgian house in Pinkney's Green, a few miles from White Waltham. Our hostess was a charming lady, a Mrs Gossett whose house and garden were straight out of *Country Life*. I am indebted to her, too, for having made me so welcome and given me the last glimpse of Edwardian England.

Sadly, dear old Brad, acting as navigator in a returning Liberator to the States, flew the aircraft into the mountains of the Isle of Arran. All were killed. My man of Arran had become my dear friend, Bradbrook. Strangely enough his story does not quite end there. It continues in the following way, though to describe it is a digression.

My Mother, since the loss of her favourite son, Kit, and her husband, had found solace in spiritualism and had occasional seances with a medium in whom she had great confidence: a Mrs Philimore of Knightsbridge Mansions, no longer standing but close to St George's Hospital. A few weeks after completing the shooting of *Ferry Pilot* my mother had arranged a seance with Mrs Philimore. When possible I would accompany her to take notes, and though not entirely convinced that I would be talking to my brother Kit and Dad, I went along.

The seance was coming to an end. Dad and Kit had made their presence known and the guide—there is always a guide for the medium, and usually an American Indian—said they would be leaving us now. Mrs Philimore was about to come out of her trance when the Indian guide came back and said there was someone who wanted to talk to Pat . . . he would try and get his name for me. Mrs Philimore stumbled on the name for a moment and then said: 'It sounds like Brad, Brad something'. 'Yes, yes', I shouted: 'Yes I know Brad. Brad, how are you?' Of all such mundane things to say. We had a cheerful chat, as though in the bar at White Waltham. Finally he said that we would win the war because our instrumentation was far ahead of the Germans'. We could see things about the enemy that he couldn't see about us. Finally I asked him whether he would like me to tell his wife that I had had this talk with him. He laughed, and it was his laugh, and said: 'Oh no. She'd think you were quite mad.' And with a final cheerful 'Cheerio', off he went. Finally, someone else wanted to say a word. Someone called Ginger. I couldn't remember knowing anyone called Ginger. 'He insists you do.' I thought for a moment, still trying to get over the mystery of talking to Brad, which shook me. The guide said: 'France'. Of course, it was dear old Ginger Corbett, Pickwick Corbett from Grenoble, shot down in the first week of the Battle of Britain. Wonderful to have made contact with him again and that in some form or another he was there.

This incident made me look at things as though I had changed a lens and was looking through the viewfinder with a different perspective. When the worldly-wise in their wisdom pronounce, as they so often do, 'that there is nothing out there', perhaps they might realise that that is all they are, worldly-wise.

I have to confess that this incident, though it remains always fresh in my memory, has not made me any better a person. I have had no great spiritual awakening, no call to the cloth and am just as frail as ever I was, spiritually speaking. But, possibly, it may have made me doubt less what may be the valuable lots in this curious rummage sale of being alive.

And so into the cutting rooms to edit *Ferry Pilot*. I was getting bogged down when my old colleague from *Night Mail*, R. Q. Mac-Naughton, took it over for me and did a wonderful job. *Ferry Pilot* was premiered at the New Gallery and went out on release as a second feature. There was now no question that we were entertaining our audiences, and when Harry Watt's *Target for Tonight* appeared, story documentary was accepted as an important part of British cinema.

I O

No escape from a dreary chore

Early January 1942. I had spent two dreary days on a building site near Bedford. An ordnance factory was being built and a film had to be made about it. A less cinematic subject would be hard to find. I had been asked to make it, and was about to report to Dal on my findings. I entered his office wondering how I could get out of this most unrewarding subject.

'How did you get on?'

'There's nothing to film, Dal. I'm sorry but what could be less cinematic than drain pipes, muddy puddles and bulldozers buzzing about? A building site is a building site. Dead as mutton.'

'Maybe . . . But it's got to be done so you'd better go away and think how. It's no good thinking it's impossible; that won't get you anywhere. Find a way of making that building site interesting. O.K.?'

'O.K. Dal.' I went down to Jo's cafe, almost below 21 Soho Square, often frequented by Joe Loss and his band. What Ian Dalrymple had asked me to do was think of a way of making a five-minute film on the building of an ordnance factory. The request had come from the Minister of Works. He was worried that the morale of the building workforce was non-existent. On certain sites, almost every day, an excuse was found to strike. He felt that a film showing how important their work was might help to encourage a more willing contribution to the war effort. That was the brief and there was no escape from it. Harry had had his Savings Bank and now I had my building site. Find the shape.

How to get the message across in five minutes? Visually, there was to be no help from the subject matter. I had spent a miserably

depressing couple of days on the site in question, my future location. It was just outside Bedford and the only interesting visual was
the forest of chimney stacks of the London Brick Company standing
stark and gaunt on the horizon. They weren't going to be of much
help. However, I had found a wonderful cockney character, a
'brickie' all his life, Charlie Fielding, a master of his craft. 'The
average bricks laid nowadays was about 400', he said. 'In the old
days we'd'a got the sack if that was all we did. Six or seven hundred
was average.' He was a natural; if only I could find a way of using
him.

A day or so later, I came across an extract in the *Telegraph* from
one of General Wavell's speeches. Its essence was that if the same
genius, energy and cooperative effort, instead of being used for the
destruction of war, were used for construction in peacetime, what
a wonderful world it would be. I cut it out. Might come in handy.

How then to make these bored labourers in the crafts connected
with building this factory aware that their time was precious and
should not be wasted as they trundled around this seemingly God-
forsaken spot? This mud flat which already looked like a battlefield
of the First World War? No wonder their morale was low.

If I were to show what a minute's production could mean to a
Spitfire and the effect of that minute's production on a marauding
Messerschmidt I might get the impact, visual and mental, I was
seeking. But, the thought of such an idea had to come naturally
from a discussion, an argument, a get-together. I would make the
camera a person, a roving reporter who went up to people and got
into conversation. When accosted, they looked up and recognised
the camera as a friend; someone who paid regular visits to the site.
In this way I could lead the conversation to the punch line—
imagine what a minute's production at (wherever) means to a
Spitfire in a dog fight. In this way the message might be put across
more naturally, reeking less of obvious propaganda. It was my only
hope and the gimmick worked, and when it came to Charlie
Fielding to argue with the camera, he was superb. As he argued,
he laid his bricks, using his trowel with the same expertise—
relatively—as Sir Harold Ghillies with his scalpel. It was a tour de

force of the bricklayer's art as well as one of the most spontaneous performances from a non-actor that I had been lucky enough to record.

He didn't let the camera have the last word. He conceded that what they were doing had to be done. But think of the waste. 'I agree with what General Wavell says', and he took out the piece of newspaper and read that speech of Wavell's in masterly fashion. The five minutes ended on an up-beat and had more to say than just war propaganda. No actor could have done what Charlie Fielding did, perform and show the craftsman's skill of a lifetime. He would have faked it, yes, but the true skill would not have been there. I had used what is now known as the subjective camera, perhaps for the first time.

Builders, I was told—I cannot vouch for the accuracy—was the only one of the five-minute series of films made by the Ministry of Information which was taken to America by their Office of War Information. A few years later the subjective camera was used again for a feature film, *The Lady in the Lake*, directed by and starring Robert Montgommery. For a gimmicky five-minute film? Yes. For a feature? No. The limited eye line is too inhibiting.

Builders was a stimulating experiment. Everyone seemed very happy with it. Like Harry Watt and his Savings Bank problem, I too had found the right shape for my building site. I had gained another notch which would lead me to *The Atlantic* and *Western Approaches*.

11

Not a remake of *Drifters* but all at sea

Shortly after completing *Builders*, Dal called me into his office. He was a shy man: words didn't flow freely. He looked up from his desk and tapped the bridge of his glasses with his cigarette holder, which usually indicated a pronouncement. He said that he had just had a visit from Owen Rutter, the naval historian and friend of Admiral Sir Percy Noble, Commander-in-Chief of Western Approaches, and hence responsible for fighting what Churchill referred to as 'The Battle of the Atlantic'. Sir Percy had recently seen Harry Watt's *Target for Tonight*. Not only was he very impressed by it but also rather jealous. The R.A.F. seemed to be getting all the attention and all the glory. It was time for the 'Silent Service' to speak up for itself. He wanted a film made but had no idea how to go about it. He called on Owen Rutter, the only person he knew who was connected with the media. He was able to tell Sir Percy that there was an official government film unit who might be persuaded to take it on. Sir Percy then asked him if, as a personal favour, he would visit this film unit and see what he could do. Hence Owen Rutter's visit to Dal and my being called in to see him as soon as Owen had left. Dal tapped the rim of his glasses again and said: 'You a good sailor Pat?'

'Yes, stomach like a horse. I discovered that quite recently on the cable ship, *Monarch*.'

'Good. Might be very important, that. Would you like to tackle this for the Admiral?'

'Crikey ... Well. Yes, you bet, and thanks very much, Dal.'

'It's not going to be a picnic, obviously.'

'No, I don't imagine it will. Has the Admiral any idea what he wants?'

'Something better than *Target*.'

'Oh, I see, just like that . . . A feature-length, then?'

'Could be . . . depends on what you're able to cook up. Owen has left a rough outline which the Admiral seemed to like, but Owen said he knew nothing about writing for the screen and that we were to look on it as something simply to get the ball rolling. He also said that whoever is going to make the film should go with him, up to Liverpool, to meet the Admiral and take it from there. O.K.?'

'O.K.'

'Here's his outline. *H.M. Escort*. His address is on the title page so make your own arrangements with Owen, and good luck.' A man of few words, perhaps, but he was fighting a continuous battle against bureaucracy so that we would remain free to get on with the job that he felt, by now, we were well trained to perform. Anyway, at the moment there was nothing more to talk about—no story line to discuss or pet idea to fight for. I left the office with Owen Rutter's treatment and a major assignment under my belt. The Crown Film Unit had been given perhaps the most dramatic subject of the war and Ian Dalrymple had given it to me.

I was both elated and deeply puzzled. It does not require the brain of an Einstein to realise that a convoy is not the most dramatic visual in the world. A hundred ships divided into four or five columns is soon digested. To find the meal was going to be the problem, for the staging of naval battles would clearly be beyond our resources or the Navy to supply the facilities. This was obvious. I went down to Joe's cafe to read Owen's outline. I still have it.

H.M. ESCORT

General Idea

The general idea of the film will be to show the working of the convoy system.

The particular aim will be to show how closely the ships under the

White Ensign and the Red work together in time of war and how the Royal and Merchant Navies together form British sea power, the merchant ships bringing the food without which the people of Britain could not live, and the oil without which her forces could not fight, taking back the products of her factories to pay for these imports: while their escort of H.M. ships protects them from destruction and keeps open the lines of communication, supported in the background by the might of the Grand Fleet. The film will show the organisation of convoy from the time the ships gather at the assembly point, and put to sea with their escort, until they are handed over in Mid-Atlantic to a relief escort of U.S. destroyers. Then the British escort will be seen meeting a home-bound and bringing it back to port, laden with food, oil and munitions of war.

The treatment will be documentary, the actors being the naval, mercantile marine and R.A.F. personnel who are engaged in the operation.

Every scene will thus carry conviction by its authenticity, and continuity will be obtained by following the actions of a British destroyer on her outward-bound and homeward passage, and of the merchant ships which fly the pennants of the outward- and homeward-bound commodores. The leading character will be the Senior Officer Escort, a commander R.N.

Outline of Treatment.

1. *Headquarters, Western Approaches.* The office of the Naval Control Senior Officer (N.C.S.O.). The date of the next outward-bound convoy to the U.S.A. is fixed. The manager of the Z shipping is informed.

2. *The Shipping Company making arrangements.* The Master of the *Leander* is given his instructions.

3. *Loading cargo in the 'Leander'.* Cases marked 'Britain delivers the goods', at the docks.

4. Quick flashes of other ships loading.

5. The ships leaving the dockside and steaming down river to the assembly point, passing the destroyer H.M.S. *Strongbow* getting ready for sea.

6. Commander A, the *Strongbow*'s Captain, receives his final orders at H.Q.

And so on until we come to the heading numbered 25.

25. The convoy is attacked by a U-Boat. One ship is torpedoed. Destroyers and corvettes attack the submarine. Oil and wreckage show that the attack has been successful. The rescue ships pick up the survivors. The convoy sails on.

Easy enough to write, these simple headings, but to reconstruct, convincingly, in wartime, in mid-Atlantic—not even to be considered.

I put the pages back in their envelope. As Dal so rightly said: it wasn't going to be a picnic. How were we to come to grips with such a vast, such a demanding subject with our limited resources and the Navy stretched to the limit? What facilities for reconstruction could they give us? Within half an hour of accepting this assignment I was almost in the depths of despair. What were we embarking upon? What was the matter with me? Carping, inwardly? What did I expect? A ready-made shooting script with every scene filmable and bursting with excitement? These pages were no more than an introduction to the all high. Owen Rutter had already made a great contribution in getting the project teed up.

I met him two days later at the Gargoyle Club. He was one of the most charming men I have ever met and I shall never forget the benevolence of his smile. He was not tall but very dapper. He put me at ease at once by telling me to ignore his notes; they were merely a means of getting the ball rolling. 'How do you want to go about it, Jackson?'

'Obviously I must get to sea as soon as possible. On a merchant and naval ship, I suppose.'

'Shows willing, anyhow', he said with a twinkle, and then made a most valuable suggestion.

'A coastal convoy'll do the trick. No point in spending weeks at sea. You won't learn any more than 48 hours up the east coast convoy and down again. I've spent weeks in a convoy—bloody boring unless, of course, you're torpedoed, and that's another story.'

'And not easy to reconstruct, either, should we want to. That's going to be our hardest problem. How to reconstruct, in war-time conditions at sea, the impression, at least, of live action—and there must be some in a prestige film of this kind, particularly when, as I understand, ships of every kind are already desperately over-worked. This is already my nightmare.'

'Yes, I can understand that. The thing for us to do is see the C. in C. as soon as we can; put the problems to him and see what he has to say. How soon can you leave for Liverpool.'

'Whenever you like . . . free as air.'

'No time like the present. I'll call him right away.' He did and was back within a few minutes. 'Sir Percy will see us for cocktails at 6.30 at Derby House, the day after tomorrow.'

That night, my sister Jocelyn helped me prepare my wardrobe for this auspicious visit. It consisted of my one and only, a pin-stripe bought two years earlier from Nichols of Regent Street for 10 guineas—a three-piece, please note. But, alas, *Lucky Jim* had not been written and we had not the inventive genius for the bright idea of passing a safety razor over the shiny cheeks of the pants or the elbows. It was all I had so it would have to do, having neither the money nor the coupons to buy a new suit. Whatever the Crown Film Unit boasted about it was not the dandy appearance of its directors. However, I needn't have worried for strangely enough Admiral Sir Percy Noble had other things to worry about. He was graciousness itself and a most impressive man. After the usual exchanges of polite pleasantries, he looked over at me and almost sympathetically said: 'So, Jackson, you're going to make this film for us.'

'I shall do my damnedest, Sir', I said, straight out of the B.O.P. Indeed, I felt like Wharton of the remove, ready to jump once more into any old breach going.

'We like Owen Rutter's script, *H.M. Escort*. What do you think of it?'

'It outlines the subject very well, Sir.'

'And?'

'In ten or twelve pages, it couldn't hope to do more. Now we have to find a story line and the characters we can care about. This means action and suspense, and for a subject as important as this, it must have these ingredients. And that is where the problem lies; to find the right conception which will include these elements and, most important of all, which are possible to film in wartime. It's no good, Sir, my writing action scenes of naval encounters which I know will be impossible to stage. And I am sure, Sir, like me, you don't want those dreadful model ships pooping away in the studio tank.'

'I quite agree with you. So, how can we help?'

'I must get to sea for a bit, Sir.'

'You've come to the right place for that. When do you want to go?'

'The sooner the better, Sir.'

'You a good sailor? Not that it matters a damn. Nelson was as sick as a dog for the first three or four days. What do you fancy? Atlantic convoy? Freetown? Capetown? You name it and we'll have you aboard in no time.'

'Mr Rutter made a very helpful suggestion, Sir, and that was that if I went up the east coast in convoy, I'd see a good deal and save a lot of time.'

Here Owen Rutter pitched in. 'I thought, Sir, that Jackson might go up in a merchantman and come down on the S.O.E.'s destroyer. In less than a week he'd have seen both sides of the convoy, so to speak.'

The Admiral considered this and took his time before answering. 'Yes, I suppose that's true ... One convoy's very much like another. On the east coast E-Boats and Messerschmidts, on the Atlantic U-Boats and Focke Wolfes. Easily transcribed by a writer, I imagine', he said with a most delightful twinkle, and added as an afterthought: 'Perhaps, Jackson, you'd like to see what the press like to call the ''Nerve Centre''—in other words the Operations Room.'

I naturally accepted and we left Sir Percy's apartments at the top of Derby House. The sentry outside the door ram-rodded to attention, as did others standing at each turn in the corridor leading to the lift. I felt that I was walking in the shadow of the Lord. Down, down, down to the deepest basement. More ram-rodding sentries until we found ourselves in the main Operations Room. A deathly hush as in an empty cathedral. The hiss of compressed air as a pneumatic communication tube dropped its despatch cartridge into its wire basket. The Duty Officer, a commander accompanied by a commodore, left the enormous chart of the Atlantic as they saw the C. in C. enter and walked towards him. A Wren on a ladder, for the chart covered a vast wall space, was in the process of pinning a symbol, quite small, in mid-ocean. The Admiral's eyes went to it at once. We walked towards the chart. He looked up at the little symbol and I saw now that it was a cross outlined in red. Very quietly, he asked: 'When did that happen, Wynne?'

'Just had news of it, Sir.'

'Hmm . . . Nothing nearer than about 500 miles . . . Let's hope they managed to get the boats away.'

'Let's hope so, Sir, with all aboard.'

'Amen to that', Sir Percy said, hardly above a whisper, and turning to me remarked: 'There's your first view of the Battle, Jackson. Not a pretty one. As you see she's caught it bang in the middle. Our nearest escort groups E and G are too far away, and anyway I couldn't afford to weaken them. Both convoys are homeward bound, crammed with Shermans for Monty. So, there you have it. We do all we can to get the convoys through, and they, all they can to destroy them. They're not lacking in courage, either. So, it's a grim battle, morning, noon and night . . . Important point to remember. It never ceases. War at sea is cat and mouse, all round the clock.'

A few days later, Sir Percy arranged that I should join an east coast convoy which was assembling at Southend. There, at the pier, I was to meet the Commodore of the convoy, Commodore Phillips, R.N.R. Accordingly, at 8.00 a.m. on 18 February 1942, I made sure that I was there, well ahead of time. It was a cold, bleak morning and snowing for good measure. The wind was strong enough to ruffle the surface of the Thames, which was the colour of slate. I mingled with the officers and ratings, waiting for the toy train to take them to the end of the pier, and as the only civilian I stuck out like a sore thumb.

'Are you Jackson of the Crown Film Unit?'

'Yes, Sir', I said as I swivelled round, and there stood my Commodore. I took his outstretched hand.

'Tony Kimmins told me to look out for you. I'm Phillips. You couldn't have chosen a better run because I've picked the *Fort Binger* to be the Commodore ship. She's a "Froggie" and she's been on the Far East run, so, with luck, bags of booze and cheroots.'

'Great', I said, as though a bottle a day man who chain smoked Havanas. He was a most genial man with graveyard teeth which in no way diminished the warmth of his smile.

'Her Chief Officer's a hell of a good bloke. Pinched her out of Bordeaux, right under Jerry's nose, at dead of night. Great feat. Anyway, welcome aboard. I hope we have a good trip.'

'Thank you very much Sir.' I felt like a 'prep' school boy and was probably behaving like one. However, I could do no more than make the best of trying to be myself, totally lacking in confidence though I was.

'Don't hesitate to ask me anything you may want to know and you'll be welcome on the bridge any time.'

'Very kind of you and much appreciated, Sir.'

Soon, we were all piling into the funny little pier train and chugging bumpily along the mile of track which would take us to the end of the pier. The rhythm of the rail beat was nothing like that of the Night Mail that Harry Watt and I had heard for so many weeks during the making of that film in 1934. Conversation was impossible during that bone shaking experience. I looked out of the window, and against the murky background the flurrying snow flakes inkily silhouetted themselves. The wind was bitter as we descended the slimy, rusty, sea-weeded steps towards the waiting pinnace. We were a mile out in the estuary waters and there was quite a chop. Thankfully aboard we sheltered from the spray under the cockpit awning.

Commodore Phillips pointed out the *Fort Binger*, and as members of her crew saw our approach they lowered a Jacob's ladder. Our pinnace was skilfully brought alongside and hands fended off as the rise and fall of the swell was several feet. Commodore Phillips prepared himself, flexed and ready, waiting for the exact moment when to commit himself to the ladder. His timing was perfect, his manoeuvre performed as casually as stepping on to an escalator. Easy: nothing to it. Just as easy as hitting a perfect drive off the first tee. I watched one or two more, confirming a growing conviction that this was not as easy as falling off a log—an unhappy thought in the circumstances. How shaming to drop into the drink without so much as having felt a deck underfoot.

Soon enough it was my turn. On the uplift I committed myself. It might have been worse. A slightly sliced approach set me swinging as on a pendulum. I waited for gravity to do its noble work and when the ladder steadied I started to climb. Looking up I saw many black faces smiling at me, hoping, no doubt, that I might provide them with a comic turn. I disappointed them and was soon clambering over the bulwarks and jumping down on to the steel decks. I was aboard and greeted by a boiling litter of St Bernard puppies, yapping and nipping with delight at my ankles—one of the hazards of marine warfare. The young ex-Chief Officer, now Captain, greeted me most hospitably and led us down to his cabin where coffee and newly baked croissants awaited us. We certainly had struck it lucky.

At 10.15 we were under way. The Commodore signalled six knots and 17 ships formed into a single line astern, separated by two cables, which was 400 yards, so I was informed by Sub-Lieutenant Hebblethwaite, the Commodore's assistant. Minesweepers were clearing the channel ahead and we were now joined by two escorting destroyers.

Commodore Phillips came down from the bridge and we paced the foredeck, as he kindly pointed out various landmarks of interest. He was irate about the bloody-mindedness of the dockers. 'If we win this war, I shan't thank them for their contribution.' He pointed out the shocking state of the *Fort Binger*. Had there been an emergency the lifeboats could not have been lowered as the drums of ropes were jammed against the unloading gear. Even on urgent repair jobs for ships required for sea it was usual to find schools of poker in full force throughout the working day. There seemed to be a complete lack of understanding from the dockers of how desperate the situation was. It was almost as though they couldn't care less who won the war. 'I had to take over a ship which had recently been constructed and as soon as I got out of port, I had to turn back. Nothing worked. The electric gear was all to hell and the steering all to buggery. And what am I to do? If I write out a report it will get so far, but as soon as it comes up against some-body who feels it may be an unfavourable reflection against himself, it gets no further. Thousands of people, in subordinate positions, whether in the services or civvy jobs, can see through the graft and are powerless to expose it, and they have to continue to support a war for which the government is making no effort to obtain maximum efficiency to back up the men at the front. It's a bloody state of affairs.'

10.40. H.M.S. *Worcester* passed us to port, going upstream. She looked pretty battered after her brush with the *Scharnhorst*. The Commodore told me that her skipper would be in very hot water for disobeying orders and not turning away. Instead, he fired his torpedoes from 3000 yards. This presupposes that his C.O. did not press home his attack with sufficient determination. So, the skipper of *Worcester* was not only guilty of a breach of discipline but was responsible for incurring damage to his ship, the only destroyer in the flotilla so to suffer. Had he sunk the enemy or inflicted damage, he would have been highly praised and decorated. But he didn't and so faced being dismissed from his ship. Certainly, she was not a pretty sight. Her mast was shot away and there was a gaping hole in her bows. Her superstructure, too, was badly peppered.

The channel here was about a mile wide, lined by buoys which seemed almost unnecessary, for it would have been easy to steer a course between the masts and funnels of the sunken ships, either side. This was grim evidence of the toll taken by the magnetic and, recently, the acoustic mines. An escort, ahead, was flying a red flag at the masthead, signifying that she was sweeping for acoustic mines. By transmitting a sub-aqua frequency comparable to the average marine engine, it was hoped that this would stimulate the mine to respond and give its all to the empty water above.

12.35. The naval control ship G 57 came alongside and on its loudhailer told the Commodore how many ships he now had in his convoy. With a final 'Good luck, Sir', it made off. We passed an old paddle steamer converted into a 'flak' ship. She had been to Dunkirk on three occasions and had brought off over a thousand men from the beaches.

We went to lunch in the Captain's cabin. It was fine to hear the French language again. The Captain and his coloured steward treated each other as comrades in arms. There seemed to be no distinction between rank or colour. They were just shipmates and respected each other as human beings: all that either expected from the other. Very refreshing. Commodore Phillips remarked on it, too, and remembered how it had struck Negley Farson in his book *Behind God's Back*. Probably the French are more evolved in their handling and treatment of their coloured people.

2.30 p.m. Two more destroyers joined our escort. We were about to enter E-Boat Alley which stretched along the Norfolk and Suffolk coast and up beyond the Wash. A patrol of Spitfires kept up their never ending flights up and down the east coast convoys.

Buoys continued to map out our course. They were spaced four miles apart, all the way to Methil, 480 miles to the north. Every day, this channel was swept as mines were dropped by the Luftwaffe at night. Those buoys seemed to be dragging their feet as they drifted past. It would be an age before another hove into sight. The monotony was already very trying. How the dickens were we going to make a film out of this?

Eventually, after several more buoys had drifted by, dinner was announced. Captain Joly kept an excellent table and each course gave us an inkling of the many trade routes his ship followed. Hearts of palm from Bali, he informed us; asparagus from Madagascar, lychees from Hong Kong and finally Burma cheroots. It was a superb meal, accompanied by Tchaikowsky's fifth symphony and a Chateau Margaux with the roast lamb. Could anything have been more incongruous, I wondered. Here we were steaming up what was considered by the pundits to be the most dangerous convoy route at this particular stage of the war, enjoying the most sumptuous meal, listening to superb music in the presence of wonderful company. It was a great experience, though it was not advancing a story line one iota. I was doing my best not to worry about that, for the moment, putting my faith in Micawber's dictum that something would turn up. It was going to need a flash, an electric storm of inspiration to come to grips with this subject. That was already painfully clear.

19 February. Breakfast in the saloon and then up on deck to see a south-bound convoy pass on the port side. It stretched miles and the barrage balloons at the mastheads were steady and not swooping about; their well-tailored rear fins were working well as stabilisers. Heblethwaite told me that our Senior Officer of Escort (S.O.E.) had had an unfortunate brush with a trawler during the night. The trawler had unwisely crossed the convoy route. Aldis lamps were flashing between our ships and the S.O.E.'s destroyer, apparently giving and exchanging information about the time and bearing when the mishap had occurred. Apart from this, nothing much to catch the eye; the Yorkshire coast slipping slowly past to port.

Dear me: how boring visually it all was. The ships hardly seemed to be moving. They pitched a bit; they rolled a bit; they showed their rusty flanks a bit, and another buoy drifted by. Another four miles had been sailed. Buoy by buoy the morning crept past and, thankfully, it was lunch time.

Everyone discussed the war or the individual in relation to the war. Commodore Phillips was wonderfully outspoken and not frightened to air his views. 'We're all caught like rats in a trap. Either conform or go to prison.' With this as an exit line, he made for the bridge. Captain Joly then told me of his fears about a possible fifth column working in the docks. When he was in dry dock, after having sneaked his ship from Bordeaux, no effort was made to get essential repairs carried out with maximum speed. Often, he would come across groups, sitting on his decks, playing cards. 'Get on with your work', he would say to them. They told him to bugger off; he wasn't their boss. He would complain to the foreman. He just shrugged his shoulders and said that there was nothing he could do about it. Apparently, it had to be seen to be believed. When it was time, eventually, to leave, the dry dock was being filled and it was only by chance that the Chief Engineer of the *Fort Binger* spotted that the valves had been left open and the ship was making water fast. 'If that isn't sabotage, I don't know what is', said Captain Joly.

Off Blyth and two new tankers had joined the convoy. The S.O.E. signalled us: 'Suggest reduce to six knots to allow buttoners to catch up.' We hoisted the signal to our masthead which had to be passed down the line. It obviously wasn't, for before long ships started to pile up, crowding each other's stern. Workings of a convoy maybe, but not very cinematic, for the effects of an un-passed signal took half an hour or so to become manifest. Cut to the soaring sea gull and then a shot of the steward emptying debris over the side, and then of course the sea gulls swoop. A buoy passes and so does another four miles.

20 February, 7.45 a.m. Pass the Isle of May and enter the Firth of Forth. An enormous amount of shipping here. Convoy being formed to leave for America. Naval Control came alongside and wanted *Fort Binger* to sail on this convoy which was to leave at noon for New York. Great disappointment from everyone: all hopes of a stretch ashore gone. But for Commodore Phillips, Heblethwaite and myself, this was where we got off. With grateful thanks to Captain Joly, we took our leave. I had met some fine people, but whether I had advanced the cause of my assignment, I doubted. Time would tell. The naval cutter took us into Methil, and after reporting to Naval Control, we booked in at the Beach Hotel.

21 February. Phoned Crown Film Unit at Denham. Kimmins trying to arrange my return trip on a destroyer so that I could see the Royal Navy's side of the problem. He would confirm on Monday.

The Beach Hotel bar was the focal point of Methil. Here were to be found officers of every rank from both the Merchant and Royal Navy. Ex-Masters, like Commodore Phillips, recalled and were now serving in the R.N.R. Here, I met the Captain and his Number 1 of the corvette *Jason*. Both had had much experience of the Atlantic. On one trip they had run foul of a U-Boat ace who had bagged 13 ships from this one convoy. He had got right in amongst it, as though the fox were lost amongst the hounds. The anecdotes of some of the Merchant Navy Masters were hair-raising, particularly some of the fiddles perpetrated against ship owners.

One Master had sold his bronze propellers in exchange for iron ones. A favourite dodge was to sign on for double the labour force than was actually used. This would be for the preparation of holds for special cargoes. The difference between the mythical and real wage bill was split between the contractor and the chief officer. Nice pickings, obviously.

Monday 24 February. Arrangements had been made for Commodore Phillips and me to board the destroyer, H.M.S. *Westminster*, whose Captain was to be the Senior Officer of Escort on a south-bound convoy. Towards evening we were driven to Methil harbour where the Naval Control cutter would take us out to the ship. It was almost dusk as we headed out to sea. There was a weird purpley light. The sea and sky seemed to merge in an overall sheen. No ripple disturbed this mystical calm as we headed towards a fleet of ships moored, haphazardly, across this oily calm.

It was dark when we boarded the *Westminster*. We were escorted below to the wardroom. It was rather cramped and the air was hazy with smoke exuding from a French stove—reminiscent of the school common room. It had those four little mica panels in front. For its warmth a price had to be paid: smog. Certainly, its flue was in need of attention, but, after all, there was a war on with more urgent matters in hand than a leaky flue. The Captain was a very quiet chap, in his late thirties, and he greeted us most charmingly. He wore his gardening flannel trousers and the oldest reefer jacket in the service, its two-and-a-half rings hanging, somehow, by a few remaining threads. He had a very quiet voice but it had timbre and his enunciation was perfect without being in the least bit blah. Every word he said was clear, no matter from what part of the room he spoke. He had just won the D.S.C. In a scrap with E-Boats, he had sunk three of them.

The Number 1, Lieutenant Hamer, made himself most affable, plying us with drinks, and soon Commodore Phillips had them all in stitches. He was great company, a fine raconteur. But only he, the Captain and the Number 1 showed any signs of animation. The other officers might have been waxworks. This was not the free and easy atmosphere of the *Fort Binger*. I felt sure it must be to do with that damned stove. How they could stick this smog was a wonder. Things, surely, were tough enough without that.

Phillips drifted off, as did the other officers, and I was left with the Captain. He was not encouraging about the Atlantic convoys. Nothing happened, according to him. The east coast was considered the toughest convoy route at the moment; that is, for brushes with the enemy. 'But, if you are sunk and have a chance of getting into the boats, there is a chance of making land in a very short time. The danger of mines is much more acute, of course, and anything under 2000 tons doesn't stand much chance and is likely to founder in a very short time.' He talked about the war and made a particular point of mentioning the tragedy of H.M.S. *The Prince of Wales*. 'As soon as we heard that she was to be sent out to Singapore we wrote her off. She hadn't an earthly.' When he left to get some sleep, he suggested that I should follow his example and indicated that my bunk was to be the wardroom's settee.

25 February. Woken at 6.30 by the rumbling of the revolving prop shaft. Stewards were scratching about and the chief kindly brought me a cup of tea and had some shaving water ready in somebody's cabin. I climbed into as many layers of pullovers as possible.

Breakfast was edible but we'd been pampered by the *Fort Binger*. Before the stove got me I went on deck for a breather. We were passing a bell buoy which tolled mournfully. A sudden and profound sadness invaded me; a nostalgia for past happiness, of childhood memories, hopes and dreams to be fulfilled. I couldn't account for the unexpected attack of the blues. It was the bell, of course. None of us ashore had heard any sort of bell since the declaration of war. The chiming of bells was to be the warning of invasion.

I paced the poop and got talking to the butcher. He was carving up great chunks of pork from his meat safe. A jovial little man with a perpetual smile, he'd been in the navy for thirty years. A pensioner recalled for service. He showed me all over the ship, including the bilges. Then, it was time for lunch.

2.15 p.m. Passed the Farne Islands. Wonderfully fine and a joy to feel the sun. A buoy passed. Another four miles of the journey. We passed them at three-quarters-of-an-hour intervals. I was not finding this slow progress easy after weeks of having been flown here, there and everywhere during the making of *Ferry Pilot*. Interesting, too, the difference in these fellows: all so reserved; hardly a word to say to each other. Obviously the result of a very demanding regime and routine of duty. Four hours on and eight off. Those four hours on, particularly at night, must drain a man. When they came off duty some tried to read for a while, but sleep soon overcame them. That damned stove, no doubt. But, entering the ward room, it was a surprise to see all these bodies sprawled all over the place as though in the last days of Pompeii, overcome by Vesuvius.

26 February. Much rougher and I hoped the 'tum' would hold up. Heavily overcast. Just ideal, so I was told, for Jerry to pop in and out of the clouds, have a squirt and pop back again. I could hear our 'Spits' on patrol against just such an eventuality. I went up on the bridge to hear the Captain in touch with his Spitfire cover. Then, I heard the Spitfires talking to each other. 'Hullo Red two. Red one calling. My power plant bum. Am returning, will wait for relief.' Up and down, round and round they went, craving, no doubt, for a shot at something. So it went on. We passed another buoy and then another. Buoy by buoy: drip by drip, that renowned Chinese torture. Boredom is a kind of torture, too. Certainly, it is the most fatiguing thing. One almost wished for a bit of action, and then I remembered what Commodore Phillips had told me as we were waiting to board the *Westminster*. 'Sometimes the whole affair seems so darn crazy, I feel like banging my head against a brick wall. You have to switch off . . . try and stop thinking. Last winter we were attacked by a JU 88. He popped out of the clouds, sprayed us with cannon. All over in a few seconds and back he popped as the Spits went after him. Over the loud hailer, I asked, ''Any casualties?'' ''Yes, Sir, third mate's copped it.'' I went forrard and there he was lying with his right lung spread all over the deck. Senseless. The Junker pilot hadn't achieved anything and yet one second of active warfare had thrown away a life. I saw the whole

dreadful uselessness of it all. It is hard to get a proper perspective until you come up against the physical impact of war for yourself.'

About noon the north-bound convoy met us and some of its escorts buttoned themselves on to us as extra defence, for we would soon be entering E-Boat Alley again.

During the last hour or so a nasty sou'-wester had sprung up, and as we were steaming almost due south our progress involved that testing cork-screwing pitch and toss, a lethal form of transport for some; guaranteed to upset the most confident tourist who rather fancies his sea legs. The hearty pipe-smoking pacer, when all around are prostrate. Before long, the dottle is knocked out, and so is he. I was neither a confident tourist nor a pipe-smoker and had few illusions about my seaworthiness. But the prospect of bacon and eggs and a fat greasy hunk of pickled pork did not seem repugnant. On the contrary, I could have tackled the lot with relish. This was encouraging. With luck, my boast was true; I did possess the stomach of a horse. If this were so, what a blessing because the thought of trying to winkle a performance out of an amateur cast interspersed by hurried visits to the gunwale seemed an impossible combination. Physically, then, I had the stomach for the job, and that was something.

After dinner that night, Number 1 and others analysed various bridge hands, bringing Culbertson to bear. One by one, they drifted off. The Chief Engineer, Number 1 and myself kipped down in the wardroom. They did not go to their cabins. In leaving them empty and locked, these spaces became air locks. In the event of being mined they would help to give added buoyancy and check the inflow of water. Extra boats, as a result, might be able to get away before the ship foundered. This was explained to me, tactfully, I thought, the following morning.

26 February. Awoke heavy and muzzy after several hours of the stove's fumigation. We were coming up the Thames estuary, the convoy in single line. We came to the boom defence where we waited until half the convoy had sailed past, and then we hopped it to Sheerness at 22 knots. She could smell the stable all right. We had an early lunch as officers appeared in the wardroom trans-

formed. In their number one uniforms and butterfly collars they were out to kill. Mighty handsome they looked, and if anyone had earned a stretch ashore and a touch of romance, each of these fellows had. The motor boat took us ashore and I tramped to the station and had an hour to wait for the first train to Victoria: an hour in which to ponder whether I had achieved anything. I doubted it. I was no nearer to having the faintest idea of how to treat this subject. The possibility of finding not only a story line, but above all, one that would be possible to film in wartime, was far away.

Was there, then, nothing to be hopeful about? I had not been sea sick. That was something. I had little idea, then, how important that discovery was to be. As for the immediate prospect . . . that was the blank page.

1 2

Blank despair

Next day, at home in Mandeville Cottage, near Pinewood Studios, I confronted the blank page. Not a pretty sight when you know that your mind is equally as blank. To describe my problem was easy enough. How was I to film this battle of the Atlantic without any hope of getting the facilities to stage it? There must be a way, but for the life of me I hadn't found it. Would I ever was the question which daily became more agonising. Days went by and still the page remained blank. Despondency soon leads to panic.

This simply wouldn't do—wouldn't do at all . . . Perhaps a breath of fresh air? Ah yes. A quick potter round the garden. Not at all pleasant, far too nippy . . . Make up the fire; getting very low on fags, bound to need another packet. A brisk walk down to dear old Dealey at the Pinewood service station; great fun old Dealey, always good for a laugh. On with the duffle coat and a quick march there and back. Might get a flash, never know your luck . . . Back again. No luck: no flash. Sit down; have another go. Get the pen to work; magic connection, pen–paper–brain; one thought leading to another. Write. Write anything; any old codswallop, just get started. 'Old Mother Hubbard went to the cupboard to fetch the poor dog a bone. Jack and Jill went up the hill to fetch a pail of water.' 'There is an oily calm. The horizon is glowing as the sun sinks. In immediate foreground a periscope breaks through the surface. We are close enough to see that it begins, slowly, to swivel. The U-Boat commander is scanning the horizon, and though his eyes are glued to the lenses, we sense him react. He sees a smudge of smoke on the fading horizon line. He gives orders to lower the periscope and sets a new course for that smoke.' Not too bad an opening image, perhaps, but then what? An inevitable attack on the convoy; torpedoes, explosions, and we're into a naval battle that even Cecil B. de Mille would think twice about staging. No good; quite beyond our resources. Have another go. The S.O.E. raises his binoculars and scans his immediate circumference of ocean. He turns to his Number 1: 'All right, Number 1. Take her down the column and let 'em know we're here. Full speed ahead, give 'em a bit of a show.' Balls, absolute balls. Think again. During the next fortnight I don't like to try and recall how many 'think again's I must have had. Time was passing at an alarming rate and there was nothing, nothing to show for it. I was in despair, a mental agony I hope never to experience again. Days of fruitless effort with only a harvest of screwed and torn up sheets of paper which, at least, had the merit of starting the fire.

I was about to start the third blank week. I was licked. I must face the fact. I must go and tell Dal. It wasn't fair to go on like this, getting nowhere and with no likelihood of my getting out of this desperate situation—this total blank. Dal would be at Pinewood. He always was on Mondays, to see rough cuts and any recent rushes. No stalling trip to dear old Dealey, this time. It is an awful moment when one has to admit defeat. I was facing it now. On with the duffle coat. The slow trudge to Pinewood Studios started. The mud was thick on the road. The tread was heavy and so was my heart. At the Five Points crossroads a turn right down the lane to the studios. On this bleak March day a sparrow had the cheek to sing away happily. I envied him. I went over in my mind the pieces of the jigsaw puzzle that went into the making of this war at sea. The convoy, the escorts, the U-Boats, the 'straggler', a ship-wrecked crew in a lifeboat, the 'Ops' Room. All these pieces I had arranged, rearranged and juxtaposed, so I thought, in every con-ceivable combination. But I could make none add up to a narrative line which was anything other than pedestrian and boring. Out of all those ingredients the right combination lay somewhere: I just hadn't had the wit to find it; to find a story line with human in-terest and, above all, suspense to superimpose over this pedestrian business of escorting convoys across the Atlantic. No matter how great the courage and the sacrifices involved, there was no escaping the fact that it was 99 per cent deadly monotonous, and it was this quality, inherent in the subject, that I had failed to overcome by my narrative ability. Never had I felt so utterly miserable and extinguished. I felt sorry for Dal, too. Now he'd have to start all over again with someone else.

On I trudged, unhappy thoughts crowding in on each other. Owen Rutter, such a hell of a nice bloke, and the C. in C., Sir Percy Noble. 'As you see, Jackson, she's caught it right in the middle.' The Wren sticking the cross into the chart. A close-up of that symbol; dissolve through to a lifeboat at sea; establish the survivors. A periscope pokes through the surface. The U-Boat commander sees the lifeboat, dismisses it as being of no importance, but at that precise moment the lifeboat is sending out an S.O.S. from its portable radio. It is picked up through the aerial in the U-Boat's periscope. Message given to the U-Boat commander who decides to use the lifeboat as a decoy. He realises that if a surface ship has picked it up, merchant or naval, he'll have a sitting duck. My God, what's wrong with that? Now we have three important elements of the convoy interacting and creating an ever growing situation of suspense. This could make sense. This could be the key. Why on earth didn't I think of it before? Never mind. Thank God you've thought of it now, not a moment too soon. I turned and went back. I couldn't wait, now, to meet my old friend that blank page.

Ten days later the first story outline was completed and this time I had a happier walk to Pinewood. Dal was seeing rushes so I left the envelope containing my opus on his desk. In bold letters I had printed:

WESTERN APPROACHES
First Treatment

It was more like the twenty-first, but that was my secret. I left the studio and walked on air, down the straight mile towards 'The Crooked Billet'. I walked on air because I felt liberated. In my bones I was confident that I had 'licked it'. Given an average bit of luck, there was nothing in the story which was insurmountably difficult to shoot . . . Poor innocent! As I had constructed the story on scenes that I knew I would have to film, I was, so I thought, going to make doubly sure not to 'snooker' myself by asking for the impossible.

The following morning Dal called and we arranged to meet at 2.30 that afternoon. He gave me no idea whether he liked the story. Before lunch I saw him fleetingly at the bar in Pinewood. He was with John Monk. I made no attempt to talk to him. Instead, I went with my sister Joss and Otto, her dachshund, who travelled in the basket attached to her handlebars as we biked to The Crooked Billet, the local, a mile down the road from the studio. Joss had been an ambulance driver throughout the London Blitz. She was a non-pussy-footing woman. She and Marjorie Maine together would have opened up the Wild West in their wagon, covered or un-covered. If you had Joss as a friend you were in luck. She was the most direct and honest woman I have ever known. If she didn't like you she thought it only fair to make that clear: that way nobody wasted any time or energy. Not surprisingly, she had enemies, but far more allies. I was to owe her a great deal before I was to be through with this little assignment. We had a game of darts, both wondering whether I was for the chop. Miraculously we got our opening double, but neither could finish, humiliatingly having worked down to double one.

Time had gone too fast and I pedalled back and got to the studio just in time and knocked on Dal's door. John Monk was still with him. Dal knocked the bridge of his glasses and looked up at me. It seemed hours before he said: 'Jolly good Pat. We've both read it. It's going to work.'

'Oh my God . . . I'm so glad . . . I'm so glad you think so.'

'You're not asking for the moon either. Apart from the single action with the U-Boat, you're not asking for anything out of the way. The sensible thing is for you to get out a shooting script so that we can make a breakdown and cost it. Incidentally, we're going to make it in Technicolor.' He could have said water colour for all the difference it made to me at that moment, so great was my sense of elation. 'So, while I get the go ahead, you get on with the shooting script as fast as you can.' And that was that. I walked on air to the door and as I was about to close it, Dal said: 'Oh, and Pat, well done'. Never before or since have I ever felt so bucked.

So, back home for the second stage, the shooting script. This requires an entirely different discipline. The initial imaginative test is over in so far as the story line and the characters to bring it to life are created. Now, it is necessary to become a sort of chess player and try and work out each move, not only of the camera but the characters in relation to the camera. Only by preconceiving these moves both of cast and camera can the art director have an idea of the director's requirements. Will a two-sided set be enough for this scene? What's the director saying that he wants? A low angled shot, the camera tracks following Orson Welles in close shot. Low angle!! That means a ceiling piece. Scene 34. A wide angled shot as Vivien Leigh walks round the room. Camera pans with her. This probably means a three-walled set with a 'floating' fourth wall. It is, to all intents and purposes, the equivalent of a score to an orchestral work. All departments, as opposed to all instruments, are able to understand the director's intentions. If deep focus is required the lighting cameraman will make sure that he has sufficient light on the rail so that he can shut down the iris of his lens to give the required depth of focus. It is no use the director suddenly getting the bright idea of this requirement when he is on the floor. If he hasn't preconceived it, the lights may not be there and precious time will be wasted until new light is added to the light rail. So it is a vital process if the production is going to be shot quickly and efficiently.

The opening paragraph of my treatment for *Western Approaches* read as follows:

As far as the eye can see there is an angry expanse of ocean. Great rollers sweep past: they are overwhelming and ominous, not because they are Atlantic rollers, but because they are not seen from the reassuring height of a ship's decks. Against the wind we hear a voice shouting: 'Keep baling, lads . . . Get out the sea anchor.' We are in an open boat amongst dim forms of drenched men straining at the oars. In the half-light of dawn there is no sense of time, only tragic isolation. The spray lashes at the men as the boat is held on the top of a wave before it wallows on its downward plunge to the trough below. On the floor boards is a lifebelt: it bears the name S.S. *Jason*. A mass of water is shipped and as it obliterates the name on the lifebelt, we dissolve through to a symbol bearing the name 'JASON' being pinned to the vast wall chart in the Operations Room at H.Q. Western Approaches, Liverpool.

The following morning that opening paragraph, transposed into shooting script, read as follows:

Scene 1. Title background of very stormy sky and sea. As the titles fade we are left with a clear picture of heavy rollers sweeping past. For a moment we are perched on the crest of a huge wave and are now plunging down to the trough below. There is a frightening sense of insecurity and of being at the mercy of the sea. The camera pans, revealing a lifeboat in which drenched men are seen pulling at the oars.

Scene 2. MEDIUM CLOSE SHOT. *The Master at the tiller. He is silhouetted against the faint dawn sky. Against the wind, he cups his hands and shouts:*
MASTER. Keep baling lads.

Scene 3. MEDIUM CLOSE SHOT *looking down on two men baling for all they're worth.*

Scene 4. CAMERA LOW LOOKS UP *at two men pulling on the oars. Spray lashes their faces. Oblivious to it they keep pulling, for their lives depend on keeping 'head on' towards the next menacing wall of sea.*

Scene 5. CLOSE SHOT. THE MASTER *puts the tiller under his arm and cups both hands and shouts:*
MASTER. Get out the sea anchor.

Scene 6. CLOSE SHOT. *Figure gropes in the forrard locker for the sea anchor.*

Scene 7. CLOSE SHOT. *An injured man with a soaking and bloodstained bandage around his head, half lying and half sitting, head and shoulder cupped in lifebelt propped on thwart. The name of the ship is clearly seen on the lifebelt, 's.s. JASON', though blood is seeping on to the lettering from the wounded man. A heavy sea is shipped, washing the name, and as the water half-obliterates it, we* DISSOLVE

Scene 8. OPERATIONS ROOM. CLOSE UP *of symbol with name 's.s. JASON' being pinned to immense wall chart, representing the Atlantic etc. etc. etc.*

Nobody can say that this makes exciting reading and so no more of it. Nevertheless, this short extract of a shooting script may illustrate how important it is to transfer prose narrative into this form of presentation. Only in this way can what is called 'a breakdown' be worked out. It enables the production manager to prepare a schedule based on what he calls his 'cross plot'. This will show him how many scenes are to be shot in each set, in how many scenes does each member of the cast appear and what are their respective script numbers. The cameraman will be able to assess the lights needed for each set and the art director their size, shape and essential props—some may only be for decor but others may have to be practical and actually be in working order for the requirements of the scene. A tedious but very essential part of film making, the writing of the 'shooting script'.

It is so easy to write about drenched men in a lifeboat, straining at the oars, spray lashing their faces and so on. It won't be quite so easy when you find yourself in a lifeboat, in those sort of seas, with a three-strip Technicolor camera, about the size of your refrigerator. It is then that you curse yourself for not having thought of a 'better way' of opening your film.

The story that I had concocted, in the nick of time, was simple enough and, in a nutshell, is as follows. Once we have established that we are going to be concerned with survivors in a lifeboat, we learn that H.Q. at Liverpool does not know a great deal about their fate: only that their ship has been torpedoed, its position not fixed as the distress call was incomplete. It is also known that a U-Boat was in their vicinity, but whether it was responsible for the sinking is not known. What is known, however, is that if there are survivors, they are beyond the radius in which any escort vessel could try and give search and, in any case, could not be spared from the protecting screen of two vital homeward-bound convoys. An enactment, almost word for word, of the scene that I had shared with the Commander in Chief, Sir Percy Noble.

We now return to the lifeboat. Conditions are easier. The sea has abated and we get to know the survivors. The Master, the Chief Officer, the young 'Sparks', a cabin boy, and a seaman with a head injury who is feverish. The Master issues meagre rations and tells the men that he intends to make for Ireland. Things could be worse because 'Sparks' has a wireless set which can send to a radius of 400 miles. They raise the sail and get under way.

In New York, a convoy is preparing to sail for the U.K. The Captain of the *Leander* is off to attend the 'Masters' Conference'. He has a word with his Chief Officer that he is worried about the ship's trim. She is down by the head by two feet, due to an enormous steam engine dumped on his forrard deck. He has a nasty feeling that it will cause trouble before they are much older. He intends to mention it at the Conference. (This is to give us the excuse for the *Leander* to leave the convoy as and when it suits us). The Master leaves and we are introduced to Griff (Chief Petty Officer Griffiths), loaned by the Royal Navy to be the gunlayer for the *Leander*. He is on the aft gun platform, checking every detail of the gun, above all that the breech block mechanism is working to his satisfaction.

The Masters' Conference takes place and is staged, almost word for word, as Owen Rutter had outlined in *H.M. Escort*, with the exception that we introduce the *Leander*'s problem. *Leander*'s Captain explains his dilemma and his worry that if the convoy has to reduce speed because of a straggler or whatever, he may find it impossible to keep station; in which case he will become a menace to his immediate neighbours ahead, astern and on either beam. The Commodore takes his points and says that should such a situation arise—naturally it will—he is to signal him and he will tell him what to do. We get to know our Senior Officer of Escort and that's that.

It is dawn; the convoy is leaving the Statue of Liberty astern.

Our homebound convoy is at sea. As a means of development, we now start to 'inter-cut' the three elements in our story, established so far. The survivors in the lifeboat, the homeward bound *Leander* and the destroyer carrying the Senior Officer of Escort; a sequence in the lifeboat, in which we get to like and know everyone better. Rough diamonds they certainly are, but their survival begins to be of importance. This sequence is followed by scenes on the *Leander*. We get to know Chief Petty Officer Griffiths. A splendid man, First World War, in the battle of Jutland and obviously a tower of strength. His Chief Officer and Master. By their way of talking, their regional accents, their bearing, we get a cross-section of Britain that no professional cast of actors could give us. They are not what they are attempting to portray. The stamp of a lifetime's work is not on them. Now to the S.O.E. shepherding his flock and encouraging a straggler to try and do better. She happens to be a 'Froggie' and the S.O.E. finds that his school-boy French just will not stand the test of time. There is a sense of the voyage progressing.

The lifeboat is sailing along happily, but we are seeing her through the lens of a periscope, and what's more, a German one. The German U-Boat commander calls over his Number 1 to have a look at it. They dismiss it as being of no interest and the Commander continues to scan the horizon. But, at this moment, the young 'Sparks' in the lifeboat is sending his usual morning S.O.S. Through the periscope, the U-Boat radio operator picks up the lifeboat's distress and brings it to his commander, who immediately plots its position. To his astonishment he sees that it is being sent from his own. It must be being sent from the lifeboat, above. He confers with his Number 1, and decides to keep station on it—a perfect decoy.

This is a diabolical situation. If the S.O.S. from our friends in the lifeboat is picked up, it will inevitably place the rescue ship in mortal danger. Devilish situation it may be but, like a dynamo, it will generate more and more suspense. And it is suspense that helps to keep the audience in their seats.

It was during my walk of resignation to Pinewood that this idea of using the lifeboat as a decoy came to me. I realised that if I used it, not only would it provide me with the suspense elements for which I had been seeking so agonisingly and which would make the story viable, but that I would also be betraying the sacred tenets of 'documentary' as currently accepted. To show an enemy periscope as seen from above the waves was within the law. But to show a shot as seen through an enemy periscope, let alone find the camera in an enemy U-Boat with the crew speaking German with English sub-titles, this was betrayal, if not treason.

I never had any qualms about it. 'The creative interpretation of reality' was the aphorism that Grierson coined about his documentary movement. As I have suggested, reality is hard to define. Send two correspondents, both highly respected for their integrity, to report on the coal strike and two very different accounts will appear, yet both are convinced of their objectivity. Reality may be seen from opposite poles. Neither is dishonest, both are subjective interpretations and subjectivity cannot be free from bias for it is part of a person's psyche and orientation to the conflicts and conditions of his environment. The camera, if it is to capture its maximum capacity to convey the most compelling illusion of reality, must be free to see what the dramatist wants it to see. To truncate its power by restricting it to illustrate a commentary is 'creative interpretation of reality' in a straitjacket. Grierson's intellectuals knew nothing about the discipline involved in shaping their themes into dramatic forms; the idea of dialogue, an acted scene, how the actors should move for the camera to the changing moods and tensions would have been unthinkable. Reportage, yes. A worker at his bench is where he belongs, and if he remains there, easy to interview. A miner at the coal face; a housewife in the kitchen or armchair, easy to handle. But to fictionalise, dramatise would be to tread on dangerous ground, and they fought shy of it.

The great documentaries which ring with truth and searing sincerity are few and far between and they come from many sources. To give but a few examples: Flaherty's *Nanook of the North* and *White Shadows of the South Seas*; Pabst's *Kameradschaft*; John Ford's *The Informer* and *The Grapes of Wrath*. These are monuments to truth and testaments to the power of drama to move hearts and minds towards the breakdown of prejudice. These lit the way ahead for me and always will. There is no message unless it makes the heart beat faster and brings laughter or a tear to the eye. The rest is earnest teaching carrying the banner of social service. All very praiseworthy but only a tiny cell in the beehive of the communicating arts.

There were U-Boats taking part in the Battle of the Atlantic, with crews of human beings, equally dedicated to their cause, equally as heroic and as much a part of this ghastly tragedy as the men in the lifeboat or the Commander in Chief. They had their place in this awful battle, an impression of which I had been asked to portray and convey with as much conviction as I could muster.

And so, back to our convoy which ploughs steadily homeward. Aboard *Leander*, in the mess decks below, the 'off watch' members of the crew are listening to the radio. An American programme is blaring forth. As the camera tracks into the loud speaker, the programme changes and becomes one from the B.B.C. One of the crew remarks that they must be over half way when the old B.B.C. starts coming through.

Up top, the weather is nasty and blowing half a gale. Just as the Master feared, the convoy has been slowed down because two ships have engine trouble, and rather than allow them to become stragglers, the convoy is trying to stay with them. The *Leander* is yawing all over the place and the helmsman is having great trouble in holding her on course. The Master has had enough. He signals the Commodore and informs him of his plight. He is given permission to steam ahead and rejoin in the morning. Thankfully, he increases speed, pulls out of his column and forges ahead.

In early morning, we are back in the lifeboat. It is a cold, bleak day. The stubble on chins is now very evident. There is a general feeling of lassitude and debility. Mouths are dry, lips being licked and eyes drooping. The Master is attending the wounded member of the crew. He cups the sick man's head and tries to get him to drink a little of the precious water. He is becoming delirious. The Master leaves him and slowly makes his way, climbing over semirecumbent figures until he finds his young 'Sparks'. He wakes him, gives him their new position and tells him to start sending. The 'Sparks' tells him, as quietly as possible, that the batteries are getting very low. The Master tells him to send as it's now or never for Alf Rawson, he fears.

Aboard *Leander*, it is a call to action stations. An aircraft is seen approaching. Griff is on the gun platform in a matter of moments and his gun crew close behind him. The aircraft starts to flash a message. Griff recognises it as a Catalina and tells his crew to stop loading. The Chief Officer reads the message being flashed by aldis from the Catalina. Below, the two Sparks are on radio watch. One of them slowly turns the tuning dial, lingering over each calibration. Half way round he tells his colleague to stop whistling. 'There's a distress—so faint, I can hardly hear it.' He scribbles the message, hands it to his colleague and tells him to take it 'pronto' to the 'Old Man'. The Master and his Chief Officer are just entering the chart room to fix the new position of the convoy to rejoin it as quickly as possible.

The 'Sparks' enters and tells the Master that he has a distress, handing him the message. He reads it and is on the 'qui vive' instantly. 'Jason . . . That's old Tom . . . How far away is he?' The Chief reads out his position as the Master fixes it with his dividers on the chart. 'Almost on top of him . . . forty miles away.'

'A big diversion, Sir.'

'I've a good mind to go after him.'

'You'll never rejoin the convoy by nightfall if you do, Sir.'

The Master looks at him, long and hard, and makes up his mind. 'Damn the convoy, I'm going after him. Alter course to 140.'

'Aye aye, Sir . . . 140 quartermaster.'

'140 it is, Sir.' A quick impression of time passing as the *Leander* makes for the lifeboat and almost certain doom, and as her bows cleave through the waves we know that each one brings her nearer to it.

Aboard the lifeboat one of the survivors is notching another day on the calendar by carving a slit into the mast. There are already ten or eleven of them. Having carved the notch, he pockets his knife and then, as is his habit, hoists himself on to the centre thwart, and starting from starboard begins to scan the horizon. Almost dead astern he sees the faintest smudge of smoke, or thinks that he does. Rather than raise a false alarm, he closes his eyes and, as though telling the beads of a rosary, starts to count on the fingers of his right hand from little finger to thumb and back again. He opens his eyes. No, he wasn't seeing things, or rather he was seeing what they have all longed and prayed to see these last ten days. A rescue ship is on the horizon.

'Ship ahoy, dead astern.'

Instant reaction from everyone: all look astern. Sure enough there is the faintest smudge of smoke which is no whispy cloud. Excitement and exhilaration know no bounds. Their ordeal is soon to be over.

'Get out the flares, somebody', shouts the Master. At that moment, the wounded man, Alf Rawson, woken by the shouts and cheering, his head perfectly clear, raises himself somewhat and finds himself looking over the starboard bow just as the U-Boat's periscope pops up.

'Periscope on the starboard bow', he shouts. It has been raised for a few seconds only to check position, and by the time Alf's shipmates look round there is no sign of it. Not unnaturally, they think that the poor chap has been hallucinating; after all, he has been delirious on occasions and so it is quite understandable that they should think that.

'There's nothing there, now, Alfie Boy', says John Walden consolingly—it was he who had just seen the rescue ship.

'I'm telling you, I saw it, plain as a pikestaff, and you can do what you damn well like about it.' He feels too ill and weak to continue the argument further.

'Don't worry about it any more, Rawson. We'll deal with the problem', the Master tells him. Rawson nods, closes his eyes and settles down once more on the thwart.

'Aren't you going to alter course for that ship?', asks a crew member rather menacingly.

'No I'm not.'

'Well why the bloody hell not?'

'Because I say so.'

'There's 24 men in this boat, Mister, and we're not risking our lives because a man who's off his rocker thinks he's seen a U-Boat. If you don't make for that ship, we'll bloody soon put someone there who will. What do you say, lads?'

'Listen, Banner. I think Rawson did see that periscope. It's more than likely because there are plenty of U-Boats in this part of the ocean. That one we heard the other night, remember? It's quite possible it's picked up our S.O.S. If it has it's quite possible, too, that he's using us as bait, knowing that sooner or later we'd bring a ship for him to sink, under our noses, and we'll have been responsible. That's a nice thing to remember for the rest of your days, isn't it . . . ISN'T IT!!!' He stares at Banner hard and long. Eventually Banner looks away. 'Well, men, are you with me?'

There is silence, several seconds of it. Indecision as the men look rather sheepishly at each other. There is an old sweat who must go back to the good old days of sail—a great porpoise of a man. He looks round at his shipmates and senses their indecision. He decides to speak for them. 'You've brought us so far, Cap'n, I think we'll stick with you to the end. What do you say, lads?'

There are more nods and affirmative grunts than those who say nothing, not quite having the desire or nerve to mutiny. The Captain looks at them, like a lion tamer dominating his animals. 'Very well . . . Now, keep a sharp look out for that periscope. If you see it for God's sake don't point, just shout periscope and that'll be the cue for us to start waving and pointing dead ahead as though a ship were approaching from there, not astern. That may confuse them just long enough for us to get a message through. Meantime we keep on our present course.'

Once again, by inter-cutting between the lifeboat, the *Leander* and the U-Boat we give an impression of time passing—the next half hour or so compressed into a few minutes. The *Leander*'s bows cutting through the water. Her Master on the bridge with those familiar binoculars, scanning the horizon for the lifeboat of his old shipmate. The lookout in the crow's nest spots it, but it is still below the horizon for those on the bridge.

Aboard the lifeboat the metal flare canister is being cut open; its shiny interior, it is hoped, will enable the master to reflect the sun, so that he can flash a morse signal to the oncoming ship . . . 'U-Boat'. It's a long shot but it's the only one left. The canister is now being flattened out into a reflector when someone shouts 'Periscope'. With one accord all stand and start to wave frantically over the bows, obviously to attract the attention of an oncoming ship.

Through the periscope it is an impressive performance and most convincingly gives the impression that there must be an oncoming rescue ship. Considering it is unrehearsed, it is, perhaps, more spontaneous, and hence doubly convincing. It certainly does the U-Boat Commander. He starts scanning from the lifeboat's bows towards the east, mercifully rather than the west. At least for the moment, the ruse has worked. Having now scanned some 180 degrees the Commander is puzzled that he can see nothing. He discusses this with his Number 1 and decides that it can only be a matter of moments. As his own horizon line is lower in the water than the men's in the lifeboat, it is obvious that they will be able to see further than he can. For a minute or two, then, this line of reasoning will satisfy him—but only for a minute or two, obviously.

Shielded by some of his men from the prying eye of the periscope, the Master is holding the canister reflecting surface and getting a blinding glare from the sun as he points it towards the approaching *Leander*, now a tiny dot on the horizon. All may yet be well for there is no doubt about the intensity of the light being beamed towards the *Leander*. Unhappily the sun decides to hide behind a cloud, a long streaky one. 'Damn and blast . . . It'll be ten minutes before the sun's out of that lot. Boatswain, chop up an oar and I'll need two shirts, white as possible for semaphoring.'

The U-Boat Commander orders the periscope to be raised. He peers through . . . The crew continues to stand, some of them on the thwarts and several are waving various garments as they look over the bows. Once more, the Commander repeats his recent scanning operation and in the same direction, with the same frustrating result. He should be seeing the ship by now. He pauses, tries to think out the problem and then slowly scans back to the lifeboat. He holds it in his sights for several seconds and then with agonising deliberation starts to scan astern, along an arc which must bring the lens of his periscope on to the *Leander*. It is only a matter of a few seconds before there is a triumphant grunt from the Commander. He calls over his Number 1 and is as proud as Punch that his decoy strategy has paid off. He has conserved his fuel and as a result can make quite sure that his last two torpedoes will be spent with telling effect. The periscope is lowered and a course laid to intercept the *Leander*. He is cock-a-hoop; of course he is.

The *Leander*'s bows are cutting through the water. That visual cliché now has a desperate significance. Members of her crew are peering over the rail at that tiny speck ahead, with its red sail, still pulling away instead of 'coming about'.

The Master and his Chief Officer are also mystified that nobody in the lifeboat has yet spotted them. Can it be that everyone is too exhausted to keep a look out? That someone is just clinging to the tiller in a semi-conscious condition? It's very possible. Who knows how long they have endured this ordeal? 'Give them another toot-toot on the siren', the Master orders.

Aboard the lifeboat, John Walden shouts back: 'O.K. O.K. We can 'ear you.' He turns to a shipmate and adds: 'Funny 'ow it goes, init . . . Been in this old tub for 14 days, praying for a ship to come along, and now we got 'er, we don't wanner.' The choicest white shirts have been tied to the bits of oar. The Master, not a young man and in these circumstances not overflowing with stamina, is helped on to the stern thwart. Supported by two of the crew he starts to semaphore the letter 'U'.

The periscope is being raised. The Commander cannot wait to check his position. He is closing. The outline of the *Leander* is almost definable but is a mile or two out of range. Aboard *Leander*, old Griff is walking forrard towards the 'Bosun's locker'. On the bridge, the Captain and his Chief still have binoculars glued to their foreheads. The Chief says: 'I think I can see movement astern, Sir.'

'So can I. Thank God for that. Give 'em another blast, Quartermaster. Let 'em know we're on our way.'

Griff meets the Bosun as he leaves his locker. 'Ullo Bos . . . I'm on the scrounge. Got a bit o' cotton waste so's I can work some grease into my breach block?'

''elp yourself, chum; bin on the starboard side, there.'

'Thanks very much.' Griff enters and the bulkhead door swings shut behind him.

On the bridge the Chief says: 'Just about make it out, Sir, I think. Yes, that's definitely an O . . . And this is an A . . . T . . .'

'O.A.T . . .', mutters the Captain.

'U . . .'

'O.A.T.U . . . U-Boat. 'Course. HARD A-STARBOARD . . . SPIN THAT WHEEL FOR CHRIST'S SAKE.'

The *Leander*, seen through the periscope, is in range. The U-Boat Commander waits no longer: 'FEUER EINZ . . . FEUER ZWEI.' A torpedo track bubbles to the surface. In the Boatswain's forepeak there is a huge explosion. The figure of Griff is hurled across the deck. The men in the lifeboat look sadly astern at the smoke trail rising from the *Leander*. They stand there, living monuments to the dead at sea.

Aboard *Leander*, the gun crew assembles, but there is no Griff. The second officer, his face half covered with shaving soap, hurries up to the Captain for orders. The Master decides to keep a skeleton crew aboard and get the rest of the men off as soon as possible. They may have another fish into them, any second.

The U-Boat Commander is anything but happy. He sees that he has not done enough damage on the enemy ship to sink her. A lucky last minute alteration of course prevented the second torpedo from hitting her. The only way to finish her off is to surface and sink her with gun fire . . . a risky business. He sees the crew taking to the boats and pulling away. This could indicate that they don't give much for her chances, or it's just a bluff. He's going to make very sure that he doesn't fall for it.

In the *Leander*'s forepeak, a burst pipe is spraying water over a large area, including the inert figure of Griff. The Chief Officer is heard calling: 'Griffiths? ... Griffiths...?' We can hear him running across the iron foredeck and entering the main hatch of the forepeak. A short corridor leads to the Bosun's holy of holies. He bangs on the bulkhead door, tries to open it but it is jammed. He looks through the little ventilating grille but his angle of vision is limited. Griffiths is lying just below it. The Chief leaves to look for him elsewhere. No sooner has he left than Griff's eyes begin to flicker. Consciousness is returning. His eyes open. He thinks he's in his bunk and tries to get up. He can't: his legs are pinned by some heavy timber which has slid from its shelves. He wriggles free and crawls to a packing case. With some difficulty he manages to seat himself; cupping his head, he tries to gather his wits. Where is he? What was he doing here? Oh yes ... cotton waste ... CHRIST ALMIGHTY ... He manages to totter to the door. It is jammed. No amount of wrenching has the slightest effect. He can hear the water rushing into the forehead bulkhead, below. It makes a frightening roaring sound. Panic takes hold of him and he sounds off, bellowing with all his might: 'Up top ... Let me aht ... I'm jammed in 'ere ... LET ME AHT O HERE. UP TOP!!!!' It is quite a while before that disciplined training of his begins to take hold. If he loses his wits, he's lost for sure. He regains control as he stands there, waiting for the breath to return. He is gathered now.

He sees a hefty oak plank and is just strong enough to pick it up but cannot gain sufficient momentum with it to have much effect as a battering ram against the bulkhead door. It overbalances him and he falls awkwardly. No escape that way. He looks around, again. He sees an old klaxon; almost First World War model. He depresses it and it barks back at him. He stumbles back to the door and holding it up to the ventilating grille sets it to bark as hard and as frequently as he can.

The Chief is moving aft, along a corridor, peering into every cabin, when he hears the barking klaxon. He knows whence that sound comes and moves forrard again. He passes a fire-hydrant station and removes the axe from the glass case and hurries on his way.

'Griff.'

'Yes, Sir.'

'Stand clear . . . Have you out in no time.' And he does.

'You all in one piece, Griff?'

'Think so, hope so Sir . . . Blast knocked me out cold. We badly hit, Sir.'

'Just abaft the port bow. We've got a chance unless she pumps another into us.' The Chief is just about to break cover and cross the foredeck when Griff checks him. He looks through a hauser fairlead on the port side. Under cover of the bulwark he signals for the Chief to join him. He nods his head below and there they see the periscope moving slowly past.

'Let's get aft to that gun. Come on Griff.'

'Watch out they don't see us, Sir.'

In the control room the U-Boat Commander sees the lifeboats pulling away. Slowly, he circles the *Leander*, looking for some sign of life aboard.

Griff and the Chief, crouching well below the shielding bulwarks, make their way aft, past the Sherman tanks amidships and a Canadian Pacific locomotive on the after deck. Soon, they are at the bottom of the companion, leading up to the gun platform. They peer through the starboard fairlead. The periscope is on their quarter and moving painfully slowly around towards her stern where they will be hidden from it by the superstructure of the gun platform. When they are hidden they climb up the iron steps and crawl on their bellies towards the gun.

'There's a shell left in the loading tray, Sir.'

'Bit of luck.'

'Save us the trouble, anyway.'

'Yeah, wonder what she's going to do with us.'

'Chances are she's going to surface, Sir, or she'd have let us have another by now.'

'Probably right . . . Anyway, nothing we can do but wait.'

'Ooh, I'm used to that Sir . . . reminds me of the Q-ships in the last war.'

The U-Boat Commander has not taken his eyes from the

periscope. Griff and the Chief do not take theirs off it as they follow its path, catching glimpses of it through the gaps in the ammunition trays or troughs spread around the perimeter of the platform. The Commander watches.

Griff and the Chief watch. Back and forth, this see-sawing, this cat and mouse game, and it may be a long drawn-out affair.

'Look, it's gone, Sir.'

'Come on Griff, let's see if the gun's loaded.'

'Better not, Sir. Oldest trick in the world. They pop it up again and catch you napping. Got to wait.'

'I can see you *have* had practice at this.'

'Hardened criminal, Sir.' They stare down at the ocean, mentally tracking the underwater position of the U-Boat, like panthers waiting to spring.

And so is the U-Boat Commander. He has not moved a muscle in that semi-crouched position at the periscope. Will he take a chance or will he resist temptation? Can he end his patrol knowing that he has left his job unfinished? He may be too proud, too stubborn, too conscientious, or he may persuade himself that none of these considerations is above the one and only: the safety of his ship and ship's company. Only time will tell and he hasn't much of it to play with. This may not be the safest place in the Atlantic. If he's going to act he must be smart about it, for who knows what may be steaming over the horizon.

Griff's and the Chief's eyes have shifted very little. Something is beginning to break the surface of the water. It is the conning tower.

'My God, here she comes, Sir.'

'Come on Griff, let's blast away at her.'

'No, Sir. She can crash dive before we get her range. We gotta get her committed: tanks blown and crew out on the casing . . . Then we've got her, Sir.'

It requires all their will-power to hold themselves in check. Here, Griff's experience in the First World War Q-ships comes to their aid. It is perhaps an agonising minute before Griff judges that the U-Boat is now at their mercy and fully committed to the surface. They jump to the gun, Griff at the range finder.

'Range? What do you think, Sir?'

'550.'

'I'll give it 500 and I'll give you an "On". Here we go. On . . . On . . . On . . . Fire.'

The Chief squeezes the firing release spring and they wait for the splash. It shoots up like a geyser, well beyond the conning tower. 'Over that time . . . Down two hundred.' Griff runs for another shell and places it in the loading tray, ready for the third shot. He adjusts his sights. Pandemonium is breaking out on the U-Boat's casing. The gun crew does its best to bring the gun to bear on the *Leander*. Another struggles to mount a machine gun in the conning tower. The *Leander*'s Captain, after the first shot, runs from his cabin, where he has been destroying secret papers, and jumps into the Oerliken gun turret, just below the wing of his bridge. Somewhat flustered he tries to come to terms with it and bring it to bear on the U-Boat.

Griff is ready to fire his second shot: 'On . . . on . . . ON. FIRE.' They wait to see the effect. They are short. 'Short that time.' He swings the shell into the breach block and runs for another.

The machine gun from the conning tower starts to fire. Griff picks up a shell and turns for the gun. The U-Boat Commander tells the machine gunner to aim at the gun. The gun shield starts to be sprayed with bullets. They are in line to cross the viewing aperture. Griff lays his shell in the tray and is hit. He sprawls across the metal deck. The Chief is immediately at his side. Griff is mortally wounded. He just manages to say: 'Up a hundred and you'll do it.'

The Chief immediately leaves him and relays the gun. The *Leander*'s Master now gets his Oerliken working and sprays the U-Boat. The Chief Officer, having reset the elevation, runs round the breach block and squeezes the firing mechanism. The shot is true and pierces the waterline, below the conning tower. The control room floods and, like the roar of a hundred drum roll, the water rises fast. The U-Boat crew abandons ship. The Chief returns to Griff. 'You got him, Griff, you got him.'

'Good . . . Tell the wife we almost made that wedding anniversary.' He dies.

We end the story as quickly as possible. The lifeboat crew is helped aboard and the two Masters meet. There is every chance that they will be able to limp back to port, if necessary with the aid of tugs. As the survivors are helped below, the engine room telegraph rings for 'Slow Ahead'. The *Leander* starts once more to move through the water. The lifeboat slips astern to become a piece of flotsam on the Atlantic.

*

And there you have it: the simple little tale. All that had to be done was to transfer it to film. As we all know, it is one thing to have the golf course laid out and quite another to play on it. Assuming that I was going to be allowed to play on it at all. The story had to be passed by the powers that be.

Here Dal obviously used his great diplomatic skills, and there is no one who worked in the Crown Film Unit who does not owe him an enormous debt. He was quite sure in what field his contribution would lie when he agreed to become our Executive Producer. He had been shown all our work and in some ways it was a new approach, a new school of cinema, as in painting or some other medium. He felt that it might have something to contribute to the war effort so long as we were left alone to get on with it. He was going to make sure that we would not be bothered and bewildered by niggling little minutes from the Films Division of the Ministry of Information and other bureaucratic bodies. He was our shining knight who was to protect us from all the clap-trap—and what's more, he did. Unless he felt that he had to, he interfered as little as possible when the creative process was under way. If you had won his confidence, he left it to you to produce the goods. He was always there to give guidance or any help he could, if called upon. If not he left you to get on with it whilst he fought for your right to be able to do just that. Never before or since has any group of film people enjoyed such creative freedom, and this is the debt that we owe him—not likely to be paid, either.

So, this story of mine, though he liked it, was going to give him some headaches. The Navy, after all, had asked for it to be made:

the Commander in Chief himself, and in Owen Rutter's *H.M. Escort* it was the Navy all the time, with personal appearances by the Commander in Chief popping up all over the place. Moreover, it is useless to imagine that the height of rings up a sleeve renders the bearer any more immune from the wish to 'have a go' in front of the camera. Nobody is totally free from the lure of it. Indeed, recent additions to the Royal Family should apply for Equity membership or take to heart Noel Coward's warning to Mrs Worthington not to put her daughter on the stage. How, then, would the C. in C. react? He was going to be asked to read a story about his battle in which he does not even appear; in which the stars are survivors in a lifeboat; a merchant ship which leaves the convoy and the protection of the Navy; and finally, a German U-Boat Commander. Well, really! It was asking a lot.

Objections did not come from the C. in C., but from their Lordships at the Admiralty who, justifiably, felt that they were not getting a fair crack of the whip. Dal defended the story, emphasising its dramatic potential, that the final situation of such suspense would have enormous commercial value as well as being legitimate to the subject. Furthermore, the writer had struggled to find a story which would not be too demanding on the Navy's resources. It was no use writing in spectacular scenes requiring facilities that their Lordships would be unable to provide, resulting in our being unable to complete the picture and a financial disaster. Better to lower their sights a little and make sure of hitting the target and portray the essence of the subject in highly dramatic form. His arguments won the day, and by the time I had completed the shooting script, the subject was 'off the ground' and the money was there. It was as though we had completed the first circuit at Aintree. Now for the second.

13

We walk the course

It was early June 1942. Dal and I were analysing the breakdown of the shooting script. We were surprised to discover that the lifeboat carried the largest number of scenes. As no one had ever attempted to shoot sustained synchronous dialogue scenes in an open ship's lifeboat, at sea, supposedly in mid-Atlantic, obviously they were going to present problems. As we would be breaking new ground, many would be unforeseen and would have to be resolved, hopefully, as and when they appeared. It would need Merlin to foresee them all and take the necessary measures to avoid them.

The lifeboat must carry a cast of about 24, the camera crew of two if not three, the 'mike' boy, someone to hold the reflector, the continuity girl, and me. Thirty-six people. Then, there was the equipment. The Technicolor three-strip camera which was as cumbersome as the average sized refrigerator. To mount it was going to be difficult in a lifeboat, bouncing about in seas that were supposed to be in mid-Atlantic. The normal tripod could not be expected to keep on its feet against every angle of pitch and corkscrew roll that the boat would obviously undergo. We would have to have an adequate towing craft which must house the sound equipment because we couldn't expect the lifeboat to take the recordist and his paraphernalia. Besides, we must be free, so far as possible, to be able to move around to alter the camera set-up after each shot. Our towing craft therefore would have three cables pulling us through the water: the microphone cable, the camera cable and the main towing cable. Quite a prospect, obviously fraught with imponderables. I asked Dal whether Technicolor had ever put to sea in a lifeboat with their three-strip and recorded sound.

'They've made a film called *Western Isle*, but whether they recorded sound we'll find out.'

'With a blimped camera and no post-synching back in the studio. Direct sound, that's the key question.' Dal was soon on the phone to Technicolor, on the Bath Road, opposite open farm lands where already bulldozers were at work on Heathrow. He asked for George Gunn, their brilliant head technician and inventor. Dal tapped the bridge of his glasses. 'George? . . . Dalrymple, Crown, about *Western Approaches*. Have you ever shot ''sync'' in a ship's lifeboat? Yes, I know about *Western Isles*, but were you shooting sync? Ah, post-sync . . . Camera unblimped. A very different kettle of fish. We have a third of the film to be shot sync and with that amount of dialogue there can be no question of post-synching. So, if you have second thoughts about our using your system, please let me know . . . Ironed out, you feel sure. Let's hope so. O.K. Goodbye.' He put the receiver down, thoughtful and troubled, and so was I. Dal tapped the ash into his tray and said: 'We haven't signed the contract with them yet. That was a perfect chance for them to wriggle out of the assignment.'

'Not too keen for us to use their system?', I suggested.

'There are only three of their cameras in the country. One on *Henry V*, the others on *This Happy Breed* and *Blithe Spirit*. We're in line for *Henry V*'s camera.'

'What seems obvious, Dal, in fact essential, is that we must be given time to have a dummy run, actually mount the camera at sea, with sound, the whole works; see what the problems are and iron them out before we start. Otherwise we shall have to do it when we're committed and heaven knows what may be involved . . . Even whether the problems are surmountable.'

'Good point. We'll try and make that a condition. But, there can be no doubt that your story in colour will be ten times as powerful so it's worth blood, sweat and tears. So, lifeboat first . . . Now, casting. Big parts, some of them. The lifeboat's Captain? Hell of a part, handling the mutiny sequence. The wounded man becoming delirious. What are you going to do, get him pissed? And the ringleader of the mutiny, a Wallace Beery type. How on earth are you going to find all these types?'

'God knows, Dal. Hang around the seamen's mission and pubs, I suppose.'

'Well, that's the way you people go about it, so you'd better keep on. You found 'em for *Ferry Pilot* so let's hope your luck holds.'

'I'll have to kick off at the Adelphi. If I can find something a bit cheaper I will.'

'You must have a reasonable base. You may have to meet all sorts of people.'

'And Dal, there's no point in my coming back until I've found at least 30 or 40 possibles and I'll have to test them rigorously.'

'That'll mean a special grant. What'll you want?'

'The full works, on the "lot". Lights and sync sound. A full unit. We've got to be sure they can face the whole bag of tricks without turning green and clamming up.'

'Quite right. O.K. then, and good luck.'

The production office arranged my travelling and hotel re-servation for the following day. This second trip to Liverpool was for something tangible. Faces and characters. Hunting for them would involve lengthy pub crawls. An odd system of casting but it had worked before and it would work again—I hoped. The only snag about the method is that it cannot be scheduled and its un-certainty is both daunting and discouraging.

14

'Tally Ho.' The hunt is on

I travelled with a new ally, Peter Bolton, who was to be my assistant: a delightful bloke with a great sense of humour. That night the Adelphi bar was filled with three-ringers and Captains R.N. and of no interest to us at that moment.

The next morning, I had an appointment with a Mr Hobbes, Senior Registration Officer for all the seamen in the port. His office in the Shipping Federation was in the dock area. He was a charming and most helpful man. We explained the purpose of our visit and left a synopsis of the story with him.

It is an odd fact that once it is known that a film unit is interested in a town, a village or what you will, a glint comes into the eye and morale seems to rise. Someone outside is taking an interest in their part of the globe. Mr Hobbes was delighted that, at last, someone was concerned about the poor old merchant seaman, who had been taking so much stick. Immediately, he gave us the run of the place and suggested that we should sit and watch the men as they came in to register. If there were a face that interested us, all we would have to do would be to wave to the chap behind the counter and he would arrange for us to meet him in an adjoining office. Then he said: 'The pub's the place, isn't it, if you want to catch them off guard . . . see them as they really are.'

'You should be in our game, Mr Hobbes, I can see that.'

'Well who wouldn't . . . must be marvellous.'

'It has its moments, Mr Hobbes, I will admit.'

'Must have, all the people you meet, places you get to see, my goodness me, and the things you must learn about the other chap's way of life. Marvellous. I'd better shut up or I'll get really cheesed off. The Angel, Mr Jackson, that's the pub for you. They all go there. Landlord's a great pal of mine. Anderson; mention my name, he'll do all he can, I'm sure of that.'

We chatted on for a while and if everyone were to be as helpful as our Mr Hobbes, the first man to receive us in Liverpool, then we were in for a very happy time, if nothing more.

He took us down to the reception rooms where seamen, whose ships may just have berthed, come to report and make known their plans; that they will be signing on again with the same ship; request a new berth and maybe put in a claim for possessions lost at sea due to enemy action. The Shipping Federation is to the seaman what the agent is to the actor. Mr Hobbes introduced us to his staff and explained to them the reason for our visit and that we would be hanging round the place for an indefinite period. If we were to give them a wink and a nod it would indicate that we would like to talk to whoever it was they were talking to. We were let into a fairly large reception room, rather like a post office with two counters. 'I'll leave you to it, Mr Jackson, and good hunting. Don't hesitate to call me if I can be of help.'

Peter and I sat ourselves down on one of the benches and waited for our stars to appear. We were a couple of hunters, in our hide, waiting for the game to appear from the undergrowth. We sat there, Tweedle Dee and Dum, for a couple of hours until about midday. We saw a fair cross-section of merchant seamen and were not encouraged that not one had seemed worthy of a nod or a wink. The best part of a morning and not a single bite. This could be a long, long siege. But at least we had discovered a way of laying it, and now it was time to lay siege to the Angel, Canning Street, not far from the Federation.

The Landlord was a jolly man, treble chinned, pot bellied and affable with every pound of his overweight person. We told him our mission. 'And about bloody time, too, these poor buggers got a bit of recognition.' More courtesies and drinks were exchanged and there was no doubt that our Landlord was both pleased and flattered to have been put in the know and that his house had been chosen for our casting H.Q. He rightly, too, foresaw pints and pints being pulled to further the nation's war effort.

'Yes, Pat, that's all right then. You and Pete sit in the little private bar there. Get a good view, you will, from there, have 'em full face, see as they wait to be served. Only got to tip me the wink and I'll shunt 'em into you. No trouble, no trouble at all. They all come in 'ere so you'll see all the talent Liverpool's got to offer in no time at all.'

'Just the ticket. Now what's yours, Mr Anderson?'

'Bill's the name, Pat. I'll have a drop of brandy with you, then.'

We stuck to our humble half of bitter, having no idea how many days or weeks this process might have to become a way of work and a daily routine. It was now about half-past twelve and the tide should be coming in. At the moment there were one or two very old 'shell backs' from the square rigger days and a bit beyond it even for one of our 'spits and coughs'. The talent started to trickle in. We'd been there about an hour and not only was our morale beginning to sag but we were nearing the critical moment when another couple of halves would have to be ordered to justify our presence in the private bar when a stocky little man, smoking a broken clay pipe, sauntered in. This was the genuine seaman's roll and he had a torn peaked cloth cap, which hung jauntily over one ear. He had the brightest browny-black eyes, like bull's eyes at 2d a quarter. He caught the eye because he was so obviously the real goods. I waited anxiously to hear him talk. He ordered a pint and a chaser. I heard every word even though he was at the far end of the bar. Bill made some quip which was received with as merry a chuckle as I'd heard in a long while.

'Bill, when you're ready.'

'Sure, Pat, what'll it be?'

'Two halves. Oh and Bill . . .' I winked in the direction of his new customer.

'Sure, two halves and an extra.'

'Couldn't have put it better myself.'

Bill started to pull the two halves and I saw him talk to our prospect, who immediately looked over in our direction, took out his pipe, pushed his cloth cap further back on his head and shook it.

'No, seriously Bob, they'd like a word with you.'

'What about, for Christ's sake?'

'They know better than I do and they don't look as though they'll do you any harm. I'll push your drinks through. Go on, man.'

'Just off me bloody boat, can't have me first drink ashore in peace.'

'What d'ye expect ... Bloody war on.'

'Bugger me ... All right then.' Somewhat grudgingly, he sauntered across the saloon, out of the door, and was poking his head round ours.

'You gentlemen wanna see me?'

'Just for a moment. What'll you have?', I said nonchalantly.

'Another chaser ... What's up?'

'My name's Pat and my colleague here is Peter. We're from the Crown Film Unit and we're up here to prepare a film on the Western Approaches. I think you might be just the person to play a small part in it.'

'ME??' He laughed, loudly and, I was happy to note, most infectiously. It was a real honest-to-God belly laugh.

'You're taking the piss.' His beady bright eyes shone mischievously and challengingly.

'No I'm not, honest.'

'Me in the fillums; never.'

'You never know your luck.'

'Luck, hm?'

'You never know. Who'm I talking to, by the way?'

'Banner, Bob Banner.'

'Hullo, I'm Pat, Pat Jackson, and my friend here's Peter, Peter Bolton.' We shook hands. His was tiny and hard as iron. I continued my sales talk.

'Would you be interested, Bob?'

'Was just saying to Bill, there, bin ashore but half an hour, hardly sipped me first drink and I'm asked a damn silly question like that—no disrespect mind.'

'May seem damn silly to you, but I assure you it isn't. I've written a part which I can see you playing very well.'

'Oh . . . What?' I waited a bit, not only to keep him frying for a moment but to make quite sure that he would understand that I was slightly pulling his leg.

'No disrespect mind . . . a mutinous dog.' He took it well and chuckled as I handed over his pint and chaser. Peter handed me my half pint.

'Cheers, Bob.'

'Good luck . . . You blokes can't be serious . . . I mean, it's a bit daft, isn't it, coming up to ordinary blokes and saying ''want to be a film star''?'

'Who said anything about film star?'

'You know what I mean. It's daft . . . honestly . . . what do I know about acting? F.A., for God's sake. Never acted in me life, 'cept the old giddy goat; done enough of that in my time. But acting, never.'

'Just as well.'

'Got no memory, never could learn a damn thing, just won't stick.'

'Won't matter.'

'Oh . . . nothing to say then?'

'Oh yes, but not to memorise, not to learn. You'll get the sense of each bit of a scene and make up your own things to say. Just as you are now. We do it bit by bit. Like building a house, brick by brick.'

'When's all this going to happen, then?'

'When I've found the other blokes. Don't want actors, Bob, we're after the real blokes who know what it's all about.'

'Oh well, I'll be back at sea in a week or so.'

'Not necessarily.'

'Eh? How do you know?'

'Because this is an official film and anyone taking part in it will be considered to be on active service.'

'Take it as seriously as that, do they?'

'Yes.'

'What about pay, then?'

'Not much more than you're getting now, plus a few allowances, maybe. I wouldn't know at the moment. You wouldn't lose but I'm not able to tell you how much you'd gain, financially. Not very much, probably.'

'But I might be bloody awful.'

'Yes, you might, but I don't think you will.'

'You gotta make sure, haven't chou?'

'Yes, so far as possible.'

'How d'you do that, then?'

'We make what we call a screen test. We make you face the camera and all the works. You'll soon know whether you're bloody awful or not, but I have a hunch you'll take to it like a duck to water.'

'And if I don't?'

'No harm done. You'll have lost nothing, you might even have had some fun. An interesting time, certainly.'

'Where does all this happen?'

'Near London. Place called Pinewood; biggest studios in England.'

'Sounds daft to me, but that's your look out, isn't it?'

'Yes.'

'Haven't got much to lose, really, have I?'

'I can't think of anything. Bit of extra shore leave seems certain.'

'All right. I don't mind. I'll have a go.'

I felt as though I'd bought the *Mona Lisa* for a song. We took his name and address and told him that we would inform Mr Hobbes, who would make arrangements for him to remain ashore on full pay until further notice, now that he was an official candidate for one of the cast of *Western Approaches*. We would notify him when his test would take place and left him to enjoy what was left of his first morning ashore. I was thrilled with the results of our first morning on the hunt. At this rate we might be able to track down the men needed for the lifeboat scenes in a week or two.

It was 30 July, almost five months since I climbed that Jacob's ladder of the *Fort Binger*. Five months in which the war could have been won or lost; the map of the world turned upside down;

millions killed and maimed, and here was I hanging around Liverpool pubs looking for seamen in the belief that I could make actors
of them. It was a ludicrous idea and an ideological confrontation
that was ever-present.

Yet, we were on an exacting operation which must inevitably
take its own time and operate within its own orbit and limitations.
We weren't producing sausages or shells whose production levels
could be foreseen and exactly scheduled. We were embarked upon
an extraordinary exercise in which we were not part of the vast
military machine; not subject to military discipline; not ram-
rodding to attention; not saluting superior rank; not reacting to the
nation's circumstances in the normal way, at all.

At a time when the energy and genius of the vast majority was
employed in destroying the enemy and his machine of war, we
were struggling in the realm of ideas, embarked upon a creative
process of dramatising part of this destructive process, and in order
that the final product should have the maximum emotional impact,
I had to emphasise the human values, the moral dilemmas, the
humanity, in fact, of this inhuman process. Was this a contra-
diction? Were we on a useless wild goose chase? Were we justified
in this endeavour? Of course, I couldn't be sure and was victim to a
constant gnawing doubt that was not good for morale. The job was
going to be tricky enough without wondering whether it were
worthwhile. I thought of *London Can Take It* and the fact that when
Quentin Reynolds, who had spoken the commentary of the film,
took it personally to the White House to show President Roosevelt, the film had had a beneficial effect on the President's thinking
towards our cause in general and the Lend-Lease scheme in particular. However, that little film of ours had taken but a few weeks
to make. This one of mine, well, God alone knew how long it
might take. At the rate we were going, years, probably. Whenever
these haunting doubts started to emerge from the cupboard I
slammed the door on them with a renewed conviction that this
assignment, this private war of mine, would be fought with no
compromise in the pursuit of realism—the greatest possible
illusion of it that our resources and abilities could command.

A week or so before leaving for Liverpool we had sent synopses of the story to various shipping lines—Elder Demster and Blue Funnel being two of them—for their comments and criticisms and, even more important, any suggestions for casting from members of their own crews. When we returned to the Adelphi there was a message waiting for me from Alfred Holt of the Blue Funnel Line. He would be pleased to see me the same afternoon.

He was a magnificently hewn man. If Epstein had known him he would have immediately ordered a massive hunk of granite and got to work. The result would have been an image of immense power. His office was of Edwardian splendour of mahogany panelling. He received me most graciously and said that he was very sympathetic towards our project and would like to help. Had I any suggestions? I replied that our main worry, at the moment, was casting and explained my reasons for wanting all the parts to be played by serving officers and men from both navies. He considered this for a moment and replied: 'Surely, Jackson, they will give very amateur performances, and amateur dramatics in a film of this sort would be a disaster.'

'That's why we give them very rigorous tests, and if they're not up to it, we soon know.' I then tried to explain how adaptable the film medium was in helping the inexperienced to give of his or her best and how quickly they gain confidence. It comes almost hourly if they are handled sympathetically. He listened politely but I don't think that I convinced him. He said: 'Hm, interesting theory . . . and it's you who are going to make them act?'

'It's more a question of asking them to use their own way to describe experiences which are akin to the story we are going to tell. I think they'll be more convincing than actors trying to look like old salts.'

'Well, well, rather you than me. Now how can we help?'

'The big bug bear at the moment is to find the men who can play these quite hefty parts.' He thought for a moment and said: 'The Captain of the lifeboat . . . I could no more learn that than I could Shakespeare, at school.'

'We do it bit by bit, Sir, like nibbling away at a hunk of cheese.

Not quite so daunting then. Can you think of a Master who could play it?'

'Several, but I couldn't spare one of them. How long are these lifeboat scenes going to take?'

'Several months, I should think, Sir. We're on experimental ground, trying to film dialogue scenes in a lifeboat.'

'In that case, I may have just the man for you. A fine Master, Captain Pycraft of the *Deukalion*, heavily damaged on a recent Malta convoy. He will be on long leave, awaiting repairs to his ship. A fatherly looking man: certainly look the part, but I don't suppose he can act for toffee. Why should he, after all?'

'Half the battle if he looks the part. I'd love to meet him.'

'I'll send him the synopsis and tell him to contact you at the Adelphi. I'm glad the poor old Merchant Navy's getting a look in. About the lifeboat; the Blue Funnel will supply it. You'd better have two. One is bound to get knocked about!'

'That's very generous, Sir. A magnificent gesture.'

'The Blue Funnel's contribution, couple of ''props''. Now is there anything else? Now's your chance.'

'Would it be possible to have detachable platforms fore and aft?'

'What for?'

'To show the lifeboat packed with survivors, I shall have to get my camera behind the helmsman, looking forrard. It's a bulky bit of equipment and to be perched above the stern will mean a platform, and it'll be a great shot.'

'You'll arrange that with my marine engineer, Mr Dickie, and he will come and see you about it. It will make the boats very unseaworthy, I can tell you that, now. In any sort of a sea, quite hazardous. If a wave breaks on it, obviously you'll ship a lot of water. Discuss that with Dickie and he'll put you wise. As and when you're ready. You'll tell him where they are to be delivered.'

'Thank you, Sir. I can't begin to tell you how grateful I am for your kindness and your interest.'

'All right Jackson. Glad to have met you, and good luck with your film.'

He shook me warmly by the hand and I took myself back to the Adelphi. I had just met one of the grand old men of England's shipping world. As solid as a rock. His line, I was to gather later, had a reputation for being hard employers—no shelter on the bridge wings; no molly-coddling whilst on duty ... must be alert and ever on the ready. The cold and the spray keep you on your toes. But everyone wanted to work for it because it also had the reputation of being just.

So far, it had been a most rewarding day. Only one cloud on the horizon. 'Can you think of a master who could play the part?' 'Yes, many, but I can't spare one of them.' This could mean that in casting this role there might be no free choice. I might be forced into accepting someone who I knew would not be right. This was an unforeseen worry, particularly so for this part which was so important. However, sufficient unto the day is the casting thereof.

Our daily routine started to fall into a fixed pattern. Until opening time we would be at the Shipping Federation and then a quick march to the Angel and Landlord Anderson's ever watchful and helpful eye. It was not long before we were known for what we were, 'talent scouts'. One day, as we were leaving the Federation, we heard a shout: 'Hi Misters!' We looked round and a fellow came running up to us and somewhat breathlessly blurted out: 'You the gen'lemen looking for blokes for this 'ere film you're going to make?'

'That's right', I said.

'Well I've been torpedoed four times and in a lifeboat for three weeks afore we was picked up. Wasna picnic, I can tell you, so I'm just the sort of bloke you're looking for, aren't I?'

'You certainly are', I said, though I knew he wasn't.

'Come on, let's have a pint at the Angel.' He was only too willing, and though it was obvious that he wasn't quite what we were looking for, it wasn't very tactful at that moment to explain that the unfortunate frequency of being torpedoed and days of misery spent in a lifeboat do not necessarily guarantee the ability to contribute a performance, or indeed anything, to the making of a film. So, along he came and we listened to his story and took his name and address. Everyone had to be given a fair hearing if and when we were approached, and we noticed that it was happening more and more. The word had got around that these two suckers could be the means towards a cushy job ashore for a month or two. This new element in our casting efforts cluttered the scene rather, but it was unavoidable, though it did waste a lot of time. But who knew when another Bob Banner might walk through the door, and this time, he could make the overture.

A few days later, Captain and Mrs Pycraft came to dinner with us. Alfred Holt was right. He looked the part, splendidly, but older than the man I had visualised. When he retired he would need practically no make-up to be the perfect Father Christmas. He was very benign, but like the Christmas pudding, lacking, perhaps, a little levity. But, judging from his guarded remarks concerning his last Malta convoy, he hadn't much to feel light and frothy about. A third of the convoy had been sent to the bottom, with his own ship under constant threat from the time of leaving Gibraltar and arriving at Malta some eight days later, and with only a few snatched hours, here and there, on duty, day and night. He was a very kind man and would bring, perhaps, values to the part which I had not foreseen. Furthermore, it occurred to me that I might have no other choice. Anyway, he might be marvellous. No man can have gone through what he had, shouldered his responsibilities, lived for weeks on end with imminence of death, commanding, apparently, as though on a peace-time Channel crossing, without enormous resources and qualities of character. There could be no question about that; the only question was how would he react to the camera, for his performance had to be more than just adequate: so much depended on it.

15

'Testing . . . Testing'

After about two weeks of this shunting between the Federation, the Angel and various seamen's missions, we had collected, or rather made note of, about forty hopefuls who had expressed their interest in and agreement to undergoing a screen test. Forty hopefuls for a boatload of around 24 gave us a discard value of 16. I had great hopes that five of them might have something a little out of the ordinary; characters from whom I would get not just the odd remark and convincing reaction shots but sustained dialogue scenes in which they would be able 'to throw the ball around'. My favourite was still Bob Banner, but I had high hopes for John Walden A.B. of 11 Arrowe Avenue, Moreton, Cheshire—a genuine London cockney, late twenties, with a face as finely chiselled as John Carradine's in *Grapes of Wrath*. A superbly sculptured face and most expressive eyes. And what, after all, has the screen actor to rely on, but eyes and voice? I did not require the great theatrical presences of the Irvings and the Forbes Robertsons. Great though they must have been, their battery of heavy guns were for other campaigns: wasted and out of place for so intimate a medium as a camera studying men's reactions to the rigours of days at sea in a lifeboat. The impression of such an ordeal could only be built up by a collected observation of minute detail in human behaviour. John Walden had a face that could register the agony of any given moment.

Alf Rawson A.B. of 105 Radnor Avenue, Welling, Kent—a good young type, alert, in his middle twenties, easy to talk to and of manner, an open face which inspired trust, and if he were to tell you that he had seen a periscope, instinctively you would believe him. He would be, for that reason, ideal to play the wounded man. But, he must be capable—and here was the rub—of conveying extreme sickness, mounting fever, babbling delirium one moment and coherence the next. Not exactly 'a cake walk' for someone with no acting experience. I explained to him, in detail, the part I had in mind for him to play, and its importance in the construction of the story. I gave him an inkling of what he would have to convey: 'From the word go, Alf, we know that you're wounded in the head, weak and feverish, your condition deteriorating daily. One night a U-Boat is heard charging its batteries. Your Captain asks for quiet. It's then that you're heard babbling away in delirium, any old rubbish you like.'

'I shouldn't find that difficult.'

'Good. But the fact that your shipmates know you go off your rocker, now and then, gives them every reason to disbelieve you when you tell them that you've seen a periscope and it's then that the real drama starts because only the Captain believes you and will not "come about" and sail towards the approaching rescuing ship, and that almost starts a mutiny.'

'Blimey.'

'It's quite a situation if we can put it across and it's you who set it up by seeing that periscope.'

'Dear Oh Lor', and you want me to do all that? I've never acted in my life.'

'It isn't a question of acting, just thinking and feeling and trying to convey what it means to you for just that moment. Between the two of us, we'll find a way of getting it across. Will you have a go?'

'Yes, if you think there's a chance I can do it.'

'I'm quite sure you can.'

'But why did you choose me?'

'Because I don't think you tell lies easily.' He laughed and said: 'I'll do my best, that I can promise.' We shook hands and I felt confident that I'd found our wounded man.

Two or three weeks later we had a list of hopefuls, and sooner or later the moment of truth would have to be faced for them and for me. Surely, we must have found a nugget or two after all those pints, swigged in the line of duty? It would be too awful if we'd drawn a complete blank. I showed my list to Mr Hobbes: the quantity surprised him. He said: 'Before they go off, would it be a good idea if we had 'em in here for, well, a little chat?'

'Read 'em the riot act, you mean?'

'A question of making them realise that while they're on this jaunt—to them—they'll be as much on duty as aboard ship. You see, it's reflex action, almost. Aboard is discipline, discipline. Ashore? Well ashore is leave, and leave is the pub—reflex action, simple as that.'

I thanked him for his helpful idea. A signpost of trouble ahead, perhaps.

The critical hour of 9.30 when the chartered Green Line bus should have deposited our seamen in the car park had passed an alarming ten minutes ago. Had they gone on a blinder and were now scattered to the four winds? I walked hurriedly back to the car park and there was Peter Bolton, waiting to shepherd his flock. A taxi drove up. Captain Pycraft got out. He had decided to come independently. He was in uniform. Thoughtful and kind; save his having to change. I went forward to greet him and asked him if he'd like a coffee and something to eat.

'Thank you, Jackson. Couldn't eat a thing. I'd like to get this over as soon as possible . . . Is everything ready?'

'Oh yes . . . But there's no desperate rush, Captain. Plenty of time.'

'When you go to the dentist, you don't want to hang around the waiting room too long. Least I don't.'

'I agree. *Country Life* and advertisements of too expensive houses aren't much comfort. Let's wander across to the lifeboat. It's made of three-ply and there's only half of it, but it'll serve our purpose.'

We started to walk across the lot. The grass was high and the birds were singing. He could see the lights suddenly switched on as Penny got a reading. I could sense his tension as he faced up to the confrontation with the camera. He walked on in silence. I thought it better for him to break it rather than risk my hitting a false note, so easily done in these circumstances. He broke it sooner than I thought. 'I did what you asked, Jackson. I learnt that first scene. I knew every word of it last night and this morning in the hotel . . . But now . . .'

'You can't remember a word of it and it couldn't matter less. As I told you, they were only meant as a guide. Your own will be far better, much greater ring of truth.' He didn't find much comfort from this and certainly didn't believe me.

On we tramped, the grasses swishing against our trousers. The lifeboat section was now a good three iron shot away. 'Funny thing, Jackson, five days out of Gib, Jerry threw everything at us, from up top and down below. It created a sort of fear that one had hopefully been trained to cope with . . . This one is quite different.'

'This won't hurt, Sir . . . There's a smiling face behind the camera and everyone is on your side, pulling for you. You'll find it'll make quite a difference. Just you wait and see.'

'We'll soon know, won't we?'

'I know already.'

By now, we were up with the unit and I introduced him. 'Penny, Kaye, Charlie, everyone, I'd like you to meet Captain Pycraft who has kindly given up some of his leave to come all this way down from Liverpool to do this test for us. I'd like you to meet Penny, Pennington Richards, our cameraman, and this Yank here is Kaye Ashe, our sound recordist who is loaned to us from the Civilian Technical Corps of the U.S.A., and Charlie Gould, his boom swinger, who will be recording your voice for us. And that's enough names for anyone at any one time. Now, Sir, I know you want to get on with this, and if you're agreeable we'll do just that. If you'll sit here in what I believe are called the stern sheets . . .'

'Very good, Jackson . . . absolutely right.'

'Thank you, Sir; homework right for once. Hat off, I think. We will assume that it was lost by enemy action. Easier for Penny to light you, you see, otherwise the peak would cast a shadow right across your face. Need a lot of light to overcome it and we won't have a lot of light when we're at sea. Now when the film runs through the camera at the right speed, Tom here will suddenly appear with a clapper board and bang it under your nose. The camera photographs the clap and the mike here records it, of course, making a mark on the sound track, on another film in the sound camera. Both run at the same speed, so if we put the two marks together, your lip movements will exactly fit the words that you have been saying. Sorry for that tedious lecture.'

'No, glad to know it. Heard so much about the "clapper board".'

'We'll start off by my asking you a few questions. Just pretend that you're at home and I'm your guest, a cub reporter, trying to get my first story and very nervous: you are anxious to put me at ease. O.K.?'

'O.K.'

'Off we go then ... Roll 'em ... And here comes the clapper board. Captain Pycraft. Take One. BANG ... Captain Pycraft, thank you very much for receiving me so kindly. I know that the first thing my readers will want me to ask you is when and how you first got the idea of going to sea?'

I let the camera run for a good six minutes and the old chap began to gather a little spontaneity, and towards the end began to show signs of becoming more relaxed. It was just possible that he might be able to adapt to all the paraphernalia and artificiality of the immediate surroundings in which he would be asked to behave naturally. It would be a question of how malleable he could be and whether he could vary inflexion, rhythm and volume. We'd soon see.

'Cut and well done, well done indeed. Most interesting. Goodness me but you've packed in a few extraordinary experiences. Now would you like a break or shall we go on?'

'Go on I think. What's next?'

'Let's see how the opening scene suits you.'

'Where I shout "keep baling lads"?'

'You're quite right, that is the opening scene. I was thinking of the one after, presumably the following morning where you give the men the "low down".'

Captain Pycraft thought for a moment, struggling with his

memory. 'I've just handed out the rations and Curtis the steward has given me what food he'd rescued from the pantry?'

'That's it, you've got it exactly . . . Let's pick it up where you say: "Now men, the position is this", and so on. Just use your own words to tell them what you think their chances are . . . Ad lib as much as you like, the more the better so far as I'm concerned because it's your thinking I want, not mine. Would you like some of us to sit in the boat as crewmen or would you rather imagine them?'

'Thanks all the same but I think I'll try and imagine them.'

'O.K. then, let's have a go.'

'Could I just have a quick look at the scene again?'

'I wouldn't . . . You know the guts of it well enough: just put your words to it and you'll be astonished how far you get and your own dialogue will be much better than mine, you see.'

'Nice thought, but I doubt it.'

'That's the fun of filming, you never know what's going to happen. Here we go, and remember; anxious faces all round you and all need reassuring. Turn 'em over and here comes the clapper board. Captain Pycraft. Scene 2. Take 1. O.K. Captain, when you like . . .'

His face went blank. He'd frozen. He looked at me quite despairingly and raised his hands in a sort of sad surrender. 'It's gone, I'm sorry.'

'No it hasn't—don't cut . . . "Now lads, the situation is this, we're in the soup but not that badly", anything you like, just to get started. I'll give you a one, two, three, go. ONE . . . TWO . . . THREE . . . GO . . .'

He shook his head, almost surrendering again. My God, but I was asking a lot, expecting a lot. How could one expect this very fatigued and probably slightly shell-shocked man to cope with this totally alien and, to him, terrifying situation? It was almost asking the impossible. He sat there, frozen again, for several seconds which must have felt like hours of torment. But Alfred Holt had asked him to do this, or at least give it a very good try. However painful, it was, after all, in the line of duty and he knew that he must do his utmost. He proceeded to do just that. He started off. 'Now men, the situation is like this. It's not too good, but it might be a damn sight worse ... I shall be giving you some rations presently and some prunes as well. Now, don't throw away the stones, keep them in your mouths and suck on them. In my experience it helps to keep away the thirst. Now we can thank our lucky stars that we got clear of the ship and, judging from last night, that we're in a stout seaworthy boat 'cos she took one hell of a bashing. From my last position, we're roughly half way across, that's roughly 1000 miles from land whether we head east or west, whichever way we go.'

'Trust old Jerry to work things to make it nice and easy for you.' I interjected his next cue and he was on to it. He had sweated on his homework, all right.

'That's the gloomy side of the picture, but don't forget that young Sparks there has got a set that will send a signal for a radius of three to four hundred miles. That's so, isn't it Sparks?'

'Aye, Sir, it's a grand wee set.' I fed him and he was away again.

'So things might be a lot worse. We'll make for Ireland. The prevailing winds will be with us and we'll be in range of Coastal Command aircraft sooner than by beating back against the wind ... Something like that Jackson, anyway.'

'Cut, and well done Captain Pycraft. What about that, fellows, for a first-timer?' The unit responded with genuine plaudits, for in truth it had been a gallant effort as well as a triumph of will power. It gave me hope, too, because I knew that I should have no other choice. The Master of the lifeboat was he and none other. Alfred Holt had made that pretty clear a week or two ago. Ships' captains were far too rare and precious birds to be wasted on amateur theatricals, unless there was a very good reason. And in this case there was; battle fatigue necessitated a long leave. Not perhaps the perfect recipe for casting one of the star parts in your picture, but it was unlikely if this were to be the only surprising thing in the making of this particular film.

'Well done again, Captain. I congratulate you, and see how

much you contributed . . . That bit about the prune stones keeping away thirst. First-hand experience and we get the benefit.'

'Second hand, actually; a friend of mine told me about it.'

'Just as valuable. We'll pinch it from you if we may.'

'All part of the service.' He was smiling and more relaxed: genuinely gratified that we were all so obviously pleased at his effort. He looked past me as something caught his eye. He caught mine and nodded his head in the direction of his look. I turned and saw Peter Bolton leading his army of recruits towards us and to their place of execution.

'Your possible shipmates, Captain. Excuse me a moment.' I went forward to meet them and I could see Bob Banner, the same cloth cap, the clay pipe giving forth its smoke signal and, even from twenty yards, his beady brown eyes gleaming mischievously and ready for anything.

'Good morning, Gentlemen . . . welcome to Pinewood, and I do assure you this won't hurt. I'll tell you exactly what I'm going to do. I'm going to ask each of you to give me a brief description of his most vivid memory at sea, and it needn't be connected with the war. And then I shall ask you to imagine having escaped from your torpedoed vessel into the lifeboat. Needn't be long. This will tell me how your voice registers and how you photograph, of course. The dentist's chair's a nightmare compared to this.'

'I don't ever go to the dentist, Gov. Too scared.' This quip came from a Don Sleeman, a cockney lad whom we'd found during our last days in Liverpool. Unfortunately for him the top row of his teeth, or lack of them, confirmed this.

'You'll make up for it, this morning', I replied, but faces were glum and it was clear that none was relishing the idea of facing the camera.

'We might as well start alphabetically. A for Armistead. Fred Armistead, isn't he here?'

'He sends his apologies, Pat; he's going to be an hour or so late', Peter informed me.

'He is the only A, then we get Banner, Bob Banner. He's the only B.'

Men in Danger (1938)

One of the girls at work in the Peak Frean biscuit factory.
Big deal: they were allowed to sing at work to overcome the
monotony of repetitive processes.

The workshop where I staged my industrial accident.

In class, 100 yards from the coal face. Manvers Main.

Ferry Pilot (1941)

Pilots, having delivered their aircraft here, there and everywhere, are rounded up by their mother hen of an Anson and are dropped off at their home base.

Philip Wills. He became the U.K.'s champion glider pilot.

Flight Lieutenant Dougie Davie of the Farnborough Research Establishment, whose *Achtung Spitfeuer* was memorable.

Flight Lieutenant Tobin of the same establishment who kindly consented to play a German Luftwaffe pilot in a captured Me 110.

Bradbrook, who played a leading part in the film. Later he joined Atlantic Ferry and on his first mission as a navigator he was killed, along with his crew in the mountains of Arran.

Joan Hughes, only twenty-one and five foot tall, just. She played in the film, flying Hurricanes and Spitfires. By the end of the war she was flying all types of four-engined bombers.

Also Audrey Sale-Barker, ski champion of Great Britain and later a duchess.

Western Approaches: the cast for the lifeboat

Frankie Edwards, cabin boy.

Tony Murdoch. Had no dialogue, but one who volunteered to come out in a force nine gale for the opening sequence.

John Walden, a Londoner. A wonderful face and gave a fine and sensitive performance.

Donald Alexander, a Kiwi.

Old Taffy, found at the Eagle. A 'Square Rigger' and round the Horn, many times. Davy Haggart his real name. No dialogue, just a fine face.

Taffy and Anthony Evans.

Jim Redmond, of the Blue Funnel Line. Played the young 'Sparks'.

Tom Major. An old round the Horn, 'Square Rigger' and a wonderful man.

Fred Armistead, our steward.

Bob Banner, found in the pub of Bill Anderson, the Angel.
The most talented natural screen actor I have ever handled.

Captain Pycraft. Master of the *Deukalian* of the Blue Funnel Line, Alfred
Holt and Co. The *Deukalian* was badly damaged in a Malta convoy. Hence
the availability of Pycraft. He would have to do for no other ship's master
could be spared. He might look the part, but could I get a performance
from him? Time would tell.

Alf Rawson (*left*), the wounded man who had to act as though in a high fever and become delirious. Not easy, even for a professional. Seeing family snaps of Duncan Cameron Bain.

Western Approaches: technical problems

The sea used for the opening sequence of *Western Approaches*, filmed first from the lifeboat and then our trawler, the *Acrasia*.

Preparing for sea. Camera mounted on wooden rails in sections which could be clamped between the thwarts, giving us the run of the boat, fore and aft. A further rail was slotted into it to give us a run port or starboard.

Almost ready to depart. Loading lifeboat with all the clobber, batteries, arc lamps, cables and heaven knows what. At high tide not too bad. At low, hell. Twenty seaweeded slippery steps, carrying one of only three Technicolor cameras in the country and get it safely aboard—nightmarish.

Our trawler attached to us with four umbilicals, the towing cable, the camera, the mike and the generator cables. When filming forrard and to get a clear horizon the trawler would veer to port and our lifeboat to starboard. But the drag on those cables, sooner or later, would pull us around and *Acrasia* would creep into shot. Cut and try again.

Not 'Three Men in a Boat': more like thirty-three men and a continuity girl.

H.M. Trawler *Acrasia*. We never saw her bows. Kay Ash, our sound recorder, seems to have seen enough of the lifeboat, astern.

All that Kay Ash ever saw of our actions in the lifeboat.

Pat Jackson gives Jack Cardiff a comforting shoulder. Imagine being responsible for lighting and getting the right exposure as well as operating the camera when most of the time you are feeling wretchedly sea-sick. A very gallant man.

By the look of things one of the cast is sea-sick just as I was about to shoot.

Our trawler, as seen from the lifeboat, before plunging out of sight into the trough. Shots for opening sequence.

That damnable flat calm. Ten miles out to sea and with no wind, we can hear all the town sounds of Holyhead: trains, traffic, dogs barking, ships hooting. The sea was a sounding board for everything. Birds and bees. Recording impossible. Five wasted days.

A tepid coffee break.

I head for home, John Walden, that wonderful Londoner, as good as John Carradine, on my right.

Will we ever get through this film? Jack Cardiff left and Pat Jackson right.

The end of a day's work. Did we manage to shoot anything? Was it just another blank day?

'Aye aye, steady on . . . Some might take exception to that.' Bob didn't miss a chance to make his presence felt. Peter raised his hand in acknowledgement and carried on.

'We've got one C—Carter—and two Ds—Davidson and Dempster.'

'O.K., that's enough for a start. Right Bob. Bob Banner, let's 'ave you, boy.'

Unperturbed, he stepped forward. Captain Pycraft was still sitting on the section of lifeboat. This was clearly the hot seat. He needed no second bidding and moved towards it. Captain Pycraft relinquished it, saying in a friendly way: 'Kept it warm for you.'

'Thank you, Cap'n.' No 'Sir', oh dear me, no. He wasn't aboard his ship, under his command or discipline. He wasn't exactly surly or impolite but there was a subtle something in the voice that suggested that the Cap'n was relinquishing his seat to his superior. In show business terms Banner's manner and bearing justified this vocal nuance. What was one man's territory was another's wilderness.

Banner seated himself and was immediately at ease, as if in the privacy of his favourite saloon bar. I went through the routine of explaining the clapper board, but in a shorter version for there was no tension to try and dispel. I didn't run more than a minute or two on him. There was no need. But those two minutes gave a graphic account of his experiences in the Australian outback and the white man's abuse of the Aborigine women. Perhaps I shouldn't have cut when I did. His account might have interested future generations of anthropologists. He was extraordinarily confident. His variation of pitch and pace was remarkable and his voice had timbre and tonal range which he knew how to use with an intuitive subtlety which was equally remarkable. This was star quality, no question about it. Wallace Beery couldn't have taught him anything.

We now tackled the scripted scene of his escaping from the *Jason*. He was almost word perfect, except that he added the odd word here and there which greatly added to the colour of the text. 'Cut. Thanks Bob, very good. Hang around please because I shall be doing some group shots of you all to see how you meld as a ship's company . . . And the next, please.'

'C. Carter', said Peter. No response. We looked around. Walking towards the studio and the car park were three figures, the ginger hair of Carter the middle one of the three.

'CARTER', I shouted. He looked, as did his companions, stopped for a second, long enough to indicate a 'get stuffed' short hand semaphore message and then continued on his and their way. I did my hundred yard dash and, sad to say, was rather out of breath when I accosted them.

'Carter, where are you going, for Pete's sake? It's your turn.'

'Sorry . . . but me and me mates here have decided there's nowt 'ere for uz . . . We'd rather face Jerry any day of the week than all that.'

'You get used to all that.'

'Greta Garbo might. But we're no Garbos. What's more, she's welcome. It's not for us, this lark, we suddenly realised. We'd rather take our chance at sea, honest to God we would.'

'What made you think you'd want to try, in the first place?'

'Well, on t' spur of moment, you can make a wrong decision. Haven't you never?'

'Of course . . . But I made it pretty plain what was involved in this film test.'

'Oh aye . . . But you never know 'til you're in it, usually up to your eye balls, like those poor buggers in t' First World War trenches. Too late for them to change mind. But it ain't for us. Not yet it ain't.'

'But this'll be a doddle compared with that, and who knows, a lot of fun.'

'Listen, Mister, we wouldn't sit in front of that thing for all the tea in China.'

'Well have a coffee in the canteen and think about it. Pity to give up without giving yourselves a chance, isn't it?'

'We don't want a chance, not 'ere, we don't. We'll take it on t' ocean. And if you can't grab that, there's nowt to be done abaht it.

Sorry if we've caused you trouble. Ta-ta and good luck.' They started to walk off.

'And good luck to you, too: sorry to see you go like this.' They turned and Carter shrugged his shoulders, gave a watery smile and a half-hearted wave. They continued on their way. There is not a lot that you can do in such a situation. At least, if there is, I certainly didn't know what it was. Manhandling and dragging, as though to the guillotine, didn't seem to me to be the correct approach towards a relaxed and convincing performance. Three good trout, successfully landed, so I thought, only to escape through a hole in the landing net. Maddening. Ah well, back to the Ds—perhaps they might be more cooperative. I certainly hoped so. And that this recent little incident was not infectious. If it were, then we faced disaster. I returned to the unit, rather more slowly than I had left it. This was, early on in the first round, a body blow which I had not foreseen.

If there were any more waverers, now was the time to find out. I noticed a few quizzical looks. 'Listen here, everybody. As you may have noticed Carter and his two mates have decided that this is not for them. If anybody feels the same way, now's the time to say so.' I looked at them, as though spraying the garden hose. None seemed keen to follow Carter's example. 'O.K., we'll get on then. Davidson, John . . . you know where the hot seat is. Just tell me what you told me at the Angel. How when you had taken to the boats, the U-Boat surfaced and the Commander spoke in perfect English.'

'Oh, and pointed out the survivors swimming towards us.'

'That's it.'

'I'll try.' We started off, and though he had a fine face and presence, he couldn't do himself justice and became monosyllabic. I came in closer on him, thinking that his face alone justified his place in the boat. I asked him to react to an imaginary aircraft flying overhead. He did this well and made me feel that he had suddenly seen it breaking through the clouds.

'Good, John. We'll try something a little bit harder. You suddenly see the aircraft break through the clouds. It means the hope of rescue and instinctively you start to shout and wave at it for a moment or two, until you realise how futile these actions are. The plane goes into cloud. Then give me a sense of let-down and bitter disappointment. O.K.?'

'I'll try.'

'You'll do fine . . . Now here we go . . . A casual glance up into the sky . . . You see it. Now shout for all your worth . . . It's gone . . . Cut . . . Excellent, John, you conveyed that very well. Thank you.' He had definitely won his place in the boat, and though he probably wouldn't be able to contribute much dialogue, never mind. They couldn't all have talking parts. I now abandoned the alphabetical order tack and started to take them at random. So, sausage factory fashion, I put them all through the mincer. I would have their faces on film and could then choose those which were not only the most photogenic but which had most vividly engraved upon them their life at sea.

Old Davy Haggart, with his grisly stubble and eyes that had long since ceased to reflect much light of day, but every line of his wrinkled parchment face helped to tell the story of his fifty or more years at sea. Old John Day, possibly five foot two inches, of the Blue Funnel Line with one fang left in his top deck, who had sailed round the Horn in square riggers, had furled the top gallants in the Roaring Forties, lived for weeks on end on hard tack and bunked down in soaking wet clothes, yet seemed hale and hearty and ready for more. Their two faces, like broad brush strokes, would contribute their fair share to the picture.

As the lunch break approached, almost everyone had had a fair crack of the whip, and a sort of natural selection had taken place, for it became fairly obvious who would win their places in the boat. The nap selections had done better than I had dared hope. John Walden was almost as good as Banner, and Fred Armistead, an hour late but on the dot, was almost certain for the part of the Steward, Curtis. The cabin boy wouldn't win an Oscar but he'd be more than adequate for the little that he had to do. I had kept Alf Rawson, upon whom so much depended, towards the end of the queue. As he went to take the 'hot seat' I had a quick word:

'Just a minute or two of any old reminiscence, then I'll cut and send all the others off to lunch so that we can have a go at the real stuff.'

'Great ... not too keen to make a fool of myself in front of all that lot.'

'You won't, but I know what you mean.'

He did his interview very well. Here again was someone with assurance and repose. Peter took the others off to lunch so that Alf and I could tackle that worrying fever and delirium problem. 'The key shot in the film, Alf, is where you spot the periscope. Let's have a go at that first.'

'O.K. Anything you say. What do you suggest.'

'You're lying on the thwart. You wake up after a bloody awful night. You have a bit of a struggle to regain consciousness. You gather your wits, try and give an impression of your mind clearing. You struggle to sit up a bit. In doing so, you happen to look over the starboard side, out to sea, and up it pops, the periscope. Immediately you're on the alert and shout ''Periscope'' for all your worth. Put that across, bonny boy, and we're home and dry.'

'I can only try.'

'Duck to water for you, you wait and see.'

Pennington Richards, the fastest cameraman I've ever worked with, had the new camera set up and lit in no time. Alf laid himself prone along the thwart.

'Al, we won't rehearse the acting bit, just the movements, so that Ted here, this chap behind the camera, knows what you're going to do; that way he'll be able to keep you in shot more easily. I'll talk you through it, just for the timing. Here we go. Asleep ... bloody awful nightmares ... Thankful slowly ... to ... waken ... Head fuddled and muddled ... Slowly clearing ... Where am I? Oh this bloodstained boat ... What's going on? Where is everyone?? ... Struggle to sit up and find out ... looking out to sea. Christ, it's a periscope ... and then look aboard for the shout ... That's it, Al, and I could see you thinking it out very clearly. You made me feel it. Now we'll do all that again on film. Would you like me to talk you through it or imagine it for yourself?'

'I think it'll help if you talk me through it, if that's all right with you.'

'Absolutely fine. Here we go then. Turn 'em over.' In went the 'clapper' and we repeated that we'd just gone through, only this time he did it even better. 'Good, Alf; convinced me. You saw it all right.'

It was a fine effort and for a first-timer quite extraordinary. It was wonderful to see the confidence flowing into him and the pleasure on his face that he hadn't made a fool of himself and that he might even have done quite well. No wonder that a few years later Johns Hopkins Hospital of Maryland was to develop play therapy for disturbed children. Within a few hours, several in this lifeboat had sensed something within themselves undreamt of before they had walked across 'the lot'.

'As we're lit for this set-up, one more shot and then you'll have earned a pint. Let's get this delirium business out of the way. O.K.?'

'Sure. Any ideas?'

'Not really; we touched on it, remember, in the Angel? Blurred speech, mumbling rubbish, your eyes won't focus on anything, your head rolls about, your mouth's dry, you keep wetting your lips, any old jabber as if you're as high as a kite, odd laughter and cackle. Mix that lot up and you'll walk it.'

'The plank, most likely. O.K., I'll have a go.' And have a 'go' he did, in masterful fashion. Astonishing. His head rolled about, he let out a cackling laugh, hysterical, almost demonic which Lon Chaney would have been proud of if only 'the talkies' had arrived when he made his original *Phantom of the Opera*. He babbled away glorious rubbish, totally incomprehensible, and just what the doctor ordered. It was a fine piece of work. I shouted 'Cut!' and we all congratulated Alf, who had clearly won the part. We broke for lunch and walked across the lot towards the restaurant bar. Alf had earned a pint and I had found my wounded man, and I felt very lucky indeed.

It had been a fascinating time and we all felt well satisfied with our morning's work. We had run off several thousand feet of film, and in doing so I felt confident that we had found the crew of the lifeboat. The actual process of making the film had almost started, and I felt encouraged. Surely, at last, we were on the way. I was thrilled, too, at the prospect of working with undiscovered and rare talent, raw maybe, but there were rich seams of it to be hewn and fashioned, I felt sure. Tomorrow, 'the rushes' would prove me right or wrong.

In the bar, I was sorry to see Captain Pycraft sitting, rather forlornly, with an almost empty half-pint glass of beer. 'May I join you, Captain, and let me get you something.'

'No, no more thanks. Half a bitter's quite enough for me.'

'Have a shorty; you've certainly earned it, and I do thank you for your help and coming all this way to do the test.'

'Rather a waste of time and your film, I'm afraid.'

'Whatever makes you say that, Captain? You did splendidly.'

'Nice of you to say so, but I'm no actor, Jackson.'

'Thank God for it. Your life at sea is stamped all over you, and no actor can give us that subtle something.'

'Ah, but they're trained instruments, you can get them to play any tune you like.'

'Quite true. They're trained to give a sustained performance for three to four hours if necessary. But they have to convince us they're sailors when we know they're not. Jack Hawkins, say, a General in a film one week and an Admiral the next. Takes a bit of swallowing. Whereas you are the real thing . . . all you have to be is yourself and that will do very nicely, thank you.'

'Ah, you make it all sound too easy.'

'Yes, I know, a bit glib. But I do promise you, Captain, that it becomes easier with each little bit you do. It becomes more real as your confidence grows, and it grows very fast.'

'I wonder.'

'You wait and see . . . I'll phone you tomorrow and let you know how it looks. I think you'll do splendidly, if you want to do it. That's the point, do you?'

'Oh yes, if you think I can.'

'I'm sure of it . . . May I pass on one tip that was given to me by a very great friend and a great director?'

'Please do.'

'The test of a screen actor—screen actor, not stage—is how he uses his eyes and voice. Is there the required thought behind the eyes and in his voice; is there music in it?'

'Music in it . . . that's interesting.'

'It's true, isn't it? So many people in everyday life, in normal conversation, are deadly dull, monotonous because they only use three notes instead of perhaps twenty. Take a simple word like "yes" . . . see how many meanings you can get into it. Little undertones of meaning, by inflection . . . sinister . . . suspicious . . . sarcastic . . . flippant . . . impatient . . . dismissive . . . Let me get you a shorty . . . tiny scotch.'

'A small Bells then . . . thank you.'

I left him to wait my turn at the bar and I could see that he was already mulling over the intricacies of voice production. This morning had been a remarkable experience for all of us. We had introduced an entirely new world to about thirty men and it was extraordinary how calmly, in the main, they had all given their utmost to adjust and adapt themselves to the challenge of this new world. It was a wonderful experience to have seen this experiment. Both wonderful and challenging for all of us, for we were about to enter upon a relationship which was to test us all to the depths of our beings and, as the Lancastrians would say, our 'stickability.'

The following day the 'rushes' confirmed that we had found the cast for the lifeboat. Mr Hobbes was immediately sent the names of the chosen who would be reserved for the film.

After consultation with our naval experts it was decided that Holyhead would be our base. The harbour there was less land-locked than Fishguard. We would require, therefore, less towing time with the lifeboats to get them free of the land and a clear horizon for filming. There was a main line to Euston, too. Mr Dickie, of the Blue Funnel, was informed and he assured us that the boats, with their platforms attached, would be in the water and safely moored at Holyhead well ahead of our arrival, giving the timbers plenty of time to expand.

No tests with the Technicolor equipment had been carried out under the working conditions that we would be experiencing as there was no camera available. So it looked as though the inevitable growing pains that we would most certainly encounter would have to be ironed out during the throes of actually being in production with the complete cast present. I had wanted to avoid this, as unaccountable delays are frustrating enough for pros who understand the reasons, but for the layman, the amateur cast, they would make their problem and mine much harder. Endless frustration is not the best way of maintaining morale.

Technicolor, however, was already taking precautions for the scenes to be filmed in convoy, on the Atlantic, so that one of their precious and irreplaceable three-strip cameras would not be risked. Accordingly, they had organised some tests to try out a new single-film colour process stock called Monopack. This stock could be used by any standard 35mm camera, the Mitchell, Vinten or whatever. So, Pennington Richards, who was to photograph the film, and Jimmy Wright, one of the bright boys of Technicolor, carried out these tests on the Denham studio tank—presumably shooting models.

Kay Ash was experimenting with recording in high winds as he knew that he would have to cope with them in the lifeboat. He had made a ball-shaped cage of galvanised wire in which he set his microphone. Over this he drew a silk stocking. To his annoyance, only the pure silk proved effective against the onslaught of the wind, almost completely immunising the mike from its turbulence. As silk stockings were articles of almost sacred rarity and the shortest way to a girl's heart, his was a noble sacrifice.

Still no release date for a camera to be put at our disposal for these vital pre-production experiments so that we could start to iron out some of the gremlins that were most assuredly waiting for us. We had to get at them as soon as possible or we'd pay for it, and the price would be high. I was beginning to feel as the Wright Brothers must have—would they ever get their machine into the air? Would I ever get started on this production?

'Dal, we must get a release date for one of their cameras. Time is getting on. Before we know it, winter will be on us before we've made a start.' We went to see Harrison, Chief Executive of Technicolor. Usual enormous desk and a fashionable nothing on it except a paperknife and leather folding blotter. All very impressive. Earliest date, due to hold ups, 14 September, a Monday. Late, but we had no alternative. Seamen, presumably happy, being fully paid, indefinite shore leave. Dear old Anderson at the Angel must have been happy, also.

Message from George Gunn of Technicolor. Having read the script in great detail, he thought we might find Griffiths, our gunner, on H.M.S. *President*, where he had recently installed one of his domes to train merchant seamen in anti-aircraft gunnery. Many good old sweats from the Royal Naval Reserve who had been called back to duty. The senior instructor was Chief Petty Officer Hills.

Whilst waiting to get started at Holyhead, this was an ideal time to try and hunt down Griffiths. His was the most important part in the film; the star part. He must know how to lay the gun; fire it; be blown up; become unconscious; regain consciousness; panic with a moment of hysteria until his ingrained discipline enables him to regain control of himself; to be shot in the chest and fall mortally wounded on to a steel deck; at death's door, give the range to the chief officer which gains the direct hit on the U-Boat; to give a final message to his wife and die as convincingly as Olivier in *Hamlet*, in convoy, in the middle of the Atlantic in wartime. Dear me, let me not think on't: it was asking a lot from an untrained actor. Don't even think about it: just go and see what's to be found on H.M.S. *President*.

Along The Embankment, about 200 yards from Cleopatra's Needle towards St Paul's, there she lay. Up the gangplank and take off your hat to the quarter deck.

'Welcome aboard, Sir.'

'Thank you, Chief . . . I have an appointment with Chief Petty Officer Hills.'

'You're talking to him, Sir.'

'Oh hullo, my name's Jackson. How do you do.' We shook hands.

'What can we do for you, Sir?'

'It sounds ridiculous, I know, but I'm looking for a gunner to play a gunner in a film we're making called *Western Approaches*.'

'Oh yes, Sir. Well I have four gunners here, Sir, and they're all very able, very able indeed. In fact, each has been responsible for training a gun's crew which have already brought down their Dornier. Remarkable, Sir, when you come to think about it. This invention of Mr Gunn's, remarkable. Would you like to see it first, or perhaps the gunners.'

'That'd be very nice, in a minute. You're the Chief Instructor here?'

'That's right, Sir.'

'I see you've got "Pip, Squeak and Wilfred" up. You must have been a kid.'

'At that time they was quite ready to be fooled if you looked more or less the age.'

'Jutland, then?'

'Yes, Sir.'

'Close run thing?'

'No, Sir. They won it, but they never came out again, so on reflection, we did.'

'When did you leave the service?'

''37, Sir.'

'And then what?'

'Like so many of us, joined the Post Office. Non-established postal sorter.'

'Good heavens, so was I.'

'Never!'

'Yes, I started in the G.P.O. Film Unit; I was their messenger boy, as a matter of fact. Well, never having had a film unit before, they hadn't a clue how to grade people. We had a chap, Harry Watt, made *Night Mail* and just recently *Target for Tonight*. He was a non-established postal sorter too.'

'Well I never, Sir . . . Would you like to meet my gunners, Sir? See how the dome works—very clever, that is. Interest you, Sir. Use of film being projected on to this white dome and the aircraft comes in on a slight parabola and flies round the dome giving our chaps a chance to follow it with this camera gun. Then we can check . . . see when they're on or off. Clever, Sir, dead clever. Genius that Mr Gunn must be. Like to see it?'

'Love to, in a tick . . . You're a gunner, too, of course?'

'Oh yes, Sir, after Jutland I was on the Q-Ships.'

'With Campbell V.C.?'

'Not in his ship, Sir, no, but in his command, of course.'

'What about you, Hills?'

'Yes, Sir, what about me?'

'To play the part of the gunner? He's called Griff, by the way.'

'Oh yes, Sir.'

'Well anyway . . .' And then, as we walked slowly aft, towards George Gunn's dome, I told him the story of what I hoped, one day, would become the film *Western Approaches*. He listened carefully as I went into some details of the scenes which involved him. When I'd finished, he remained silent for a moment or two as though mulling things over. Then he said: 'Yes Sir; sounds all right. Could happen, too.'

I didn't disguise my delight, for this was genuine reaction from a reliable source. 'Would you like to play it, Griff—sorry, Chief?'

'Nice of you to ask, Sir, but I don't think they'd release me. This invention here, well, it's knocking them down, as I said.'

'But you're doing a teaching job here, and though you obviously do it brilliantly, it could be done by someone else, couldn't it?'

'Oh yes, Sir, nobody's indispensable, as we all know, and I'm certainly not.'

'So, if we could get your release from their Lordships, it'd be all right with you?'

'Oh yes, Sir, it'd be in the line of duty on another deck, if you follow me.'

'And you'd be prepared to come down and have a test at Pinewood, and it will be a very testing test, as you will have gathered?'

'If I'm ordered to do it, I won't have much choice, will I, Sir?'

'There's no question of your being ordered to do it. It's simply a question of whether you'd like to have a shot at it or not. All you have to say is yes or no. If it's no, you'll hear no more about it. So, which is it to be?'

'Yes, and thank you very much for asking me. I'll do my best, and I can only hope that I don't let you down.'

'I'm quite sure you won't.'

And he didn't. He did a wonderful test. When he let himself go berserk on discovering the bulkhead door was jammed, he terrified the life out of us with his hysterical shouting and banging. To see the way he took hold of himself to regain his composure was a fine piece of acting in the purest sense, and further confirmation of the amount of talent that seems to be lying dormant in so many people: talent, that is, which can be moulded and adapted to the needs of the camera. I am not referring to the more classical expression of that talent which the stage demands. That is of a different mould.

Had the *Guinness Book of Records* existed then, C.P.O. Hills would, during his onerous test, have written himself into it for the understatement of the year. We wanted to experiment how he would give the impression of being lifted off his feet by the explosion. We had a small charge of explosive prepared and on cue he managed a miraculous form of levitation. No Olympic gymnast could have contrived a more realistic interpretation of a body being hurled into the air. It, or rather he, came to rest in the darkness of the set and I let the camera run until a quiet and very respectful voice was heard to say: 'I'm sorry, Sir. You'll have to stop now, because my leg's on fire.'

That was the sort of man he was: one of the finest I have ever met. I shall always be in his debt and shall always treasure his memory. He had a strong yet sensitive face, he stood six feet tall and every inch of them was assured and upright. He knew the order of things and what made the world spin. He was no pussy foot and the fact that, to some extent, he had been conditioned to add a 'Sir' after most of his sentences in no way diminished him in his eyes nor anyone else's. It was a form of address that was as instinctive as fighting to his last gasp in the face of the enemy if called upon to do so . . . Fighting injustice, too, to the bitter end if he felt that to be his duty. He had been one of the ring-leaders in the Invergordon

Mutiny, in 1931. The injustice of the service pay cuts was undermining the morale of the service he loved and he fought to get things put right, and they were. He was a very special man.

The rushes, the following day, confirmed that we had found our gunner, Griff. And what a find. He had been a gunner and had gained experience in the First World War in Q-Ships, a similar situation to the one which was to be the climax of our story. Imagine casting directors trying to find such a character in *Spotlight*, the bible for professional actors.

16

Faltering steps, again

In a much happier frame of mind, I prepared to leave for Holy-head. Jack Cardiff, Technicolor's cameraman, and Pennington Richards had already gone ahead with Kay Ash and Charlie Gould, the two American sound chaps with their Western Electric system, hopefully to get some of the inevitable problems sorted out. Penny went to learn from Jack the mysteries of Technicolor's three-film strip camera, each strip sensitive to its own primary colour and each passing across its allotted facet of the prism set in the camera. In the studio, when the camera is reloaded, the prism is taken out with reverential awe. Rubber gloves are donned. A deathly hush descends as a dust sheet is thrown over the camera and the operator enters this almost antiseptic area, not to carry out a heart transplant, but to remove the prism and make sure that each of its three facets is clean, clear and free of any dust particles. I couldn't quite see these clinical conditions being carried out as we bounced about in a lifeboat. However, that was their problem—or was it?

With a hefty expanding suitcase strapped to the pillion of my 500cc Royal Enfield, I roared up to Euston to catch the 9.00 a.m. to Holyhead and joined the rest of the unit on platform one. Charlie Squires was there, the finest 'prop man' in the business, all five foot of him: a cockney through and through and the most gifted of the 'cheekie chappies'. He said to us: 'When we gets to Crewe, I don't want none of you coming out of the buffet without you have a cup in your pocket. We're going to need them.' Then there was Harry Tupper, master carpenter, our 'stand-by' chippie and a tower of strength. And Roland Stafford, 'boom boy', who would be holding Kay's 'mike', squatting on the deck of the lifeboat: rocking about, it would be hard to keep a boom or pole out of shot. Two grips and a van driver made up the rest, not forgetting Phil Ross, continuity girl.

The flag was raised: the whistle blew. The 4–6–0 locomotive gave its first grunting puff, wheel-slipped, spurted steam on to the track, gained purchase and inch by inch we drew away towards Holyhead. We were on our way, and with a bit of luck would be 'turning over' for real on 18 September, the following Friday.

A few hours later, I am ashamed to say a few tea cups to the good from the buffet at Crewe, we pulled into Holyhead, and there was Gerry Bryant who was to be Production Manager, waiting to greet us. He had had a triumphant time, having arranged all the billets for our seamen. Some of the landladies had not been too keen, apparently, but Gerry's persuasive powers had won the day.

Installed in the hotel and with Gerry on the pillion, we went in search of our two lifeboats, moored, so he told me, in the inner basin. In the care of a naval rating, they had been politely awaiting our arrival, with planks now fully expanded. And there they were, each with its magnificent platform attached, quite large enough to house a string quartet and a conductor. Not surprisingly, the trim of the boats was slightly out—very much out. The tide was out, too, so that they lay a good 15 to 20 feet below the jetty, and I could recognise Penny, with two other blokes, in most gingerly fashion descending a flight of heavily seaweeded steps. They were carrying something that looked like a cabin trunk. We propped the motorbike against the harbour wall and walked nearer to the scene of operations.

I was about to call down but thought better of it. Their concentration was intense. It had to be, for their tread on the wet seaweed was as if on banana skins . . . They were aboard now and started a slow-motion hurdle race as they lifted their load and themselves over the thwarts on their way to the platform, in the middle of which had been bolted a steel mushroom-shaped affair, like a giant golf tee.

'Presumably the three-strip camera', I said to Gerry.

'In its location blimp and not a hundred per cent sound-proof, Jack tells me. He's hoping the wind will blow away the camera noise.'

'Let's hope he's right. Hell of a rise and fall of tide.'

By now Penny and his mates were on the platform, teeing up their cabin trunk. The trim of the boat did not require a spirit level to tell us that it was very wonky: bows almost out of the water. 'Counterweight forrard . . . put that right', I thought, grabbing at any straw. Now that the trunk was secured, I felt it safe to hail Penny and we made our way down the treacherous steps and climbed aboard—our floating studio for several days to come, no doubt. I was introduced to Jack Cardiff, and clearly a nicer chap one couldn't hope to meet, and his focus puller, Eric Asbury.

'We thought we'd just go out and see that everything's working O.K.', Jack said with disarming insouciance.

'Splendid idea . . . We may as well come along for the ride. At least we'll help bring the bows down.'

There was a shout aft: 'Let's know when you're ready and we'll come alongside': this from a runnerbean of a young R.N.V.R. lieutenant who was hailing us from a strange motor yacht affair which one would expect to see above Boulter's Lock, cruising gracefully up and down the Cliveden Reach. She did not inspire confidence.

'All set', shouted Jack and the runnerbean disappeared into his wheel house. His engines chugged: a rating let go fore and aft and scrambled back aboard.

'This is H.M.S. *Tyella*. Kay's aboard with Charlie. We're going to run sync, just to make sure', Penny informed me.

'Good idea.' *Tyella* inched alongside. A rating boarded us with a tow rope which he hitched round the lifeboat's davit hook, hinged in the bow, and then, almost in Burghley fashion, hurdled over the thwarts and took hold of our tiller. *Tyella* moved forward as we fended off from the barnacles encrusting the harbour wall. We were soon round the buff and heading for the main basin, a fine harbourage, a miniature Scapa Flow. Kay appeared on the stern of the *Tyella*, beaming with geniality as he stood ready to hand the camera and mike cables to Eric. Handling his precious wire cage, housing the mike, he shouted a warning: 'For God's sake don't ladder me stocking. If you do, the wind will climb in.'

We were pulled alongside by our rating, hauling on the tow rope. The cables were handed over. We pushed ourselves astern and, when well clear of the prop, Kay started to pay out at the same speed as the tow rope, and when separated by a cricket pitch-and-a-half, all was made fast. The camera cable was now in place and therefore connected to Kay's batteries, as was the sound camera so that both were locked in a three-phase flow of power. Simple as A.B.C.—so far.

The main harbour wall was perhaps half a mile long and equally far away. It was a magnificent late summer's afternoon with scarcely a ripple on this inner harbour water. The seagulls were squawking away and soaring above and, from our point of view, dangerously low, for at that height they would be flying into shot and give the game away as there are no gulls in mid-Atlantic. We could always scare them away with a shotgun, I supposed.

'Pat . . . Gerry . . . Sit in the foreground, will you. I want to see if I can get a tolerable balance to expose for the sky and your faces.' He came forward with his exposure meter and Eric ran out a tape for his focus. Jack asked Penny to get a reflector board working on our faces as he had to have more light on them to balance the hot sky. If he exposed for the sky, our faces would be too dark, and if for our faces, the sky would burn up. We could feel the heat of the sun on our faces when Penny had the angle correct. We were approaching the open sea and a slight ripple started, enough to affect the reflecting angle of the sun which was no longer a constant, and we could feel the heat varying in intensity on our faces, and therefore the exposure problem for Jack. If the light were to remain constant, the angle of reflection had to adjust to the size and the rhythm of the wavelets. Neither is ever the same and our faces must therefore have been sending their own form of morse code. The choppier the sea, the worse the problem would become. How noisy was the camera going to be? Vital that we discover as soon as possible. Within this short time it was already clear that every shot taken in these conditions was not going to be easy, and the thought of having any ruined was intolerable. We were now passing the lighthouse of the main harbour wall and were heading out to sea. We were ready to turn over for the first time under conditions with which we would be competing for however long it would take to film these lifeboat scenes. I held the mike out of shot in my lap and Gerry prepared the clapper board. I asked Kay, over the mike, to turn us over. The power came through the submerged cables and we were running. Jack shouted speed and Gerry clapped the board. We spieled some rubbish for a minute or so and then cut. We had turned enough to tell us whether the mike had picked up the camera noise. The waves were now a couple of feet high, certainly no more. Then, for no reason at all, the *Tyella* started to turn for home. Nobody had asked him to do so. This was a test run, for heaven's sake, and at this moment our clear horizon line gave us little more than an angle of 90 degrees—hopelessly restricting. I spoke into the mike: 'Kay, will you ask the Lieutenant why we are turning back?' I waited, but no reply came. We continued to turn and were now broadside to the waves and soon heading back into the harbour, the stern platform now facing the oncoming waves. We had been bouncing about a bit for ten minutes or so and, at this moment, Jack became very seasick. At such a time one has only to recall a bad Channel crossing, when people so stricken wish nothing more but to die.

Poor Jack seemed to reflect this desperate longing. It is so unfair that some should be blessed with stomachs like horses and others so sensitive to the ocean wave. Thankfully, though, he would only have to endure this misery for a week or two until he had taught Penny Technicolor's mysteries. It would physically be impossible for anyone daily to endure such a battering and at the same time be responsible for photographing and operating for a film under conditions which, clearly, were not going to be easy for the most hardened of sailors. It was unthinkable. I was thankful, therefore, to see that Penny seemed to be of the horse variety. And then we were pooped. Whether by the seventh wave I have no idea, but certainly a playful one which suddenly got it into its head to clamber aboard the platform, swirl past the camera, and empty itself into the lifeboat—a readily available receptacle, after all.

This was a most uncalled-for invasion of our proceedings until I recalled that Alfred Holt had foreseen the likelihood of such an occurrence and warned me of it. I now understood why the skipper of the *Tyella* had turned back. Dear me. This had been a useful if sobering canter down the course, and I can't say that it encouraged a state of euphoria. Very much the reverse. Within half an hour we had already encountered problems enough: problems that should have been ironed out by pre-production preparation, and here we were like a bunch of enthusiastic film society amateurs trying to tackle a production and its concomitant problems that were enough to make the great Cecil B. de Mille think for a moment or two. True, he had separated the Red Sea, but that was something that we did not have to tackle. I took little comfort from that as I contemplated the weeks that lay ahead. As we were towed back into harbour, I realised that we were in a mess; there was no doubt about that. I felt like a golfer who had played the first few holes in par and now finds the deepest bunker on the course and is facing a ten if not worse on his card. Not a pleasant feeling, and yet, in a way, I knew that this situation was almost inevitable and I had foreseen it. We were not helped by the fact that the Technicolor equipment could only be released to us at this late date.

This combination of factors had put me, my unit and cast, shortly to arrive, in a very dicey situation, so it was not without a certain justification that I felt . . . well and truly bunkered. As for Jack Cardiff, poor chap, his prospect was not very rosy, either. There is nothing more unpleasant than a bout of sea-sickness. He was facing this every day, from now on.

'There used to be a thing called Mothersill against sea-sickness. It's supposed to do the trick; a lot of people swear by it', I said to Jack as we approached the inner basin and our mooring.

'Wish to God I could—doesn't do the trick for me, I'm afraid.'

'Local chemist may have something. This crossing to Cork's worse even than Newhaven–Dieppe . . . that can be a swine.'

'No good, Pat, thanks all the same. I'm just one of those cases.

Only have to look at it . . . I'm not even sure that I'd be a hundred per cent on the Serpentine, so the odds, you see, are against the local chemist': he said this with a smile of resignation, facing the inevitable.

'You mean every time you go out . . .'

'Fraid so . . .'

'Heroic, that's all there is to it.'

'Get hardened to it, I hope . . . Why should it be so much worse at sea? . . . Make a beast of yourself ashore, it's oops and over. At sea, the memory seems to linger on a bit.'

'Brandy any good?'

'Hardly has time to linger; just a waste.'

'Dear Oh Lor', you poor old sod.'

'So long as I don't give the wrong exposure, that's all that matters . . . Don't worry, I won't. You didn't hear the camera, did you?'

'No . . .'

'I did, but I think with duffle coats and extra padding we should be O.K. We'll need lights, though.'

'But that'll mean a genny' (generator).

'I think I can get away with a couple of "inky dinks" run of batteries. Reflectors are too unreliable.'

'Yes, I could feel the difference when Penny had the angle and when he lost it. Quite a temperature change.'

'Which could mean a whole lens stop, if not more. That could change your colour quite a bit. And it's not only the sky we have to worry about; the movement of the boat brings the reflection of the sea into consideration.'

'Hence the need for a steady and reliable light source for the faces. And these "inky dinks" are, what, 250s?'

'That's it, but they're enough to give me a stop that'll hold skies and faces in a tolerable balance, and if we are a little out, the labs will be able to adjust. With three colours you can juggle a bit, but not all that much.'

Tyella cast us off and the rating steered us round the bluff and made us fast. The tide had risen so there were not so many of those treacherous steps to climb. Unloading was a much simpler matter. The van was waiting to take the gear back to the hotel, and as it drove off with the crew, I went to make my number with H.M.S. *Tyella* and her runnerbean skipper, who turned out to be a very welcoming and friendly person. It was good to see Kay and Charlie again, and before very long we were all on christian name terms and were soon able to get down to brass tacks, and I didn't hesitate to bang the first one home as I said: 'Jim, no doubt Kay and Charlie have given you the gen on the script.'

'Yes, I've read it. Should make a jolly good movie.'

'If we can make it.'

'Quite. You're going to have your problems, I can tell you that.'

'You don't entirely surprise me. Such as?'

'For a start, you'll have to take off those platforms or they'll sink you. In no sea at all, you saw what happened.'

'Yes, I did. O.K., so we take off the platforms and then you can really take us out?'

'Yes, reasonably far.'

'How far is that?'

'How far do you want to go?'

'Jim, you know the story. We're supposed to be in mid-Atlantic.'

'Yes, I know.'

'So obviously to be free of land creeping into shot we must have the widest, uninterrupted horizon line of clear ocean as possible.'

'Naturally, I realise that and it will all depend on the prevailing conditions: tides, wind, its strength and direction. We'll have to see how we go day by day and hour by hour.'

'Do you mind if I ask you, not exactly a personal question, but a very direct one?'

'Fire away.'

'Is your boat up to it?'

'Quite frankly, no.'

'Being an interested party, may I ask why?'

'Quite simple. The draught is too shallow, the top hamper much too high and we're underpowered. With too high a sea and wind behind it we'd capsize.'

'I see . . . quite the most encouraging news I've heard in a long time.' We had to laugh because the baldness and simple frankness of his admission was humorous in a black fashion. 'Seriously, Jim, what you have just said, from my viewpoint, is like the kiss of death. Here we are about to start a film which the C. in C. has himself ordered, and he gives me . . .'

'Me . . . I know', Jim said with a disarming smile, and then added: 'What you need for this job is a trawler, of course. Trouble is they're all mine sweeping and a cleared mine can save a ship. Unfortunately, the brutal fact is that your filming operations can't.' He shrugged his shoulders, indicating that there was nothing more to be said. He was right, and then as though to soften his assess- ment, he added: 'It's more than likely that the C. in C. wanted to give you a trawler, but the situation may have changed since then.' He nodded his head towards the ocean: 'Things are a bit dicey out there, at the moment; that's why every spare trawler and drifter is on convoy duty, as rescue ships. Priority again. Saving life must be more important than filming, however good yours may turn out to be.'

'Of course, of course', I said, lamely. He had laid it on the line in simple, straightforward fashion. I obviously wasn't looking the cheerful Christmas card robin, and he added: 'Cheer up, Pat; we'll manage somehow. I'll do my damnedest to give you the widest horizon I can. But, for the reasons I've given you, if I can't, I bloody well can't. O.K.?'

'O.K. Jim, and thanks for being so frank.' We shook hands and I jumped on to the jetty. What I had just heard made me wonder whether the project were even possible. The odds against seemed to lengthen as every hour went by, and as every day went by it seemed that we would get sucked deeper and deeper into the mire—pull out now, then, or be in it up to our necks. We were in it up to our necks . . . Ah, but were we? Should I phone Dal now and advise him not to go ahead or, at any rate, not to go ahead unless we were guaranteed adequate and proper facilities—a trawler or drifter? What would that achieve? I had just heard, and for the most convincing reasons, that there was none available. A face-saving form of official cancellation: 'Due to the lack of adequate and available facilities through the exigencies of war, the Ministry of Information very much regrets that it has had to cancel . . .' No. Too much was at stake: the Crown Film Unit's reputation, the Ministry of Information's, the Minister's, and on down the line until little me. If I were to recommend such a course of action for the most logical and sensible reasons, the chances were that I would be replaced. Cowardice, if not exactly in the face of the enemy, but of a tough assignment, which was just as bad. I would never live it down. Therefore, I would not phone Dal. However hopeless the undertaking seemed, I must go ahead. I had no alternative. I was trapped.

With this series of happy thoughts to mull over I wandered back to the hotel and was more than ready for a pint and the jolly company of the unit. It was not possible to remain gloomy very long in the company of such blokes as Penny, Jack Cardiff and Gerry Bryant. Soon everything seemed possible and with such a unit we would win through. It had been an eventful day and it was not over yet, not by any means.

The last train, with a connection from Liverpool, had pulled in but there was no sign of Banner. Gerry, Peter and I started to scour the train, loos and luggage vans, thinking that he might be 'sleeping it off'. No sign of him.

Here we were on Thursday night, 17 September 1942 and due to start filming the following morning. The entire flock was there, safely gathered in their pens, except for Banner, the black sheep, and he, of course, would have to be the star. It was as though I were about to start a remake of *Tugboat Annie*. I had Marie Dressler safely stowed away, but what was she without Wallace Beery? Just overweight.

We must try the pubs again. Peter Bolton found him. Banner must have been influenced by *City Lights* because, in Chaplin fashion, he was found asleep on the war memorial, purring away as innocently as a babe in a manger. He was soon ready for a welcoming drink at the hotel. Before long, with his old cloth cap perched on his forehead, his pipe belching away, he marched into the hotel as if he owned it. For all he knew or cared it could have been Buckingham Palace. He would be himself, his un-compromising self wherever he was and in whatever company. He had set his sails and he wasn't going to change them no matter from what direction the wind blew. He'd got by, hadn't he, and to no one had he bent his knee. He was Banner and bugger the lot of you. As usual, he talked very well and very amusingly, but he did have a rather disconcerting habit of taking his pipe out of his mouth, not to be more articulate but to spit on the carpet.

17

A non-starter for a start

UNIT CALL. On the Jetty. 8.30.
CAST CALL. On the Jetty. 9.00.

I did not have one of my best nights, and when the alarm went off at 6.45, I was wide awake—had been for some time. What was the weather like? I went to the window and pulled back the curtains. It was promising in so far as it wasn't raining and it wasn't blowing a gale. Luck, but then it was the 17th when we arrived and I like 7s. It was seven months since I trundled down Southend Pier. Holy heavens, we were going to make a start. We would be turning over and this time it was for real.

Shortly, we would be making ready and down those treacherous steps would go the two heavy service batteries. The two lamps. The camera. The blimp. The film magazine cases. The light cables. The 24 members of the cast. The three on the camera. Two electricians. The mike boy. The continuity girl. And finally, me. Almost like a factory outing, only instead of 'the chara', a lifeboat.

It all went quite well; that is, it was about 10.30 before we were ready to leave the jetty and then, of course, we had the delicate business of transferring towing cable, mike cable and camera cable from the *Tyella*. This went well, too. It was now 10.50 by the time we were being towed towards the harbour mouth. Then and only then would we have a chance of going for our first shot. I had explained to Jim why we had not taken off the platform. We had to have the camera mounted on it so that I could get an establishing shot of the full complement of men in the boat. The only way to get it was to have the camera in almost the same place as it had been for our first canter down the course when we were pooped. If pooped once, why not twice? A very fair question and we hoped that we had found a very fair answer. During the intervening two days we had not been idle and our combined wits had resolved that the answer was a little counterweighting. To bring the rear platform up out of the water we must bring the bows down. Obviously! Any fool could have thought of that. Exactly, and nobody is denying it. But how to find the counterweight? It would have to be very considerable to have the required effect on a floating boat 28 feet long with thirty people aboard. What was so irritating was the fact that when in the stern position from which we were to film, it couldn't matter less if the platform were trailing in the water for that was spent water: it had passed us and could do no harm. It was when we had to be turned round and towed back into harbour that the situation became critical. What had been astern was now in the bows and the platform became an easy slipway for any wave to come aboard. With batteries, delicate cable terminals and electric motors, this could be disastrous.

To bring this nautical exercise to fruition we had luckily come across a great ally in Captain Mackenzie who was in charge of the L.M.S. terminal dock area. He was not under naval control. He was his own boss of his area of the port. He had also been with Captain Scott on the *Discovery* on his last ill-fated voyage to the Antarctic. He was a fine man. He saw what we were trying to do and was determined to do all in his power to help. We borrowed all the short ends of steel rail in three-foot sections that we needed, and as we kept on coming back for more and more, he said: 'You'll be reacting like a punch-drunk heavyweight with all that aboard.' Maybe, but it was the only way to get these vital establishing shots. First the one with Captain Pycraft astern, shooting over his shoulder, showing his crew and the injured man lying forrard stretched out on the thwart. And then the reverse of this from the bow showing the Captain in the stern. Two vital shots to open the lifeboat part of the story. I was determined to get them if it took all day. It was for these that Alfred Holt had so generously ordered the platforms to be built.

And now, having left our parent ship with umbilicals attached, camera and mike cables, we were about to go into production. The harbour wall was still a hundred yards away and our approach was slower than usual because *Tyella* had never before pulled the lifeboat fully loaded. We were loaded, all right, and, as Captain Mackenzie had foreseen, sluggish, to say the least, rather like a bargeful of newly dredged sludge being towed out to be emptied. But, we were getting there. I took a final look through the view finder. It was a superb shot. The whole length of the boat. The Master, back to us, in foreground and his men grouped around: the shot to establish the lifeboat part of the story. I needed perhaps thirty feet of it, twenty seconds, and to get them, all we needed was for *Tyella* to move out of shot and no seagulls to swoop down into it.

We passed the harbour wall and were heading out to sea. 'O.K. Roland', I shouted. Roland, in touch with *Tyella* via the mike, relayed to Kay, and Kay to Jim, the skipper, who put his helm hard over to starboard to get clear of the shot. Jack, anticipating the few seconds required to run us up to speed, gave the signal to turn over, and Roland relayed to Kay. We were running. 'Speed.' The clapper board appeared. '*Western Approaches*. Scene one, take one.' Bang. 'Action', I shouted, not that there was any action, but the men looked intently at their skipper and he valiantly went through his lines. 'Cut', I shouted, triumphantly.

'O.K., Jack?'

'Fine for me.'

'We've got it. First shot in the can. Well done everyone. We're off. We've started.'

It was nearly midday. It had taken us the best part of three hours to shoot ten seconds of film: ten seconds out of the 90 minutes estimated time that the film would run. If we continued at this rate of progress . . . Better not continue that line of thought. Not at all helpful.

If we could now get the camera into the boat from the platform and start to work on our reverse angles on the Captain, we'd be getting somewhere. But the equipment was so awkward to handle, hard enough ashore, but bouncing about on a platform at the end of a lifeboat? However, I thought it worth mentioning and broached the subject with Jack. 'What do you think, Jack; dare we try and get a new set-up in the boat?'

'Reverse on the Skipper, you mean?'

'That's it.'

'Low enough to miss the platform?'

'If necessary, yes.'

'Pity to miss any of the sea background, isn't it?'

'We'll cover the master group shot later. Go for the close shot cover.' Jack looked at his focus puller, Eric. He put paid to any such foolhardy idea.

'I'm sorry, Pat, I didn't bring the wedge or any rostrums. I thought it was agreed we'd go back to set up again.'

'It was, but what I hadn't realised is the time it takes to get us here when we're so heavily loaded.'

'Without them I don't think I could keep the camera steady enough and we've nothing to build it up on.'

'O.K., we've no option. Roland, tell Kay, original plan, back to harbour.' We sludged our way back into the inner basin. Dear old Harry Tupper had the bolts off the platform and the whole affair hoisted on to the jetty in no time. But setting up was a lengthier problem. Shallow rostrums had to be built up to just below gunwale height and locked together, the top hat or giant golf tee screwed into place in the exact position required: by no means the work of a few moments. Time and good weather were being wasted. If I'd been a nail biter I'd have been down to the quick by the time the set-up was fixed, and while this was going on, spare hands emptied the short rail lengths against the harbour wall in case of future need. Captain Pycraft sat most patiently on the stern thwart so that we had the perfect set-up on him to play the scene in which he had been tested at Pinewood. It was now almost half past twelve and by the time we got to our 'shooting grounds' it would be well after one. I decided to call an early lunch break to get a good run at things in the afternoon. All back at 1.30.

Everyone played fair and was back on the dot. The tide was now almost high, making loading much easier. We were soon all aboard and the taking on of umbilicals went very smoothly. We were after a well balanced group shot with Captain Pycraft, facing camera this time, with his Chief Engineer on his right, sitting alongside on the stern thwart and both surrounded by crewmen. This was a wide angle shot requiring maximum sea horizon. This time, shooting over the stern, we had no problem in getting *Tyella* out of the shot, because she was behind us, ready to tow us back into harbour, or would be, that is, when she had got us into the right position. We passed the lighthouse and were doing very nicely. The weather looked set and there was a nice little breeze freshening to help blow away any likelihood of camera noise being picked up, and there was hardly more than a ripple on the water. We looked set to bite into the opening scene. To my astonishment and for no reason that I could understand, *Tyella* suddenly decided that she had come far enough and proceeded to start turning in order to head back into harbour. We couldn't have been more than two or three hundred yards from the lighthouse. I took the mike from Roland and spoke into it: 'Kay, could you ask Jim why he's turning so soon?'

I waited for Kay to relay the message and Jim came out of his wheel house with a loudhailer. 'Just received news of freshening winds; can't risk taking you out further.'

'Kay, will you tell Jim that I can't shoot in a flat calm. I might as well be on the round pond.'

'You don't have a six knot current running on the round pond, and that's what you've got here.'

'I can't make do with this, Jim.'

'You'll have to.'

'Is this the best you can do for us?'

'Yes.'

'Then we might as well go back and call the whole thing off. If you saw this on the screen, Jim, you'd make fools of us all.'

'I'll try and give you another hundred yards or so, and that's the limit.' He went back into the wheel house and I could almost see the steam rising from him. If this was an indication of what was to come in terms of his cooperation, we were in real trouble, and in spite of what he had told me the other night, I now really wondered whether he wasn't pulling the wool over my eyes. We were still in a toddlers' paddling pool when he turned us again. It was this or nothing. I remembered the advice of my dear old friend, the great George Pearson: 'If a scene's any good, the only thing the audience will be looking at are the eyes of your artists'. I could only hope that the scene was good enough, because we were in a flat calm.

At 2.30, an hour after having arrived back from lunch, we were ready for our first real 'sync take'; an acted scene. Everything was right. No ships on the horizon and no land. We turned over and when I heard Eric say 'speed', I shoved the board in front of the camera. '*Western Approaches*. Scene 2, take 1.' Bang. 'When you like, Captain.' And off he went, and very confidently. He'd reached the line, 'from my last position we're roughly half way across, that's a thousand miles from the nearest land', when, from nowhere, down they came. Seagulls, having been scavenging elsewhere, now decided to pay us a call and swooped down into shot. I had to say 'Cut'.

'Sorry, Captain. You were doing splendidly but those damn gulls have given the game away.' He smiled resignedly, but he was gaining confidence, and that was very important. The birds were now wheeling and dealing in determined fashion. Jack came up with a brilliant suggestion. 'Ask Kay if *Tyella* has any scraps they can throw over the side, but keep some in reserve for when we're turning.' Roland relayed this to Kay and Kay to Jim, who came out of his wheel house, no longer steaming, and waved agreement to the plan. Until the screaming and wheeling mob overhead could be enticed elsewhere, there was no way of advancing our cause. Soon a rating was throwing tit-bits over *Tyella*'s stern. One gull spotted them and flew off. Others followed. Soon we were clear and we started to roll once more. Take 2. Bang. We got through the whole take, including Pat O'Malley's feed line: 'Trust old Gerry to make it nice and easy for you'. And on to the end. It was a two-minute take, and probably more.

Our tails were up. This was progress. We were biting into it. We went for a close cover shot on him and I thought it would be tactful to explain why, having been congratulated on having done the scene so well, we were about to do it all over again. 'Captain Pycraft, having just done that scene so well, I'm going to ask you to do it again on a different lens. You will be in close-up, you see, and this will enable me to use bits of it to give greater emphasis as and when it's necessary. When you answer questions and point to the young sparks. It's what we call cover shots, so that we can make it all more interesting. O.K.?'

'Whatever you say. Just tell me when you're ready.'

'Won't take long.' I shouldn't have said that because by the time Eric had opened the blimp (more complicated than the cabin trunk), changed the lens, run out a tape and closed up the blimp, a good five minutes had gone by. Then all was ready. The sun seemed to want to cooperate, the gulls were still happy behind *Tyella* and we were off again. 'Scene 3, take 1. Clap. When you like, Captain.'

'Now lads, the position is this . . .'

I saw Eric start to gesticulate as he continued peering through the camera but pointing towards the horizon. I was intent on watching Captain Pycraft, and was unaware until Eric's gesticulations that a bonfire seemed to be burning in the distance over his camera right shoulder. 'Cut', I said, despairingly. 'Sorry, Captain, but a damned great puff of smoke has suddenly appeared on the horizon.'

He looked round. 'That's the Irish mail boat from Cork. Be half an hour for that to pass by.'

'Bastard bloody thing . . . What a time to appear. Jack, do you think it'll be out of focus enough, not to notice. Can we risk it?'

'No, I'm stopped down too far. Focus'll carry to the horizon. If we could get the stern over to the left, say even ten degrees, we'd be clear, I think.'

Captain Pycraft looked over his shoulder and saw that Jack was right, and made the following seaman-like suggestion. 'Get an oar out either side, midships. Back water on starboard and pull on port and you'll swivel enough to get a clear shot.'

'Thanks, Captain, we'll try.' It took time to get the oars free from everybody, the cables and general toot. They were lengthy affairs, these oars, worthy of the Roman galley ships in *Ben Hur*. Then there was a hunt for the stretchers and more dancing around as they were placed in their slots set into deck boards. Without them to pull against, the oarsmen would have no chance. Unless they could pull and push with all their might, they would have no effect on our fully loaded boat. It needed two men to each oar before the stern responded and swivelled us into position. But it had taken us a good ten minutes, and though the desired result had been achieved, the Irish mail boat had sabotaged our efforts. The smoky streak, like a watercolourist's brush stroke, was now washed across the horizon, as though a convoy might appear at any moment—hardly the effect that we wanted at this stage.

'Let's shoot the smoke, Jack. It'll be useful for the end of the film. The *Leander* rescue sequence.' Captain Pycraft moved out of the way and we took a shot or two of the approaching smoke. Useful 'cut-ins' maybe, but a damnable interruption when the Captain was all keyed-up, word perfect in his own mind and beginning to feel his role so well.

'Suppose, Jack, we go for the shot of Pat O'Malley, when he says to the Master: ''Trust old Gerry to work things out to make it nice and easy for you''.' We had a look at Pat from where the Master was sitting, but the Skerries lighthouse, perched on a massive outcrop of rocks, would have been growing out of Pat's left shoulder. In order to get a clear horizon would have involved a tricky manoeuvre across the mail boat's path. In the time that would take, it would be a tight squeeze, almost as bad as throwing the opening double on the dart board. It was not encouraging constantly to be confronted by these ridiculously restricted angles in which to try and work. At best, little more than ninety degrees, unless *Tyella* could be persuaded to become a little more adventurous. Further speculation on trying to find something to shoot was interrupted by *Tyella*'s loud hailer: 'I am pulling you closer inshore. We're in the shipping lane.' Without more ado, we were towed towards the shore line on our port side. To say the least, it was souring.

And so, in this demoralising and desultory fashion, we limped to the end of our first day of shooting. By the time the mail boat had passed and we were back in position, the light had completely changed. The gallant Captain Pycraft redid the scenes that we had so happily and so successfully completed earlier so that we had the 'master scene' and his close shot of that scene shot in both sunlight and grey skies. Whatever the weather tomorrow, we would be able to continue. Our opening shot, taken from the stern platform and which had taken so much time and trouble, had only been shot in sunshine. If it were cloudy tomorrow it would not match, be of no use and end on the cutting room floor.

This first day, then, had set the course on which we were to do battle. Most of the obstacles, we hoped, were clear to see. Did they give us a sporting chance? I was not alone in doubting whether they did. Once the novelty of being filmed wears off—and it wears off very soon—there isn't much left, unless you are the star. But, hanging around and waiting your turn to do your little bit, by which time those lines, so sure a few moments ago, have flown . . . well, it's bad enough in the comparative comfort of the film studio, but not so funny bouncing about in a lifeboat in all weathers. Total disillusionment in the whole endeavour could very easily set in. Even the most hardened 'pro' of stage and screen would have found his patience sorely tried and his physical stamina tested as never before. But for raw seamen to stick it, without the tradition that 'the show must go on' and who would be asked to sit there perhaps for several days without the camera being able so much as to take a peek at them—it would be asking a great deal. Hardly surprising if their loyalties started to shift more and more to the pubs of Holyhead rather than the lifeboat outside the harbour wall. There were storm clouds ahead all right, and deep depressions.

Phil Ross, that gallant continuity girl, who was to sit for months on end, throughout the winter, sometimes five and six hours, and finally write a log of each day's events. Her comments are as objective as any record could hope to be. Here is her account of our second day.

Diary. Sat Sep 19. Shooting days: 2.
EXT. Lifeboat.
Sea and sky grey all day. Low clouds. No sun.
Slate scenes 5–10. Estimated screen time. 2 mins 2 secs.
Script scenes. 37. 39. 42, 44, 46. 39A.   TOTAL 5
                                              EXTRAS 1

Shooting from 10-15 to 5-15 at sea.

Late starting getting gear together and leaving quay. Seagulls constantly settling on sea and spoiling background. Delay over sound on two occasions, due to salt erosion on terminals creating 'shorts'. Very depressing this happens so soon. Also for changing camera position from built up pedestal to one on floor boards for closer angle on Master at tiller. More delays moving lifeboat around to avoid land, convoys and ship's smoke. Service boat had to tow lifeboat some distance along coast on this account.

Our third day's shooting was a washout, just when we hoped to get into our stride. It rained incessantly and the wind blew at gale force. As we had only a hastily erected tarpaulin under which to shelter, I had no intention of killing the enthusiasm of my amateur cast by having them hanging around too long and for no good reason when the weather showed no signs of improving.

Our fourth day wasn't much better, and neither was the fifth— but during the sequence of its many frustrations I realised that unless we could find a means of being able to alter the camera set-up more easily in the lifeboat, we would be here for a lifetime. Facility to move the camera was priority number one. We returned to the harbour around 5.00 p.m. and for a variety of maddening reasons had not shot a single foot of film. Our patience and stamina were going to be given a very thorough test.

When the boat was secured, I waited my turn up those slippery steps to the jetty, and there was dear old Harry Tupper and Charlie

Squires, smiling down and anxious to know how we'd got on. Harry was the same type of man as Chief Petty Officer Hills. They don't come better in any walk of life. Harry talked rather slowly. He was never to be hurried about anything, but always thorough and efficient in everything. He had a keen and kindly eye and carried never an ounce too much on his six-foot frame. 'How did it go today, Pat?'

'Bloody awful, Harry. A real balls-up.'

'What, more gulls?'

'We'll never be without them.'

'What then? Camera noise?'

'Didn't get that far . . . No, Harry, we've got to find a way of setting up that blood-stained camera. After the first shot, we were over half an hour getting a new set-up. It's like moving your fridge and anchoring it, at a tilt, mind you, on the kitchen floor. That's what we're trying to do out there. Bloody madness, and there was the light, absolutely perfect, no gulls and a clear horizon. Stinking fish, Harry . . . chocking it up and trying to hold it steady. Anything more idiotic . . .'

'Any ideas, Pat?'

'No . . . Only that we ought to be able to shove it forrard and aft and port and starboard.' I suited the action to the words.

Harry watched and didn't say a word for a moment or two, and then, very quietly, he said: 'Why don't we make it do . . . just that . . . Pat?'

'If you could, wonderful. Any ideas?'

'Yes . . . We'll mount it on rails . . . like those short bits we got from Captain Mackenzie, only we'll make 'em in grooved wood so's you can bolt 'em, section by section, into the seats, as you go along, like. If you want to get up to the bow and you're in the stern, we'll screw the whole set into place and shove it forrard, and then if you want to look back, unbolt the rails in shot and dump 'em on the floor 'til you need 'em again. To get you port and starboard, I'll mount the camera on a tray affair set in its own side slider. You'll be able to move camera all over the boat, then.' I looked at him as if a halo were already shining round his head, for if he could construct such a device he was indeed our saviour. If ever there were an example of how much a director relies on his unit, here it was. Harry Tupper, master carpenter, had solved one of the problems that should never have arisen.

As I have said, these fundamental production and technical problems should have been resolved in plenty of time, rather than expose a production unit and, far more important, an amateur cast to what was going to be a siege of endurance in finding ways and means of how to shoot the film. 'How long do you think it'll take, Harry?'

'I'll make a start now . . . More timber tomorrow. Quick as I can, Pat.'

'You bet . . . Thanks Harry . . . Wonderful idea.'

Wednesday 23 September; sixth day. This progress report has the stigma of 'Screen time: nil'. Other comments make discouraging reading, and what poor Dal must have thought when he read them I shudder to think. Clearly he would have to get hardened to them. For example: 'We made four takes on the long shot but had to cut on takes 3 and 4 due to gulls flying into picture.' Gulls do not take direction and sadly soon tire of tit-bits thrown overboard, that is, scraps from wartime rationing. 'We found the camera wouldn't work because the battery connection was wet. Returned to the quay in a rain storm.'

Thursday 24 September; seventh day. Incredible. We advanced by 27 seconds of screen time. A few little problems presented themselves; a dip-stick to check our reserves of patience. A random selection of them, for example:

- Two invasion barges careering round our background just when we were ready to shoot.
- *Tyella* refused to go outside harbour due to strong tides and currents.
- More ships kept getting in the way.
- Bright sky and sun too strong for Jack Cardiff to get a balanced exposure between faces and hot sky. Had to wait for cloud cover to cut down on brilliance.

However, it wasn't all doom and gloom. The camera crew was reinforced by the arrival of a new focus puller, a young Dutch lad, de Buy, who was most efficient and of horse stomach variety. Bob Banner, too, put on a superb cabaret act. As we were being towed back for another run at a take, Banner felt that things needed livening up a bit. He sang three songs, brilliantly. The first he called 'In a Persian Beer Garden'. It was a send-up of Saint Saens' Ballet Egyptien. He broke into a falsetto and moaned like a mad mullah. This remarkable rendition was followed by an irreverent interpretation of the Salvation Army song: 'I'm glad that salvation is free'. Finally a real winner which had us all in fits:

> A German clock maker to England once came.
> Benjamin Snook was that clock maker's name.
> He searched every street and he searched every lane
> and rang on his bell any old clocks to mend?

This led to a sing-song chorus and we all found ourselves joining in. It was all infectiously joyous thanks to Bob's verve and vivid rendering. I was determined to build a sequence out of this act of his. It was so apt for the story—a dispirited boatload of survivors who needed to be perked up. I couldn't wait for the chance to film it. But, for the moment, it was a luxury that had to be kept on ice. When we had made some real progress and eaten into the scripted scenes, then would be the time for luxuries of this sort. But, I had no intention of leaving this location without having put that act of Banner's safely on film. There was no doubt the man had star quality. He was a real find and he would make an enormous contribution. It was a lucky day when we ran into him: the best stroke of luck that the picture had had, so far. Phil Ross told me that he was, with the greatest coherence, explaining to her Einstein's theory of relativity. His range of knowledge and the extent of his reading was astonishing, she said. Nothing would surprise me about him. Though, I must say, his spitting on the hotel carpet most certainly did.

With luck, Harry would have our camera rails ready in a day or so, and this would speed things up—I hoped.

Friday 25 September; eighth day. Screen time: nil. Morning rained off. Afternoon we had troubles getting the half lifeboat section mounted on rockers, supposedly, but it took us the rest of the day to make the damned contrivance work. But, at least, it would help in the future.

Saturday 26 September. Another blob. Screen time: nil. One blob after another. The progress report on this day's events is too depressing. It appears that we took the utility van after returning to harbour and started careering around the coast of Anglesey trying to find a more suitable location than Holyhead. Phil ended her report with a charming statement: 'The lunch is still un-satisfactory'. Nine days of shooting and we had two minutes and twenty-nine seconds of screen under our belts. If that weren't alarming enough, here we were bouncing around the countryside like a troop of scouts looking for somewhere to pitch the tent for a camping weekend. Back at base a cast of twenty officers and men and an entire film unit were waiting to get to work. It was mind-boggling in its imbecility.

I envied Peter Bolton, at that moment, being the life and soul of the party, cracking jokes and being very funny indeed. Just as Banner was, yesterday. He lifted our morale considerably and Peter contributed greatly to our well-being. But, I feared that we were being sucked deeper and deeper into that bog and I didn't know in which direction to turn or what course to set. We were in this dire situation through an inability to prepare and I resented it, deeply— being made to look and feel an amateur nincompoop. I'd been pooped once and that was enough. I could see no other course but to keep going and hope to get unstuck, even though we were 'in it' up to our knees. Nine days of production for two minutes and twenty-nine seconds. It was a record, and a shaming one. By the way things were going, we'd be well over our knee caps, to-morrow.

Sunday 27 September; tenth day. Not completely in the 'dog house'. Phil ends her daily report with: 'No delays or mishaps'. We got one minute and nine seconds of screen time. Not much, perhaps, but more than the total of the last eight days. Conditions were uniquely in our favour. Skies not too hot, watery sun, no strong tides or currents, no high winds, no ships and no gulls. Mercifully, they had taken the day and flown off. Had we been able to move the camera easily, heaven knows what we might have achieved. But, nevertheless, at the end of the day it was a fine feeling to put a pencil through the completed scenes. Done—safely in the can, always assuming, of course, they were given a clean bill of health from the 'labs'.

Scenes 164–66, done. The young Sparks tapping out his morning message: boat's position and S.O.S. Scenes 180–81, done. The Sparks about to close his portable radio into its specially designed suitcase and being persuaded to give it one more go. 'You never know who may be listening.' He agrees, with the proviso that he must preserve his batteries. 'They don't last for ever.' Scene 174, done. The journalist, Tosti Russell, known as Carter in the script, answering the Master's quip that he will have a good story for his paper when he gets home. Not a wasted day, though perhaps not a lot to write home about; at least something was achieved, and however minimal that was to us, during these trying growing pains, a godsend.

Monday 28 September; eleventh day. Dog house. Screen time: nil. *Tyella* is no use to us. She props up the harbour wall as she has her tanks cleaned out. Jack Holmes has come down from Pinewood and with Gerry Bryant and Jim of *Tyella* they take the utility van and go Boy Scouting for another possible camping site: Pwllheli, this time, to see whether it might offer a less landlocked harbour. Too late, the unit cried. All this should have been done months ago. I shoot on the quay, trying to get a few shots on the half lifeboat section-rocker set.

Tuesday 29 September; twelfth day. Screen time: five seconds. *Tyella* is still propping up the harbour wall, having her tanks cleaned. They must be very dirty. I am left to fiddle about on the rocker set . . . Too much of this and I shall go off mine.

Wednesday 30 September; thirteenth day. Screen time: two minutes eight seconds. *Tyella*'s tanks are clean but she has to have her monthly check-up and take on stores. This house-keeping act of hers took until 11.00 a.m. and, with a beautiful day going to waste, was a maddening delay. We got to sea only to discover an Admiralty inspection boat moored bang in the centre of our operating area—a small enough bit of ocean without having that obstacle thrown against our sight screen. We shall make this film in spite of the Navy. They must have forgotten that we were trying to make it for them. Obviously a total lack of comprehension of each other's problems.

We were set up for a long dialogue scene with Tosti Russell chatting to Banner and the Master, and it ran for about two minutes—a bit over. He was doing splendidly but, through no fault of his, we had to keep cutting. The usual combination of problems. On take one, which was going perfectly, a Spitfire roared across the sky and deafened us all, as well as ruining the take. On two subsequent takes the sun went in and the exposure variation would have been too great; by which time the sea got up too high for *Tyella* and we had to return to harbour in the hope that when the tide turned, the sea might go down somewhat. I felt sorry for poor Tosti. He had done so well and, through no fault of his, had not managed to have a completed take in the can.

We tried again in the afternoon, and conditions were more favourable. But Tosti could not repeat the excellence of his morning's efforts. Not being a professional, he could not equal the seeming spontaneity of the morning. But we got a complete take, though privately, I knew I would have to retake it as his voice suddenly developed a maddening minor intonation. It was useless to continue and we could not change the camera position. He had had enough for one day. Anyway, by 4.45 the light failed and we returned to the quay. An encouraging day in that we had put over two minutes in the can. If we could make this a daily average, our progress would be tolerable, considering the working conditions. But more encouraging was dear old Harry Tupper, waiting at the top of the steps: 'Pat . . . Got a minute? . . . Got something to show you.'

'Don't tell me . . . You've made the rails?'

'Just get some holes drilled into them thwarts so's we can bolt 'em in place.' We went over to the bench he'd built himself. Neatly stacked were twelve grooved wooden lengths of our rails, each as long as the distance between the centre points of the thwarts, and then he showed me his masterpiece. 'This is the important bit, Pat . . . This bit takes the camera . . . sort of tray arrangement, but it slides sideways, the whole width of the boat, and these are the rails that slot into the fore and aft rails . . . Now you'll be able to go right up to the bow, and if you want to look back at the stern, Pat, all you got to do is unscrew the bits that'll be in shot . . . Should work all right, Pat . . .'

'Wow . . . I'll say it will, Harry; you're a genius . . . Can't thank you enough. The hours that this'll save us . . . My God, I'm grateful . . .'

'Let's see if the bloody thing works, first, Pat . . .' Without more ado he took his bag of tools and descended the slippery steps and climbed aboard the lifeboat. Soon he was drilling holes into the thwarts so that our permanent way could be laid, as and when required, down the length of the boat. As he was doing this, Jack and Eric bolted the camera's top hat-cum-golf tee into the centre of the tray which was set into its own cross-boat rail. It was wider than the actual beam of the boat. This would allow us, if necessary, to look into the boat from a set-up just outside the line of the gunwale. Masterly . . . When all was ready, we put all the pieces together and had the enormous pleasure of playing trains in our lifeboat. We could shove the camera wherever we wanted. Our tails were up. Our chances looked better.

Thursday 1 October; fourteenth day. Screen time: two minutes forty seconds. This is much more like it. Home railways a joy and we were soon into our stride. We were at work on the third lifeboat sequence of getting to know everyone. Tosti Russell starts a lengthy conversation with Bob Banner and it was a lengthy scene. Sadly, the camera assistant committed the unforgivable sin of allowing us to run out of film during a take. This was the ultimate crime. He should have known the length of the scene and what footage of film it would require, and he knew, or should have done, how much film he had left in his magazine. Ninety feet to the minute—360 feet is four minutes' worth of scene. On this simple basis of calculation he should have known that he had enough before he committed the unit to a take. To have allowed us to run out in these circumstances when the preparation for every shot was a minor conquest brooked of no appeal against 100 lashes or keel hauling, whichever the guilty party preferred. However, the camera crew, all three of them, in the slight cross-wind, found the corkscrew movement of the boat too much for them. They were succumbing in turns. So, the threshold of punishment changes and values have to be reassessed. Indeed they do, and all three had our sympathy and respect for the gutsy way in which they stuck it out. Both Eric and Jack suffered almost daily without complaint or lack of enthusiasm once the nausea was over.

But our progress was encouraging. So much so that we ran out of film before lunch and had to return to harbour earlier than I would have liked. By the end of the day, we were not far short of three minutes of screen time. Even Elia Kazan is on record as saying that three minutes in studio conditions is good going. Tortoise-like we might be, but, thanks to Harry, we all felt that we could get there, in the end.

Friday 2 October; fifteenth day. Dog house. Screen time: nil. *Tyella*'s tanks again. Some sort of adjustment required. We'd have done better with *The African Queen*. Anyway, that morning she would be of no use to us. We made the unit call for 2.00 p.m. *Tyella* really was causing quite enough trouble, and now there were signs of trouble brewing with the seamen. Four of them had not responded to the unit call of 2.00 p.m. Pat O'Malley, Tony Evans, the old 'shell back' 'Taffy' and sadly, Bob Banner. Peter Bolton went off to scour the locals and tracked them down to 'Skerries'. But they would not or could not be winkled out. I went and had a go but they were too far gone to be of any use. I told them to report to the office at 6.00 p.m.

This was a worrying situation. Once they had been established as part of the lifeboat's crew, their absence would not only be noticed on the screen but create havoc to the entire enterprise. They had become indispensable and they were certainly not so dumb not to have recognised this fact. They had us over a barrel. We were undefended and vulnerable on every flank.

They reported to the hotel at 3.30, and though they apologised for their non-appearance, they then asked for more money. As I feared, a blackmail situation. I told them they had made an agreement and so far as I was concerned they and I would stick by it. They went off and there were storm clouds in the making. No question.

We then held a unit meeting. It was generally felt that Pat O'Malley was the ringleader and that I should sack him. I was against this. I told the unit what Mr Hobbes had said to me at the Shipping Federation. We could all understand that it was difficult to make the switch from rigid discipline aboard ship to this job of hanging about, getting wet and cramped for hours on end, with the prospect of a limp lettuce sandwich with a bit of spam for lunch. Difficult to maintain an active interest when for some, the camera had not even looked in their direction. Instead of service discipline to make you toe the line, only the matey atmosphere of a film unit to keep you up to the mark.

They had all behaved very well during these first two damnably difficult weeks during which, it had to be faced, they must have thought that they were being handled by a bunch of bungling amateurs, not having foreseen even a few of the problems from which they and we were all suffering. Frustration and boredom are dangerous customers in the best of circumstances, but in these, devilish. Our only hope was to try and build a sense of genuine comradeship.

It was the only way: our only hope. We could not dragoon these men; pull rank; put them in irons for insubordination. If after two weeks, after a bit of a bust-up, we started a sacking procedure, I'd soon end up with an empty boat. There would be more bust-ups to come—bound to be. We must find a way of learning how to ride them. Unless we did, our cast would slowly disappear.

Saturday 3 October; fifteenth day. Screen time: three minutes three seconds. Three minutes: this was almost studio standard. We were slowly getting on top. Banner today was wonderful. Just as well we did not over-react to yesterday's little 'contretemps'. He gave a fine performance in describing how he got away from the ship after it had been torpedoed. What was interesting was the way in which he used the script to give him his guideline and then ad-libbed—what I so hoped would happen. They were not imprisoned by the inhibition of learning lines. They used them simply as guides for their own thoughts and forms of expression.

Scenes 31–35: Bob describing his escape and his mates reacting to his account. Scene 30b–30c: Alf Rawson established as the wounded man and his account of leaving the ship. A most encouraging day, particularly after yesterday's set-back.

18

'Dead slow ahead'

On Thursday 8 October, we had bad news over the rushes. Two good dialogue scenes which had not been easy to shoot were ruined because the faces in the foreground were under-exposed and the background sky too hot and hopelessly over-exposed. After seeing them in rushes it was obvious we faced new problems, especially for poor Jack Cardiff, and goodness knows, he had had enough to put up with as it was, bearing up under the physical strain of his daily ordeal at sea. Now, light problems. Either too much of it or not enough: either too red or too orange; either too bright or too dull, and all four ingredients being mixed up into a nightmarish goulash as the day proceeded—for the light ingredients changed as quickly as the night sky at sunset. Somehow, he had to juggle with these so that the faces did not look as though they had been washed in tomato ketchup or were waiting to play the ghost in *Hamlet*.

Not unnaturally, as we left the cinema, he was a worried man. So was Penny, who immediately understood Jack's problems even though they were in Technicolor—in some ways a system more able to overcome exposure problems with three films to bear the burden of any mistake, rather than just one in black-and-white.

Back at the hotel, like a tolling bell, Jack said: 'Those ''inky dinks'' aren't up to it. I'm going to need two mini arcs: du-arcs, and that means a ''genny''.'

'Oh my Gawd', I said, but soon realised that his needs were everybody's, even though they meant delay for us all.

'If you need them, obviously you've got to have them, but where on earth do we put the ''genny''? *Tyella* can't take another paper clip with Kay's stuff aboard, and Jim would never have it bolted to his deck', I said.

'Be no good anyway. Bound to hear it. Be the end of ''sync'' shooting', Penny said, stunning us into gloomy silence until he ventured to suggest: 'There's only one place it can go and . . . that is the second lifeboat!' Jack's powers of deduction were equal to this simple equation.

'Keeping *Tyella* out of shot is bad enough without sandwiching a lifeboat between us. We'd be lucky to get a shot a day, and it's no news to you that even that's a struggle sometimes', I said.

'We'll put her astern when you're going to shoot over the bows and sandwiched when you shoot over the stern.'

'Oh come on, Penny, it takes us long enough to get to sea as it is without threading a necklace of boats together.'

'There's no other way, Pat', he said.

'But as it is our progress would put a tortoise to shame.'

'Better a snail's pace than no pace at all', Penny replied, and his simple logic brooked of no argument except a further doubt of mine. 'But we'll probably hear the ''genny'' in the lifeboat?'

'Not if we house it below the gunwale', Penny said.

'But that'll mean cutting out some of the thwarts and that'll ruin the boat!', I said.

'Let's face it, by the time we're finished with them, all they'll be fit for is bonfire night.' The realistic Penny summed up the situation with brutal candour. I hated the idea of butchering one of Alfred Holt's boats. It seemed an abuse of his kindness, but if it had to go, it had to go. We were in a nasty situation and well we realised it. 'To quote old Pycraft, the situation is this: unless you get more light, Jack, the production comes to an end. That's it, isn't it?'

'Yes, virtually. I mean, we can run film through the camera as if to show willing, but when we know it's going to be N.G., what's the point? Just make us look ridiculous. Through nobody's fault, we're beginning to look that already . . .' I took their glasses, deeply troubled, and went to the bar. Now we were in it up to our necks.

As I took our drinks back, another nasty thought hit me. 'I'm not trying to be a wet blanket, but are we sure that we can get a ''genny'' into the lifeboat?' I looked at Penny and then Jack and back at Penny, as though on the centre court.

'Ah', Penny said, 'I've seen a ''genny'' somewhere, a little petrol-driven job that'll give Jack about 50 amps; just enough for his two du-arcs. But I'll have to hunt it down.'

'That means you'll have to go back tomorrow?'

'It's our only chance, chum. If Jack gets these conditions again, and he's bound to at this time of year . . .'

'Do you think you can track it down fairly easily, this ''genny''?'

'Might have been in a garage at Croydon or even Tooting, where I used to use some of their equipment. Anyway, the model exists and I'll find one somewhere.'

'So, everything depends on whether you can find it . . . What an incredible situation.'

He left the next morning to start his search upon which the fate of the film depended, leaving us to limp along in the three-legged egg-and-spoon race against the elements and *Tyella*. Our log shows that she continued to be the villain of the piece. It was 12 October and she held us up the whole day having new water tanks fitted, and half the next. Two days later it was wind and gales. No shooting. The next day *Tyella* trouble; sea too rough. And the one after that she was having a new dynamo fitted; and then we all took a most necessary two-day break.

We returned on Monday, 19 October with batteries recharged. We arrived at the quay at 9.00 a.m. to find the lifeboat half-full of water. It took us until midday to bale it out. In the afternoon *Tyella* fiddled about in the harbour mouth. This state of affairs could not be allowed to continue. I would go to Liverpool and put my problems to the C. in C.: it was the only way out of this hopeless situation. Mines or no mines, if the Navy wanted this film made, then they must stop treating us as poor relations and come to our aid. However, it was not all gloom and doom because when we returned to the quay there was Penny, smiling as though newly minted and like an officer of the Raj with his foot, not on his first tiger, but his 'genny'. He had provided us with one of the essential tools to finish the job. Now, it was up to me to get the second. I hurried back to the hotel and called Owen Rutter. The number was ringing and luckily his voice answered: 'Owen Rutter.'

'Owen, I hope that I'm not calling you at an inconvenient time; it's Pat, Pat Jackson.'

'Hullo, Pat, how's it going?'

'Could be better, a lot better, and that's why I'm calling you. I need to see Sir Percy. Could you tell me the correct procedure for me to ask to see him for a few moments.'

'I think you'd go through his Flag Lieutenant. He's one of your fraternity. Peter Lupino, nephew of Lupino Lane, I think. Would you like me to call Sir Percy for you?'

'I hate to put you to the trouble, but anything that would save time, I'd be most grateful.'

'What's your number.'

'Holyhead 24.'

'I'll call you back as soon as I can. Shall I give any hint of your problems? No . . . On second thoughts, it'll be better coming from you. All I'll say is that you have urgent problems that you'd like to discuss with him. How'll that do?'

'Fine.'

'O.K. I'll get back to you as soon as I can. So long.'

'So long.' I didn't dare leave the lobby and paced up and down, rehearsing what I was going to say to the C. in C. The message was so simple that I didn't need much rehearsal, and though I am no actor, I doubted whether even I could fluff it. The phone rang, but it was not for me. I remembered my trip up the east coast and Commodore Phillips telling me how important it was to keep to the swept channel—'You see what happens if you don't'—and then his pointing either side of the channel where avenues of masts from sunken vessels lined both sides in the estuary waters of the Thames. I must not let that affect my attempt to get the help we needed. The phone rang again and this time it was for me, and it was Owen.

'Pat, I'm afraid the Admiral is not available for a few days. He's in Washington . . . Naval conference.'

'Oh my God.'

'Bad as that, eh?'

'Yes, Owen, to be frank.'

'Oh dear, I am sorry. Anyway, I spoke to Commodore Mansfield whom you met, remember; very helpful in explaining the new convoy system. I told him you had problems and need to see the Admiral as soon as possible. He promised to convey your message and be in touch as soon as possible. He will, too. Nothing more I can do, I'm afraid.'

'Thank you, Owen, for what you've done. I suppose his deputy wouldn't be able to allocate us a trawler would he? We've been given a craft, you see, that just isn't up to the job.'

'I see. How very depressing. But I don't think it would be very tactful. I think you'll just have to sweat it out for a few more days.'

'O.K., Owen, and thanks again for your help.'

'So long, Pat, and good luck.' Nothing more to be done except put a good face on it and rejoin the unit. Always very supportive and great company.

The next day, 20 October, we went to sea and bounced around for a couple of hours and hoped for the light to improve. In between spasms Jack read his exposure meter and shook his head: 'Until we get the du-arcs, no go in these conditions'. The men looked as dejected as we felt. They were sticking it remarkably well. Admittedly, simple logic must have told them that these endless days of frustration were better than being torpedoed, but even that reasoning can wear a bit thin. Still no call from Commodore Mansfield. An unemployed actor waiting for the phone to ring couldn't have felt more discouraged.

The following day there was plenty of light and plenty of sea, too. No sooner did our 'bête noire' put her nose out of harbour than she turned hard for home: broadside to the waves for only a few seconds and we heard the crockery come crashing to the floor. Poor old Jim, it wasn't his fault that he was in command of a craft that was fit only for the Serpentine, and though he lost some of his favourite records in this manoeuvre, I lost my last vestige of patience with this state of affairs.

That night, after the rushes, we showed the cast and hotel staff *Ferry Pilot*. It may not have been an Oscar winning film but it was, at least, a finished product and had its moments of visual interest and excitement. There is no doubt that this showing had an effect. If nothing more, the sandwiches next day were almost palatable and the seamen entered the boat not as though they had been press-ganged.

However, one look at the sky made us change tactics. The weather looked as though it were going to be similar to yesterday's, and rather than waste time and this suspicion of new-found enthusiasm, I decided that we'd row out to the second lifeboat which was moored in the outer harbour, as there was insufficient space for a permanent mooring in the inner basin. We were awaiting the arrival of our two arc lights and their electricians. We would put a crew aboard to row her back into the inner basin so that we could house the precious 'genny'. It was, as it turned out, a delightful diversion. With four pairs of oars now and then working together, we bore down on our other lifeboat, transferred a crew, and the two boats made a race of it for the basin. Henley had come to Holyhead: a diversion that helped to bring us all together into something like a united band.

Safely moored below the crane on the jetty, Harry Tupper descended and our sister lifeboat suffered the indignity of losing her two central thwarts. Then, our 'genny' was reverently lowered and made secure. Penny poured in two gallons of petrol and hand cranked the thing into life. The two little du-arcs standing innocently on the quay were connected by the two 'sparks', Young and Coy, who had arrived on the morning train ... N.A.T.K.A. regulations—an arc a spark or a spark an arc, whichever way round sounds better—and lo, there was light. Never was a more spontaneous cheer uttered. Jack grabbed the first two faces he could find and set them against the greyest of grey skies and bathed them in light. A quick meter reading told him that he would now be able to get to work no matter what sort of weather the fates were to throw at us. He was in business: we were in business, photographically speaking. If we could only become sea-worthy, we had a chance. Meantime, if only at a snail's pace, we must make our necklace of boats work. All we needed now was for the phone to ring from H.Q. Liverpool. So please, Admiral Sir Percy Noble, Commander in Chief, come back to base because my unit, my cast, my story and your film could so easily founder without trace.

Meanwhile, Gerry Bryant was not having a happy time. He, too, had his problems which needed the most rarified diplomatic skills. One of the cast had had one, if not several, too many. He managed to stagger back to his lodgings and somehow got himself to bed. The next thing he knew was that . . . it was on fire: not just smouldering, but flaming. He sobered up pretty quickly. With no running water in his room he looked into his 'goesunder', and to his extreme annoyance and disappointment found it to be empty, so he used his personal apparatus to extinguish the trouble, no doubt thankful for the extra pint or two. Some might describe such action as that of a man with remarkable presence of mind. Not so his landlady and, when Gerry went round, first thing, to pay the rent, he found her anything but friendly. In fact she was in danger of catching fire herself. Her description of this gallant member of my cast was not flattering. She ordered Gerry to have his things packed straight away as she would not tolerate such a XXXX ZZZZZ + + + + + + person in her house, one minute longer than necessary. She was getting into her full stride, remembering that her mother tongue was Welsh—a pretty language, they tell me. Gerry, a peaceful sort of chap, stood his ground manfully and waited, in the hope that she must stop some time. She did, and believe it or not, he found the right words—and the right compensation—to mollify the lady, who was now prepared to give the man a second chance and herself the chance, indeed the likelihood, of more compensation. 'It was a bit dodgy, old boy, because she was becoming very militant and threatened to bring all the other landladies out in sympathy . . . send all the seamen packing . . . Could have been very awkward indeed.' In such a manner and with such little incidents, the production limped along.

The next day was Saturday 24 October. It was fine, but there was a breeze. We had been just over a month fighting our growing pains

. . . Resisting them rather than overcoming them would perhaps be a more accurate description. Today, however, all installed and ready to go by 9.30, we felt that, at last, we had the means and had learnt how to come to terms. It was galling, therefore, to discover that *Tyella*'s crew was still at breakfast. The loss of his favourite records must still have been rankling with her skipper. Certainly, nobody could accuse him of being a hundred per cent dedicated to our cause. I contained my temper as best I could and went aboard. 'Jim, are you on our side or not?'

'There's a gale warning. I shall have to get permission from the base.'

'Well perhaps you'd be good enough to do that right away. The weather's perfect and I can't stand by and see it go to waste unless there is a very good reason. Meantime, I'm going to phone H.Q. Liverpool.' I left and hurried back to the hotel. I phoned Owen Rutter who kindly gave me the number of Derby House. I put a call through immediately. A voice answered. 'Derby House. Who is speaking?'

'Pat Jackson, the director of the film *Western Approaches* which I am making for the Commander in Chief. I need to speak to Commodore Mansfield urgently.'

'One moment, Sir.' I waited several seconds.

'Commodore Mansfield's office.' I identified myself again and a Wren's voice answered: 'I am very sorry, Sir, but the Commodore will not be back until Monday.'

'I see . . . Could I speak to the Flag Lieutenant, please?'

'One moment, Sir, I'll get you transferred.' I heard her wiggle the contact up and down and say: 'Transfer to the Flag Lieutenant, please'. Then several 'burr burr burrs' and a voice answering: 'C. in C.'s office.'

'Could I speak to the Flag Lieutenant, please?'

'Speaking. Who's that?'

'Pat Jackson . . . I've worked with your relations Wally and Barry Lupino at Welwyn Garden way back in 1932.'

'My father and uncle . . . ghastly quota quickies.'

'I was only the loading boy—hardly out of nappies. Anyway, I'm at Holyhead and trying to make this film for the C. in C. We're in trouble and need his help. What chance of seeing him urgently?'

'I'll call you back as soon as I can. What's your number?'

'Holyhead 24. Are we talking of today or tomorrow—your calling back?'

'Say noon, today.'

'Would 1.30 be convenient? I'm hoping to get to sea and a few shots in the can before lunch.'

'O.K. . . . Will do. 1.30. So long.' I charged back to the quay, and as they saw me running round the quay, *Tyella* started up and was ticking over as I jumped aboard the lifeboat with the glad tidings to everyone that the Admiral was back. 'We may yet get a trawler . . . Meantime let's see if we can get something more with this thing.'

We were going to start shooting a new sequence—the part of the story where John Walden, sitting on a forrard thwart and leaning wearily against the mast, thinks that he hears an aircraft. He looks up out of his half-slumber, spots it and shouts to the rest as he points to it, darting in and out of the clouds. For a moment, all hell breaks out as everyone shouts and gesticulates in a frenzied attempt to attract its attention. But, it disappears for good.

I wanted to show their dejection at having their hopes so quickly raised, only to be dashed in a few seconds. John had a few lines at the end to sum up all their feelings. We would be shooting over the bows so Penny was installed in the second lifeboat which we would be towing well astern of us. It would be out of shot all right, but whether out of ear-shot remained to be seen, or rather heard. Harry Tupper and Charlie Squires were a willing crew to help keep her in station: Harry at the helm and Charlie to fend off. We rehearsed the scene as we proceeded towards our restricted shooting area. John had it perfectly. By the time we had reached our restricted shooting grounds the sun had gone in. The cold descended with a shock as sudden as a cold shower. The two du-arcs were struck and a wonderful light burst from them. Jack countered its brilliance with a slightly bluish filter. We were now ready for a take, whereas yesterday, against these grey skies, no balance would have been possible. Now Jack was in control and, like a painter, could mix the palette that nature provided him in all its moods and variations. Here were the first real signs of progress. But cold of this intensity was something new and I could see that John was shivering so much that there was no disguising it. It is very hard to remain mentally alert feeling the cold, and John certainly found this to be the case. His memory refused to function. We got the take after six attempts, and that meant that we had had to manoeuvre three times; like a horse refusing a jump, he has to be turned round and taken back for another run at it. We managed two takes per run in, but a horse is a single, albeit four-legged, unit. A necklace of three boats, the lead one being none too sea-worthy, undergoing a similar process is a time-consuming business. Everyone had had enough. We returned to port.

I was in plenty of time to pace up and down the hotel lobby, and a few minutes past 1.30 p.m., the phone rang. It was for me. I catapulted into the box.'

'Jackson?'

'Yes.'

'Lupino . . . The Admiral will be happy to see you at 11.00 next Monday, 26 October.'

'God bless you, Sir.'

'That would be nice. Thank you. How's it going down there?'

'Room for improvement.'

'Be good to hear a clapper board again. Must winkle a day or so and pay you a visit.'

'You'd be most welcome.'

'When you get to Derby House, ask for me and I'll come and collect you. Look forward to meeting you on Monday.' The heavens had opened. There was a chink of light.

I grabbed a sandwich and hurried back to the quay. The unit was already in the boat but there was only one member of the crew aboard *Tyella*. For the second time that day I fumed aboard. This time the delay was through nobody's fault. The coxswain had received a telegram informing him that his wife was dangerously ill. Jim had had to go to the Base Commander to get his coxswain compassionate leave. There was nothing to be done but wait and twiddle our thumbs. We were becoming experts at it. We disembarked and paced up and down the jetty. It was then that we discovered that our dear and intrepid continuity girl, Phil Ross, had secret ambitions of becoming an astrologer. She came up to me as Jack and I turned back to the boat. 'My sweet', she said, 'I'm afraid Neptune is wrongly aspected with Mars, in opposite houses; it'll be quite useless this afternoon.'

'Thank you, Phil, for those few kind words. What do you suggest we do; pack it in?'

'You might just as well.'

Jim was seen striding towards us. We all climbed back aboard. *Tyella* was clearly going out to show her paces, for the wind was much higher than anything she had ever considered meeting before. Could the fact that I had phoned Liverpool have anything to do with this surprisingly gallant performance on her part? Once more we were towed out to our patch. The arcs struck up and the 'genny', being well down-wind, was as silent as a mouse. Splendid progress, and the two lifeboats were riding the swell as confidently as though Britannia still and unquestionably ruled the waves. Not so poor old *Tyella*; one sniff of this disturbed brine was too much for her. She turned for home, and as she exposed her broadside to the waves, we thought she was going. Jim, poor chap, had proved his point. He wasn't a malingerer. He had done his best with what was given him and it wasn't his fault that the craft, as he said originally, just wasn't up to the job. Yes, Phil, Neptune was clearly wrongly aspected with Mars. It was quite useless, this afternoon.

19

S.O.S. to the C. in C.

The following day, Sunday, gave us no hope of filming. It bucketed down. I caught the 7.30 p.m. to Liverpool. I had been tempted to visit the Admiral in my filming uniform, a Cornish fisherman's jersey. I'd bought it at Mousehole whilst being first assistant to Harry Watt, filming *The Savings of Bill Blewett.* Anyway, fond of my jersey as I was, it was hardly Savile Row. Neither was my 'One and Only'. But it was the best I could do. As a mark of respect, out it had to come for, perhaps, its last appearance.

It was a lonely journey, and so was the Adelphi with its vast and cavernous reception rooms and half-empty dining room. I escaped to my old H.Q., The Angel, and spent a jolly evening with my loyal friend Bill Anderson, and mighty good company he was, too.

At 10.30 the following morning I left the Adelphi and started out for Derby House. Was I about to ask for the moon? The remarks of *Tyella*'s skipper unhappily came to mind: 'A swept mine can save a ship. Unfortunately, the brutal fact is your filming operations can't. Saving life must be more important than filming, however good yours turns out to be.' Once more I had to concur. All I could do was ask for help. If I didn't get it, there was nothing more to be done except face the fact that in carrying on under the existing conditions we'd be old age pensioners before we finished the film.

Two 'blue jackets' with green gaiters stood with their fixed bayonets outside their sandbagged sentry boxes either side of the steps leading up to Derby House. I wondered whether they'd say 'Halt. Who goes there?' and point a point at my belly or ask for a password. But no. My innocence proclaimed itself loud and clear.

They didn't even have the courtesy of altering their eye line as I walked between them and climbed the steps into Derby House. I entered and was immediately challenged. 'Your pass, Sir, please.'

'I'm sorry. I haven't a pass.'

'Nobody can enter without a pass, Sir.'

'As I said, I haven't a pass, but I have an appointment with the C. in C. at eleven hundred hours and I have no intention of being late for it.' I was given the once, if not the twice, over which, to say the least, I found unnecessary. 'Petty Officer, phone the Flag Lieutenant immediately, will you, and tell him that the director of the film *Western Approaches* is here. My appointment with the Admiral is in exactly six minutes.' Irritatingly unimpressed, he hailed a blue jacket, standing 'at ease' under one of the archways, north, south, east and west of the reception hall.

''ere, you, Thomson, come 'ere, and smart abaht it.' He was, and received his orders: 'Tell the young lady at reception to phone the Flag Lieutenant that there is a . . . gentleman to see him.' It was an oral triumph on his part for never have I heard that classification pronounced with such scathing emphasis. I reminded myself that he was only doing his duty, but with such relish in going far beyond its normal call. A moment later a cluster of knotted gold cord, dripping from a shoulder, caught my eye. It reminded me of the receptionist of the Palace cinema, Eltham, for its première opening with *The Mark of Zoro*. I was eight at the time and those golden bits of twisted sash cord must have affected me at that tender age. Here they were again, decorating a sprightly young officer with jet black hair and the brightest eyes, shining mischievously, as though the whole paraphernalia of war was nothing more than a delicious pantomime at the local Hippodrome. Under full sail and all penants flying, he bore down . . . 'Jackson?'

'Lupino?'

'Just in time.'

'A little local difficulty, took time to overcome.' He led me into a lift. Last time I went down into the depths. This time also, but not so far. A good deal of 'ram rodding' to attention along the corridors until, like Alice, we found ourselves outside 'The' door.

Lupino knocked, opened it and announced me: 'Mr Jackson, Sir'. And there stood the great man. He was looking down at the vast wall map of the Atlantic, at that battle: 'A grim battle, morning, noon and night ... It never ceases.' He turned and I shall never forget his gracious smile of welcome.

'Ah, Jackson ... How's it all going? Tell me all about it.' He indicated for us to be seated and then, to put me more at ease, said: 'I liked your story, by the way. And though we don't feature in it quite as much as Owen Rutter's original outline suggested, I well understand the reasons. You made me care about those men. It's a good yarn and very believable.'

'Thank you, Sir. Most encouraging.'

'Well now, I know that you haven't come all this way to hear that. You have problems, I understand. I have Commodore Mansfield's memo and Lupino told me that you urgently wanted to see me. Tell me all about it and take your time. We're not rushed.'

'Thank you, Sir. Briefly, we have had many technical problems to overcome. Never before has a Technicolor camera, which is very bulky and awkward to handle, been put in a lifeboat to shoot dialogue scenes. So we came ill-prepared: not through negligence but through lack of resources. We couldn't get hold of the Technicolor equipment earlier, because *Henry the Fifth* and *This Happy Breed* had first call on it. As soon as we could, down we came, and we met these many technical problems which should have been ironed out beforehand. So a combination of circumstances was against us. On top of this we discovered that the craft allocated to us was simply not up to the job. Only last Saturday, its poor skipper, trying to take advantage of the good weather, took us out in seas which normally it would have shied at, and in turning back almost capsized.'

'Dear me. How long has this been going on, Jackson?'

'The realisation that she wasn't up to it?'

'Precisely!'

'Since almost the first day, Sir.'

'Then why on earth didn't you let me know earlier?'

'I should have, Sir. Inexperience on my part is the reason. That, and having seen what mines can do—that's when I went up the east coast, and I'd rather understood that every available trawler was either sweeping or acting as a rescue ship, so it seemed only right and natural that we should put up with what we were given. Our filming couldn't save life; these ships could.'

'Yes, quite understandable . . . Go on.'

'Now, Sir, I realise that unless we are given a sea-worthy ship, we haven't a hope. Our lifeboat, with all the equipment aboard, will take anything; so will the cast and the technicians. But we're supposed to be in the middle of the Atlantic. At the moment we might as well be on the Serpentine or that studio tank, which, if you remember, is the one thing we didn't want, Sir.'

'I do, and you're quite right. So without a trawler you can't proceed?'

'No, Sir.'

'Well, clearly you must have one, and quickly.'

My heart missed a beat. He pressed a switch on his desk intercom. A voice answered: 'Yes, Sir?'

'Ask Commander Wynne to step in, please.' Whilst waiting, he kept the conversation flowing and courteously asked: 'How are these raw seamen doing as actors?'

'I think—I hope you're going to approve, Sir. Some are doing better than others. But if we've created the right situations for them, in the end, like the professionals, they'll be as good as their material, Sir.'

'Interesting observation . . . Drama well conceived and well written makes the going that much easier for the actor?'

'I think so, Sir.'

'Yes, never occurred to me, but of course you're right, but don't ask me to learn *Hamlet* . . . Ah Wynne, I'd like you to meet Jackson, here. He's making this film for us at Holyhead—or trying to. We've given him a duff craft. He needs a trawler.'

'Ah, yes, Sir?'

'Down at Gladstone dock, I saw half a dozen seemingly doing nothing but propping up the harbour wall. We can spare one, surely?'

'I . . . I have . . . That is, off hand . . . I am not . . .'

'Have one sent to Jackson's film unit at Holyhead with the utmost despatch. This film has to be made. Lupino, see that the orders are sent out from this office at once, and you, Wynne, see to it that it's made effective right away. Immediately.'

'Certainly, Sir.' He nodded to me and left.

'There you are Jackson.'

'Wonderful, Sir. I don't know how to thank you.'

'You don't have to. We've asked you to make this and we didn't give you the tools. Now we have, and good luck. If you have any further troubles, you are to get in touch with me at once.' He held out his hand. I took it and gave him a formal little bow, the only salute and sign of respect permitted me. I floated out of his office with elation. Now we had a chance. As we walked along to the lift, Lupino said: 'Utmost despatch and order made effective immediately sounds as though you'll get it tomorrow, but it'll take several days.'

'Oh, that long?'

'Yes, it's not quite like posting a letter. I expect it'll mean stripping some equipment, re-allocation of crew and revictualing—quite a rigmarole. Thought I'd warn you in case you thought we'd ratted. What are we today?'

'Twenty-sixth.'

'I wouldn't expect her before November the fifth.'

'Splendid . . . We'll have a bonfire and rockets all ready for her.'

'How about lunch?'

'Good of you, but I think I can catch the 12.45 to Holyhead.'

'Quite a glutton, aren't you?'

'I'm kicking myself that I didn't ask to see Sir Percy before . . . Could have saved so much time and frustration for everyone.'

'You mightn't have got it, then. What you said was right. They are like gold dust. The way you put it was bang on. So I wouldn't worry—water under the bridge: spilt milk and all that.'

'Yes, quite right.' He showed me to the door, and as we shook hands, he said: 'You've got my number, and if you think I can help in any way, just give me a buzz. So long, and good luck.'

'Thanks, and if you can get away, come and have a trip in our lifeboat . . . Shortest cut to being sea-sick there is.'

'Delightful . . . Can't wait.' I had time to send a telegram to the unit. 'HAVE GOT A TRAWLER. PAT'.

20

The *Temeraire* to the rescue

It was to be 9 November when our *Temeraire* steamed into Holyhead. I couldn't wait to get aboard and introduce myself to her Captain. He was a massive Yorkshire man and had been trawling out of Hull all his life, and his ship was called *Acrasia*. The unit had gathered round and were looking her over with delight. She was the realisation of all our hopes that the frustrations of the last weeks were now over. I asked the Captain to come down and meet the unit. This he most willingly did. And when it came to Phil Ross, her auburn hair down to her shoulders and her perky impish smile beaming up at him, he was struck with awe as he swallowed her hand in his massive fist. 'What's thy job, lass? Not putting paint ont' this mob, surely?'

'Not quite, Captain. I sort of keep the log, keep track of things, the day's events. Quite complicated, really. You'll see as the days go by.'

'But you don't get int' boat with all this lot, do you?'

'Certainly I do.'

'How many hours are you out there, lass?'

'Depends on the weather. On a good day, five or six.'

'I've never heard the like. How long you been doing this?'

'September 18th we started; about seven weeks I suppose.'

'My word, but I reckon you've earned the V.C. twice over.'

'And so say all of us, Captain', I added, and meant it.

'Now what's to be done today, like?'

'We have to get our equipment aboard, if that's all right with you.' And then we explained our bits and pieces of equipment and what each one did, how and why. We put him in the picture so far as it was possible, and from his occasional blank stare, he would have identified better with us if we had walked out of a circus tent in our various garbs: clown, juggler, trapeze, equestrian, but this lot? A bit rum, no question.

At the end of the day Charlie found himself and his sound camera somewhere down in one of the holds—none too salubrious—whilst Kay lorded it, perched imperiously astern, his recorder nestling in a cradle that Harry knocked up for him. He would be looking down loftily on us poor lifeboat people, bouncing about below some forty yards astern. But, for the first time, we were housed under one roof, that is the 'genny' and sound were together on the same ship. Our necklace days were over. The second lifeboat had been a martyr and nobly sacrificed her midriff to our cause.

That evening, we all had a pleasant get together at the hotel bar and were able to explain our problems more clearly to the trawler's Captain, and I was not slow in letting him know that he had been chosen as a result of my meeting with the C. in C. If we had not hooked him before, he was well and truly 'on' now.

A few days prior to our recent weekend break, we had got to know a very likeable Dutch minesweeper Captain, who was temporarily stationed at Holyhead. He wore a telling ginger Van Gogh beard and lived in the outskirts of the Hague. By a strange coincidence he knew friends of mine with whom I had stayed before the war. We had struck up quite a friendship and I saw him walking into the bar. He had presence, no question. He carried himself with an inner authority—quite impressive. I went over and offered him a drink and we started to chat. He spoke outstandingly good English and I complimented him as I said: 'I do envy you your English. If I could speak a second language half as well as you speak English, I'd be very pleased with myself.'

'If you were Dutch, you'd have to.' We laughed, even though it was the well worn cliché, but it prompted the next question: 'How's your German?'

'Ah, that really is my second language.'

'Better than your English?'

'Yes. I have been taken for a German, in Germany, many times.'

'Have you!!'

I told myself: 'he doesn't know the script, all he knows is that we're filming. Nobody can have told him that we need a German U-Boat Commander who must speak German.' I was not going to have phoney clipped foreign accent English. I had made this clear in my original treatment and shooting script. I asked him: 'How long are you going to be here?'

'Two days, probably. Why?'

'Because I need someone to play a German U-Boat Commander who speaks in German. I think you could play him very well.'

'But I have my ship.' And then it was an almost word-for-word repeat of what I had said to Chief Petty Officer Hills on H.M.S. *President*. I assured him that I could get him leave if he were right for the part. Would he, therefore, be prepared to do a test first thing in the morning? He agreed immediately and seemed delighted at the prospect. We went into a neutral corner and went over the scenes in which he would be involved. He chose the scene on which to be tested and it wasn't a silly choice. It is when he realises that the S.O.S., just received by his radio operator, came from the lifeboat he had just spotted through his periscope and decides to use it as a decoy. It is the most important scene in the film: the fulcrum on which suspense slowly develops and builds into the inevitable climax. I asked Phil to get the scene typed so that he would be able to mull over it. I then gave him the usual message that I didn't want him to be word perfect, only clear about the content and what he had to say to convey it in his own words. We left it at that, and he too, as soon as Phil returned with a copy of the scene.

I told Jack of the plan and we decided to do it in our hut so that we would be free of weather hazard, and then explained our plan to Harry Tupper, who saw at once what was required. 'That's all right, Pat . . . I'll drop a swivelled broom handle from the roof, for his periscope, with an eight by two for his handles. How'll that do?'

'Harry, it's a poem.' He smiled; his smiles were long maturing but long held.

The following morning our broomhandled periscope was in

place and our hut became our test studio for the Dutch lieutenant. He did splendidly and I knew that I had found our U-Boat Commander. It had been a rigorous test and at no time had he appeared ill at ease. It was out of the camera and canned up ready to be despatched to London on the 11.45 to Euston. Another important role had been filled. We were all elated at our morning's discovery and, with new fields to conquer, happily sardined into our lifeboat. At 1.30 we moved from the quay, fending off round the bluff of the jetty as *Acrasia* carefully took up the slack and then two members of her crew paid out the full length of our tow. From that moment the production moved into a different gear and was in overdrive.

Our old landmark, the lighthouse, was soon forgotten as she drifted astern: our old shooting grounds only a painful memory, for we were on the ocean wave—and no mistake. We were beyond the shelter of the Skerries to the north-east and we were getting into the real thing. This was no cheat. We began to feel the full force of the wind and the waves were beginning to look quite convincing. Yes, this was something like it. It was magnificent. Over the gunwale to port, walls of water as though to engulf us reared up and magically passed from view as they slipped beneath and, with subtle variations, to be endlessly repeated. It is one thing to see waves of this height from a channel steamer, rather different from a lifeboat whose free-board seemed almost non-existent. But, once assured and amazed by the buoyancy of the boat, the exhilaration was unforgettable. Now we could justify our painful christening and put visuals on the screen with a compelling realism never before seen.

But, before long, it seemed that a scythe was working through the boat. A moment before, all eager and upright; now, a dozen or more bent double over the gunwale to port and starboard. These seas were higher than anything previously experienced and it wasn't only members of the unit who were suffering, but the seamen, also. Many who had spent their working lives at sea and who had never suffered before were suffering now. They were used to a 'long sea' with a great distance between the waves, as though moving to an adagio. This was vivace and staccato . . . Uncomfortable. Our tow rope would slacken as we dipped over a crest and then not only tighten but pull us up and over the next oncoming wave. Our progress was anything but smooth: a series of jerks, in fact, rather, I imagine, like being a dog on a lead and being pulled past every likely looking lamp post. It was hardly surprising that this was proving too much for too many.

We had set up on our way out, on a two-shot of the Master, his Chief Engineer seated beside him. He is confiding his worries about making a landfall on the west coast of Ireland: 'A treacherous coast, rocks all along it, and if there's a high sea running, and at this time of year there usually is, well, Chief, it'll be just too bad'. The Chief tries to reassure him that they'll be picked up long before that situation arises. With this wonderful sea background it would look quite something, and it was a tight little scene. I waited for poor Jack not only to recover from, in these conditions, an inevitable spasm, poor chap, but to give me the signal when he was happy with his light and exposure. He checked it and nodded. I was about to say 'turn over' to Eric, but he succumbed and chose the port side. Light was right: sun free for another minute or two, but you can't shoot without someone looking through the view-finder. He was as quick as he could be and there's no trade union agreement on how long such an ordeal can or may take. Nothing to do but wait. But not everything is prepared to: the sun, for example. However, it looked as though it would cooperate for several minutes.

Eric gallantly returned to his focus and Jack to his finder and both gave me the thumbs up. 'Roll 'em, Kay', I shouted, loud enough, because Roland Stafford was only a few feet away with the mike, just below Captain Pycraft and Mr Russell, playing the Chief.

'Speed', shouted Eric. I pushed the clapper board in front of the camera: '126, take 1'. Bang. 'When you like, Captain.' And the gallant Captain started out in most convincing fashion. I was hooked, anyway, and then like a Jack in the Box, up popped Roland.

'So sorry, Pat.' He just made it to the gunwale.

'Cut', I shouted, and Kay, in the trawler, hearing all our groans and grunts through his ear phones, switched off.

Hm . . . It was not going to be plain sailing, even now. And here was the irony. At last, we had been given the means of doing justice to the subject and this unforeseen problem presented itself. The question still remained unanswered: could we do justice to this subject? Nobody can legislate for the behaviour of people's stomachs: yet, clearly, they were going to be a controlling factor in our rate of progress.

In the good old days of sail, sailors with delicate stomachs suffered misery for the first week or so and by sheer brutal conditioning got over it. But my poor sufferers were in the same category as those unhappy at the prospect of a Channel crossing. There can be scarcely one of us whose memory is not seared by that one ghastly crossing between Folkestone and Boulogne. 'I thought I was going to die, indeed I hoped I would', is a comment that I have heard many times. This unhappy prospect now had to be faced by many of the unit, every day, until we finished the lifeboat scenes, which accounted for nearly half the picture. Not a pleasant prospect and not a happy blend to combine with an already highly complex creative process. The question of whether we should have been doing it was not our problem: ours was to get on with it. But, within the first hour of being at sea with my longed-for trawler, it was going to be a mixed blessing for some.

Roland recovered and was now back in position, on the deck, and holding the mike just below the Captain and the Chief. The sun was still obliging. I looked round at the camera crew: they were hanging on, just. I chalked up 'take 2' and asked Kay to roll. We got the shot. It was superb. The sea, piling up behind, looked threatening and wonderful, as we see-sawed with the horizon. We went for another set-up, mid-ships, and having adjusted our rail sections, moved the camera forward and got another good take in the can of Bob Banner, sitting by the mast and ad-libbing as he chatted up the journalist, Tosti Russell. We were looking forrard, with the red sail bottom foreground and the spray breaking over the bow. We were sailing almost under our own power, with the *Acrasia* way off to starboard. Captain Pycraft held us off on this course just long enough for us to get the scene, and then the pressure of the towing cables, power, camera, mike and rope pulled us hard to starboard. But by then we had the scene in the 'can', and splendid it was. If we could carry on like this we would justify those awful early fumbling weeks.

We went for another shot which meant moving all the equipment on the floor boards so that we had room to move the camera and arc lights. Dan picked up one of the batteries, but slipped as a large wave hit us. He dropped the battery on his foot. He was obviously in great pain: a camera battery is no featherweight. I took the mike and told Kay to ask our Skipper to make for port, and explained the reason. We took Dan Gaffney to hospital and, happily, there were no bones broken.

That night, Jack, Penny and I held a cabinet meeting. I started the ball rolling by saying: 'What do you think, Jack? Things are going to get tougher the further we go into winter, and we're hardly a third through these lifeboat scenes. The arrangement was that "as and when" Penny would take over and you must let me know when you've had enough.'

'We're in an odd situation.' This spontaneous, simple understatement gave us a laugh and Penny said: 'Let's face it. Nothing has gone according to plan. I was supposed to be taught the system by Jack, sure, but I've been more useful chasing up the "genny", and now, nursing it, and if that goes we all go because I've no idea where we'll ever find another.'

'How do you feel about it, Jack?'

'We've no other solution but go on as we are. Don't worry about me. I'll manage.' As there was no alternative, that's what had to be done. The siege continued, admittedly with new weaponry.

On our third day with the trawler, Phil notes that we got five shots in 12-foot seas. 'Soon after we had started back the tow rope broke as it was too short (owing to our short electric cables) and had been subjected to extreme pressure and tugs in the heavy seas.' It certainly had, being pulled past those likely lamp posts that I mentioned. Our only hope of getting back, unless we resorted to our own sailing ability, was to hope our power cable from the 'genny' held. It did.

This was a hop-scotch sort of production. No sooner was one problem solved than another promptly popped up. Many a fretful night resulted, and how to get one particular shot was the cause of many. It had been niggling me, like persistent toothache, since day one. It was the shot of the periscope appearing for a second or two which Alf Rawson sees, after bouts of delirium. He awakes: his head clears and he looks over the gunwale, spots the periscope and shouts 'Periscope to starboard'. All aboard look but, of course, it is no longer there. Alf is raving again. No one believes him except the Captain. It is the start of potential mutiny.

The periscope pops for a second or two and submerges.

So easy to write, but script writers are not faced with the problem of bringing to the screen what they have written. I, on the other hand, was now hoisted on my own pen. I had not fully appreciated that a periscope popping up and down needs a submarine under it with a crew of a hundred or so, their commander to raise and lower it at the exact spot and all for six feet of film; two seconds. Yet those six feet were a tiny cog in a complex piece of machinery, and without them it would not come to life. How to get a submarine? I tossed and turned and then wondered how we would ever stage the battle between the merchant ship and the U-boat. Heavens above, the simple scenes in the lifeboat were trouble enough. Oh well, sufficient unto the day were the problems thereof.

Miracle of miracles, of its own accord, drifting in on the tide, it seemed, appeared a submarine rounding Holyhead lighthouse. Down tools, phone the Port Commander. 'Come and see me.' He introduced me to the U.48's captain, a Lieutenant R.N. in his twenties. Yes, of course he'd help. Only too pleased. He boarded the lifeboat, peered through Jack's viewfinder, with Alf Rawson leaning over the gunwale in the foreground.

'Yes, I see exactly what you want. I'll get as near as I can and keep circling round you. We're bound to get into the right position once or twice and I'll keep shoving the thing up and down. We'll do it tomorrow before I go on patrol at 10.30. O.K?'

'You bet, and I couldn't be more grateful.'

'Not a bit; pleasure. Any snags, light a red flare and I'll surface to check.' Off he went, leaving me purring. A nightmare less.

Phil Ross's log tells me that, sure enough, we were on station at 10.30 with U.48's supply ship *Lord Middleton* in attendance. U.48 submerged and 30 or so pairs of well-focused eyes searched the nearby ocean on the starboard side. Any moment now . . . must be . . . Where is the thing? Are we blind? Not a thing. 'There it is', a seaman shouted. Without binoculars he had wonderful eyesight. I couldn't see it. Minutes went by. We'd have settled for a walking stick. But delirious or not, there was nothing for poor Alf Rawson to spot. Something was wrong. We lit a red flare. Up he came. This part of the plan was working perfectly. Through his supply ship we signalled 'nearer, much nearer, please'. Down he went and that was the last we saw, of anything. Over the water came the supply ship's loud hailer message. 'Sorry, time's up. Better luck next time.'

To this day I wonder what went wrong. Perhaps a tide race below stairs set against him or other circumstances too complex to explain.

We returned to base and I was resigned to that persistent toothache. And there, on the jetty, was dear old Harry Tupper, the one and only 'stand-by Chippie', always keen to know how we'd got on. He knew how important this shot was. He could see immediately that we hadn't got it.

'No luck then . . . Pat?'

'No, Harry. I don't know what went wrong. It all seemed so simple. We saw the perishing thing once . . . it was miles away.'

'Never mind . . . Pat . . . We'll get it somehow.'

'Rustling up a submarine, Harry . . . Not like hailing a taxi.'

'Not easy either . . . Pat. Not in London. Not nowadays.'

'Can't think what went wrong. It all looked so easy. No problem, he said. Had it all worked out on paper.'

'Things look easy on paper, Haig must have thought, planning his battle of the Somme. If he'd been with us, he might have thought different.'

That brought me back to relative values with a bump.

'Miracle any of you survived that day, Harry.'

'Lucky to be here, I know that . . . Still, that won't get us this perishing periscope, will it? Don't you worry, Pat . . . we'll get it . . . somehow.'

What a wonderful man. So were they all, the way they rallied round, shared the problems, giving me such support. I am permanently in their debt.

A few days later, after another none-too-successful day, I climbed up the slimy steps to the quay and there was Harry, as usual, with his quiet, confident smile. 'Got a minute, Pat? . . . Got something to show you.' As though presenting me with a baby for christening—not far wrong—he offered me a strange-looking wooden device. It was a periscope. His periscope. A beautifully painted wooden pole, shaped at the top with a recess, grey, to represent the lens. It was mounted on a miniature surf board, angled forrard at about 30° downwards with a projecting proboscis. Aft was a similar-shaped tail-piece angled slightly more acutely. Both could be adjusted with wing nuts.

'What I hope'll happen . . . Pat . . . when we pull it along, this one, in front 'ere, will take her down and when we pull 'er a bit 'arder the back fin'll pull her up. Question of getting the angles of fins right and the speed, to sink 'er and pull 'er up . . . Pat. If it works, nappoo to the sub.'

'If it works, Harry, I'll have you canonised.'

Immediately, we put her through rigorous trials. The Harbour Master kindly lent us his launch. Harry, as though at the Round Pond, floated his craft and attached a long length of insulated light cable to it which he paid out as we slowly proceeded across the inner harbour. Harry indicated a slight increase in speed. Rev by rev it increased. We focused, hypnotised, on Harry's craft. As though conducting the London Philharmonic, Harry again indicated a slight increase in speed. Wonder of wonders, his craft started to submerge. It submerged upright. As the speed increased it surfaced, upright. Oh, Harry Tupper. What a man. Now we could complete the mutiny sequence. Once more, Harry had come to my rescue, just as the trawler had. But the trawler had a virus.

'The following morning, we were ready to leave the quay, all assembled in the lifeboat, when the Skipper called out from the trawler that he was on his bottom and couldn't get off it for half an hour as he had a 12-foot draft.' 'At 12 o'clock he was ready to go to sea but his engineer had had an accident. Some part of the engine blew off when someone sat on the safety valve.' These incidents and the hold-ups that they caused were a test of everyone's already sorely tried patience. But a quite unexpected problem was waiting round the corner for us. It occurred in a manner that nobody could possibly have foreseen. Our original camera had been recalled by Technicolor for routine servicing and been replaced by one which in comparison was as noisy as a sewing machine. Had the weather that we experienced continued, we would probably have been able to continue working. But it didn't. Abnormal times hit us. A calm, a breathless calm descended: not a whisper of wind, not a breath to blow away the noise of this new camera or the 'genny'. We went dutifully to sea. Day after day we pointed up and we pointed down. No matter which way we headed, still this deadly hush and calm. Five miles out and the noises of the town carried across the water, a most efficient sound board for the trains shunting, the clock tower and the hoots and toots of cars and the sewing machine of a camera, and finally, the 'genny'.

The enforced idleness of those days when everything else was so perfect was indescribably painful. Mounting frustration and fury made me feel like an over-pressurised boiler about to burst. But, just as all good things come to an end, so, mercifully, do the bad. Light winds returned to take us out of our doldrums, and with *Acrasia* we went ahead at twice the speed.

Diesel fumes had been the cause of much of the seasickness. We noticed that ribbons of oil slicks had been floating past us. *Acrasia* had been pumping out her bilges for a good part of each day. When I explained to her skipper that we were the recipients of a nauseating stink which was causing havoc amongst cast and crew, he stopped at once. Gradually our worst sufferers became hardened and had hopes that their worst days were behind them. The cast, too, became more and more liberated with this new-found freedom of horizon and honest seas. I tried to take full advantage of it by more and more improvisation. It was thrilling to see these men becoming more and more relaxed in front of the camera, arguing about this and that, revealing more and more of their true personalities and characteristics. I probed deeper and deeper. Too much, in fact, and Dal had to pull me up, very sharply: 'Hi. Hi. All very well, all this ad-lib stuff, but get on with your story. Get back to it.' He was quite right to crack the whip and bring me back on course.

Happily, Jack and Eric were beginning to suffer less, and two or three days were now going past without so much as a tremor or change of colour. Marvellous. But, sooner or later, that opening sequence had to be faced: that purple patch of prose, as Maugham would have described it, still had to be filmed. In my original story outline, knowing that eventually I would have to shoot it, I had been indulgent enough to write: 'As far as the eye can see there is an angry expanse of ocean. Great rollers sweep past. They are overwhelming and ominous, not because they are Atlantic rollers, but because they are not seen from the reassuring height of a ship's decks, but from an open boat amongst dim forms of drenched men.' Yes, sounds all right. Now go and shoot it. I had been wondering how, ever since we got here. I knew that we would have to include the gunwale of our lifeboat in our set-up as proof that there was no cheating; that we were actually in the boat. The camera would be about midships and with a wide-angled lens we would clip the gunwale, leaving the rest of the screen clear for my 'purple patch' of great rollers sweeping past. As and when!!

On 5 December, as soon as I woke up, I could hear that the time had come for us to tackle it. The wind was howling as it had never before. A gale was in full force. After breakfast—rather light for me because I wondered whether my hitherto impregnable defences might crumble—I met Jack on the jetty and he readily agreed that the day had arrived. He said that he would get set up with an unblimped but heavily mackintoshed camera whilst I went to see the Skipper. We were on Sam and Pat terms by now, and the crew, having been given stills of themselves and their ship, were on our side.

Sam saw me coming aboard and was there to greet me. 'Shan't do nowt today, Pat.'

'Sam, that's what I want to talk to you about.'

'You're not thinking of going out in that, are you?'

'Yes.'

'You're daft.'

'No.' We were shouting against the wind even in the lee of the jetty wall. 'Got to have a chat, Sam.'

'Come inside, lad.' He took me into his cabin. I said: 'Sam, I only want to go out for a minute or two. Let me explain. This film we're trying to make is at the request of the C. in C., that's why he has sent you and your ship to help us. I told him the ship we had before was useless because it couldn't take us out in anything like a sea.'

'That isn'a sea, out there, it's a bloody cauldron.'

'It's certainly rough. Now he's given us the facilities and it's up to us to get the film, and the only tough part so far as you and me are concerned is today's work. It's the opening of the film, you see, Sam, and we've got to hit 'em in the eye, straight away. I'll read it you, so's you know what I'm talking about.' I read it to him and I could see that the visual he had conjured up for himself had also hooked him.

'If we can get it, Sam, it'll be magnificent.'

'Aye . . .' He stroked his chin. 'Aye, would at that.'

'All I want is to be among those waves for five minutes, no more, and we'll have our opening.'

'It's a big sea out there . . . Don't reckon you know how big.'

'Only for a minute, just to show the audience that we are in that boat in those seas. If we can prove that to them we've won 'em. We're half way there.'

'I'm not disagreeing with you on that score . . . It's risky, and I'm responsible for you.'

'But Sam, these lifeboats can take anything.'

'Don't be daft, lad. You'll take 'em head on. I'm not worried about that. But sooner or later, I've got to bring you back, and unless I can turn you in the trough, you'll take it broadside and you know what that could mean.'

'We've got to take that chance, Sam; there's no other way.'

'You don't know what you're saying.'

'Sam, if you won't do it for me and you want an order from the C. in C., by God I'll get it, and I can, don't doubt it.'

'No doubt you can, but you won't have to . . . But I won't have that lass in t'boat. That I won't have.'

'I shall ask her not to come, but she won't listen, I can tell you that right now.'

'Why not? You're t'boss, aren't you?'

'No Sam, not as you are because of your stripes. We're not under any service code of discipline. She'll do what she thinks her job demands of her. Her pride. I can't take that from her however much I want to. I can't order her not to do what she thinks, in this instance, is her duty, and neither can you.'

'You're a rum lot and no mistake . . . Never known the like.'

'Thanks Sam.'

'Let me know when you're ready. I'll double the length of tow, erst I'll pull you straight through that lot.' He nodded towards the ocean.

I went back to the hotel and saw Captain Pycraft, who was just finishing his breakfast. I told him of my plan and that if he were agreeable I would like to get some shots of him at the tiller for the opening sequence of the film. Without a moment's hesitation he said: 'Of course. When do you want to leave?'

'Half an hour suit you?'

'Perfectly.'

'O.K., Captain. Fine. See you down there.' I saw Phil getting her things together into her voluminous shoulder bag. I said: 'Phil, we're only going out for a few rough sea shots: be about ten minutes, no more. No point in your coming. Catch up on your notes.'

'I have already, my sweet. Thank you. Where the camera goes, I go; that's my job.'

'Maybe, but I am telling you that the camera can very well do without you, this morning.'

'My sweet, don't be stupid. I'm coming and that's that.' She slung her bag over her shoulder and was off for the quay. 'You're t'boss aren't you?' Like hell, with that indomitable woman, God bless her. No point in making a great song and dance. More pressing issues to worry about and I did a Pontius Pilate on that one and went down and into the seamen's hut. Several were there. Alec the ginger haired, always steady and reliable amongst them. I said: 'We're just going out for those rough sea shots that we need for the opening of the film. I'd appreciate three or four of you, but this could be considered bordering on an unreasonable call, so, fellows, I'll leave the decision with you.'

I went out on to the quay and followed Captain Pycraft down those slippery steps. The tide would be out. Phil was already in the boat, as were Jack and Eric, who also had insisted on coming, even though Jack was going to do the operating, ready to snatch at a likely visual. I stepped into the boat, looked up and those four or five seamen, as though it were a normal day, climbed into the boat. Our central 'set-up' enabled us to cover the Captain, and allow enough foreground to have a figure falling across foreground and the gunwale. This could be a moment of great dramatic emphasis, if we could get it. The camera was bolted down as never before because we were in new territory and there was no time to go to night school to work out calculus and the forces that might be thrown on the bolts of that top hat, our giant golf tee.

Sam was on the move and nosing his way out of the inner basin. We fingered our way round the bluff until we were in the Scapa Flow of our inner harbour, a mile or so away from the lighthouse. *Acrasia* took up our slack and, once in contact, slowly paid us out, letting us drop astern some 50 or 60 yards. I looked at Captain Pycraft. The tiller was firmly under his arm. He stared ahead at walls of water rolling into the inner harbour. Sam was steering a course which would take us out of the shelter of the outer wall so that we would make our approach to take the full force of wind and waves directly on the bow. The lighthouse, that old, familiar landmark, appeared and disappeared again as clouds of spray enveloped it. If we could convey the savagery of this scene it would be sensational. We crouched by the camera, amazed by the beauty of it.

As we drew towards the open water, the height of the waves increased: they were now getting so high that when their crests swept past, they hid the land from us. Jack had noticed this, too, and had already turned on those foaming wave tops breaking past us. I looked towards the *Acrasia*. Only her masthead was visible, and then up she popped like the giant racer of the 1924 Empire Wembley Exhibition, a visual that as an eight-year-old I had never forgotten. She was up and over and gone again. We slid down into the trough. Our tow rope slackened for a moment, lifted from the water and tightened like a rod of steel. We were catapulted forward towards a mountain of water rearing above us. Up we went. I caught a glimpse of the lighthouse and realised that we were looking down on the main jetty. It quickly disappeared as we ploughed down into the trough. I'd wanted rough seas. Here they were. Enough to last me for some time to come. Jack was shooting away, spraying the camera around, as though it were a machine gun. I saw Sam on the starboard wing of his bridge, looking back at us. He turned and looked ahead. I looked at Pycraft. He held that tiller as though in a vice. He, too, was looking dead ahead. *Acrasia* appeared again, and as she started to climb, Sam turned hard a-starboard, hoping that he, not us, would take the wave broadside. She was executing a climbing turn, like a Christiania, only uphill. I thought of poor old *Tyella* almost capsizing in a five-foot wave. What of *Acrasia*? She was half way up, and still turning as she climbed that wall of water. Before the crest broke she was able to present her port quarter and the full force was dispersed along an angled flank. Down she plunged and buried herself in spray. She was not a trawler for nothing and soon popped up, right as rain. She was heading back as we were still heading out. We passed each other on the top of the next wave. Pycraft had not altered course. He held the tiller dead ahead. Our tow rope was now looping across and through the water, his eyes darting from it to the on-coming wave and back again. The factor to be reckoned with was not the wave, ominous though it was, but the tow. He must be in line with it before the slack was taken up. Then it would become like a rod and jerk us round with untold power, and if that happened when we took the wave broadside . . . it was a combination best avoided. Our timing for our turn depended on the behaviour of the tow. The oncoming wave must look after itself and, hopefully, us as well. We started our slide to the valley and Pycraft rammed the tiller hard over. We were turning hard a-starboard as we started our climb. I was on the weather side, watching Jack as he peered through the view finder. I looked, hypnotised, at the wall of water breaking down on us. The next thing I knew was that I was leaning over the lee gunwale, as though about to offer up. I had felt nothing. The kapok padded lifejacket had absorbed the shock of my having been catapulted from one side of the boat to the other. The seamen were picking themselves off the deck. Jack was still turning and Eric was protecting the camera with a tarpaulin. We were in line for home and Pycraft was now set against those mighty rollers, astern.

Twenty minutes later we were home and dry. Waiting for us was an unexpected telegram from Technicolor to remind us that their camera was not insured beyond a three-mile limit. The end of the telegram said that 'the last remaining three-strip colour film in the country is already in your possession'. That left us with reserves of about 2,000 feet, enough for two or three days.

However, we were not going to let that depress us. More would be shipped in from the U.S.A., we felt sure, in time for our needs. Nothing was going to depress us after our morning's excursion, knowing that we had seen and, what's more, filmed visuals that were magnificent. We were chuckling with delight and the joyous expectation of seeing those rushes that we felt sure would knock us for six.

Four days later we saw them, and we were bitterly disappointed. Converting a three-dimensional image into a down-graded two-dimensional was a truncating and miserable process, diminishing the impact of what we had seen into insignificance on the screen, or so it seemed with the memory of the real thing still fresh in our minds. We could do no more and would have to make do with what we had for the opening sequence of the film. Our trawler had made it possible and she had behaved superbly in getting us those shots, and though she was our saviour, she suddenly became a threat, and a very dangerous one. In her innocence she carried aboard a virus which was slowly infecting my lifeboat survivors, my cast and particularly my 'star', Bob Banner. Aboard *Acrasia* was a crew of 15, each entitled to a daily ration of rum. A tot of navy rum is about equivalent to two doubles, and quite a depth charge. These tots, daily totted up into a bottle, became a most viable commodity, and there would be 15 of them. A ready market was soon found for them.

I had been noticing, I thought, an increasing smell of rum in the lifeboat recently, and my tiny mind had not imagined the cause to be so near at hand—the other end of our tow rope. Innocently, I imagined that they had had a well deserved snort in the pub during the lunch break, but as most of our lunches were spam sandwiches at sea, how naive could I have been! I was now no longer sitting on a thwart in the lifeboat but a powder keg, and the fuse had already been lit.

Ashore a few days later, during the lunch break, Donald Alexander, a tall, fine looking Kiwi, the first man I found in Liverpool, came into our hut and said that he had been elected as spokesman. The men had decided that they wanted overtime. Last night they had worked until 6.30. Don was a likeable chap, a bit of a sea lawyer, but one couldn't blame him for that. I remember his saying to me once, as we were being towed back into harbour and discussing the day's work and the film in general: 'Of course, most of the time for us, it's a balls aching business. All this hanging about . . . bouncing about . . . might be in a shot, once in a while. Hell, none of us want to become film stars. Whereas for you, well it's your life . . . all this mucking about is a means to an end. If you pull it off and the film's any good, could mean a lot to you. Whereas for us, we might see ourselves on the screen for a couple of seconds: so what?'

He had a point. I hadn't read it in exactly those terms, having been too preoccupied with the challenge to consider the fruits thereof. I thought for a moment before answering: 'Yes, Don. I hadn't thought of it like that, but, yes, you're right. But, mind you, it cuts both ways. If it's a flop it's "good night nurse".'

'Yes, but that's in everything.'

'Not at all . . . plenty of safe careers around where, if you keep your nose clean and don't say "boo" to a goose, you'll end up with a knighthood and a fat pension.' He laughed and agreed. Nevertheless, he had made a valid point. I liked him, and we had mutual respect.

I have Phil's progress report on the episode. It reads as follows: 'P.J. said he could not settle this until he had re-read the agreement. Then Bob Banner returned from the town roaring drunk, and staggered about the quay arousing the other men into a state of mutiny. P.J. went into the hut and ordered them to board the lifeboat. He pushed two of them out of the hut and a free fight was about to start.'

I remember entering their hut. Yo-ho-ho, 15 men's tots. Bob Banner was laughing, rocking backwards and forwards, his beady 'bull's eyes' gleaming with malicious joy . . . If we could only have switched productions to *Treasure Island*, here was the personified evil of Long John Silver, and not in the shape of Robert Newton. Bob, who had contributed so much, had given such a fine performance and been the mainstay of credibility in the lifeboat, was now a laughing, drunken, maniac. 'I knew we'd break you in the end', he sneered, laughingly.

I remember pulling him out of the hut on to the quay. I don't remember going in for another. Bob had made no attempt to hit me—he was probably too drunk. I saw Pat O'Malley coming up and standing at the ready beside Bob and Tony Evans. I saw our head sparks, Frank Brice and Harry Tupper, and other members of the unit hurrying to join me. One punch thrown and we would have been at each other cat and dog, only worse. I was full of rage and disgust that an intelligence such as Bob's could so easily be reduced to this. But I was not so blind with rage not to realise that if I started, all our collective efforts, theirs and ours, would be gone. We would never be able to work again. If one of them threw a punch, well . . . then we were in it. But they did not; they were waiting for me to start, and that I was not going to do. But an example had to be made and authority established. Like committing Hara Kiri, I sacked Bob Banner on the spot, and Pat O'Malley for being drunk. I told the others that if there were any further trouble, they would be sacked and that I'd make sure that they returned to the Shipping Federation with a record that would haunt them for the rest of their lives. I had to give them some sort of shock and the realisation that I had the power to do that and that they were putting themselves in a situation tantamount to dereliction of duty.

The psychological reasons that had brought about this situation were obvious and very understandable. Boredom, in the end, is everybody's killer and they had had plenty of it. Don Alexander's words were ringing very true.

I was now in the absurd situation of having had to sack my star, knowing that I could not complete the film without him. My old friend Mr Hobbes at the Liverpool Shipping Federation might be able to help, and how well he had foreseen these troubles: 'It's a question of making them realise that while they're on this jaunt they'll be as much on duty as aboard ship', and his other comment about conditioning: 'When they're aboard, it's discipline. Ashore is leave and leave is the pub. Reflex action, almost.' I phoned him as soon as I could and explained my problem about sacking my leading man and still needing him.

'Oh dear. Awkward.'

'Very.'

'When's he leaving?'

'When he's sober enough to collect his cards; later today, I imagine. Any ideas, Mr Hobbes?'

'He'll have to come here to sign on. He's registered here, you see. He may go to ground for a few days, hibernate with an almighty blow-out until his money runs out. Can you manage without him for a few days?'

'I'll have to. Trouble is, he's rather a key person.'

'Let's hope he surfaces soon and comes to register for another job.'

'Then what?'

'I'll just say he's already registered with you and until a

satisfactory release form and his discharge papers, he will be unemployable and classified as a deserter. He'll sober up quick enough then. Come to his senses and realise that he'll have to go back and finish his duty with you people. Awful waste of time for you.'

'We've had to harden ourselves to that, I'm afraid.'

'How's it going, apart from this little blow up?'

'Mr Hobbes, if I tried to answer that, it'd take time. We'll get there . . . under "jury rig".'

'I'm sure you will . . . Good luck. Leave this with me, we'll work it out.'

'Thanks, Mr Hobbes, most grateful.' I hung up. If making films involved all this, there must be easier ways of making a living. A dentist, perhaps? That takes brains, of course.

It was to be a week, thanks to Mr Hobbes, before Bob Banner returned to the fold. He came sauntering down the quay, his usual, debonair self. He was still cock of the walk and we met like old friends, as though nothing had happened. The old twinkling smile was back. The evil had gone out of him. He was back to normal. His spat was over until the next time and, with a little bit of luck, we would be finished with this location before that happened. And so it was. Two or three weeks later, having filmed 393 shots, we left for Pinewood. It was 12 March. We had been nearly six months bouncing about in Alfred Holt's lifeboat and only a third of the film was in the can.

The convoy sequences and the climax, the duel with the U-Boat, were formidable obstacles to be cleared before the winning post was in sight. Two important hunks of the film still out there waiting for us. Surely they couldn't be as bad as the lifeboat? Could they?

I could not leave Holyhead without expressing my gratitude for one miracle which happened just when needed it. I owed it to Nora Lee. She had trained at R.A.D.A. and, though she did not go on the stage, she recognised charisma and talent a mile away. What would Humphrey Jennings have done without her? She discovered his entire cast for *Fires Were Started*. What would I have done? She discovered two stars for me. The Master of the rescue ship *Leander*, Captain Kerr, and his Chief Officer.

I had come to the final shot of my lifeboat survivors being picked up by the *Leander* and now had to shoot the final scene when the two captains meet. But I had no Captain to play the Master of the *Leander*. An aldiss flashed from the harbour. A Captain Kerr would like to board *Leander*. I had never met him but Nora had and tested him. She had found a star and after 55 years I humbly salute her for her invaluable contribution, She was talented and fun and always will be.

2 1

The White Swan from Norway

The studio scenes were a doddle. Three to four minutes a day of screen time in Teddy Carrick's wonderful sets saw the interior scenes safely in the can and then, true to form, an unexpected problem appeared on the horizon. No British shipping line would take us on the round trip to New York. The excuse was that there was insufficient accommodation. When we assured them that hard lying meant nothing to us, hammocks anywhere would do very well, this failed to lower any gang plank. For several days we were at sixes and sevens. Once again it was our Flag Lieutenant Peter Lupino to the rescue. Having kept his ear and nose to the ground, he had picked up the whiff of something: a scent, he assured me, that would be worth following. It led me to a Norwegian ship, the *Samuel Bakke*, berthed in the Manchester Ship Canal. Her Master was Captain Olsen. His ship also carried some passengers in peacetime. Peter had already sent him a signal that the C. in C. would consider it a great favour if he could give any help to the Crown Film Unit in the making of their official film on the Battle of the Atlantic. Would it be convenient if the director came and discussed the matter? Captain Olsen replied in the affirmative, and after a call from Peter, I left for Manchester.

The following morning a taxi deposited me alongside the *Samuel Bakke*. She was a magnificent white ship. An ideal heroine; the swan of the Atlantic, risking her life as she sails to rescue the men in the lifeboat. What could be better? Perfect casting and her white hull, what an advantage when seen through the periscope of the threatening U-Boat. What a find. Would she let us aboard?'

I climbed the gangplank. The last one was up to the *President* where I'd found Griff, and what a find he was. Now, would history repeat itself? At the top I was greeted by the Chief Officer. Six feet four, must be, and a mouthful of gold teeth. He spoke not a word of English but he knew the sound of his Captain's name in any language. He showed me into a most handsome saloon, lavishly panelled.

I thought: 'we could do a lot worse. This is de luxe.' Captain Olsen soon appeared, a Humpty Dumpty of a man with a warm welcoming smile and only one gold tooth, double chins, a decided paunch and all adding up to a most genial Norwegian version of Mr Pickwick, and he spoke very good English—an added bonus. When he had made me feel at home, he opened the proceedings by saying: 'I am asked to see you by the C. in C., who tells me that I may be able to help you and that he would be grateful if I could. How can this be?'

I explained as briefly as possible. He listened, his face a mask. I was not gaining in confidence that I was serving my cause well. I concluded by saying: 'Your ship will, of course, feature very strongly.' He picked me up, immediately.

'How?' He had shown me his Achilles.

'She is the ship that saves the men in the lifeboat and she sinks the U-Boat. But before that, the U-Boat circles her many times, trying to determine whether she is really abandoned, so we shall see her as though through the periscope. She should look lovely, sitting there like a swan. We're making the film in colour, you see, Captain.'

'How many of you want to come?'

'Ten, Captain Olsen. I do hope that that's not too many.'

'No, we could take more if required. But if you want to come on this voyage you will have to hurry. We leave in four days.'

'You will take us?'

'If you can be ready in time, yes. I am sure we shall get on fine.'

'Captain Olsen. My God. I don't know how to thank you. I am most grateful. We all are.'

It was a scramble, but on 24 July all ten of us and the equipment were safely aboard. We were without the three-strip camera. Technicolor couldn't risk the loss and we were going well beyond their three-mile limit. We had a single-strip Vinten and were forced to use this new untried Monopak film stock. Good or bad, there was no other. Nothing to be done, therefore, except hope that the results would be usable. The more serious drawback, however, was that all our exposed film had to be processed in Hollywood and then sent back by air. How long it took to get back to us didn't matter so much, but how long it took to get to the labs in Hollywood mattered a great deal. The exposed film was very sensitive to temperature change, and though we would send our outgoing rushes from New York by air to Los Angeles, there was no guarantee that there would not be endless delays in some airfield in the mid-west where the temperature at that time of the year could be well into the nineties. Our film, then, would be well and truly cooked long before it had ever smelt a developing bath.

Our first evening aboard was a gala occasion. Hills, in his Chief Petty Officer's uniform, was perfectly at ease sitting with the 'four ringed' masters. His serenity and poise were great to see and he was happy that all his studio scenes were behind him. He knew, too, that they were good and that his performance had pleased everyone. He had never been lacking in confidence and his indoctrination to performing for the camera had done nothing to diminish it. Very much the reverse, and the same applied to Captain Kerr and Chief Officer Baskeyfield, playing the part of Rogers. All three had performed better than I could have hoped, and so we were all in high spirits as we sat down to table in the sumptuous saloon. Captain Olsen produced a banquet for us. The smorgasbord, for starters, represented a week's rations. An enormous roast leg of lamb then followed, with cheese and sweet to follow. After over three years of rationing, one had forgotten that such meals could exist. Even now, I have not forgotten that wonderful feast that Captain Olsen spread before us. It was a very kind gesture, even though it very nearly pole-axed the lot of us. There was no doubt: we had struck it lucky.

The round trip to New York had its moments, taking five to six weeks. Leaving the Mersey we headed for our rendezvous to take up our station in the convoy; like a pack of hounds to the meet, ships were dotted all around with the same idea. Then, the fog descended and wrapped us in its wet blanket for ten days. A white-out for ten days of fog horns ahead, astern, to port and starboard. Not the best of starts with a quarter of the film to be shot on this return trip to New York. We were in a fast convoy of ten knots. We had been sailing for 268 hours, roughly 2,680 miles. Liverpool–New York approximately 3,250 miles. That left us with two to three days' outward bound and we hadn't turned a foot of film. No point when we could scarcely see our hand outstretched.

On the eleventh day the fog lifted and, having been cooped up for so long, we went wild and shot everything in sight: ships wallowing, rolling and pitching. Bow waves, the wake, the log wheel turning, the sun sinking, the Master pacing, all those 'might come in handy' shots.

With no deck cargo we couldn't start on the final sequence of Griff and Basky, the Chief Officer, making aft towards the gun. They would be using the locomotives and tanks and heaven knows what to shield them from the U-Boat's periscope. Those shots must wait until we were homeward bound.

The following day we docked in Hoboken as dusk was falling, the skyline of Manhattan reflecting in the dark mirrored waters of the Hudson River. An hour later it lit up like a forest of Christmas trees, every tree alight with candles and coloured balls. Fifty-five years ago I saw that wondrous sight. I see it now, and not one candle has gone out.

*

A tank was being lowered into the forrard hold. A Mikado railway locomotive was being swung inboard and was slowly lowered on to the deck, aft. Our props were arriving. Our homeward-bound set was being built around us. The *Samuel Bakke* was disappearing under these huge items of deck cargo. More tanks were being lowered into the holds, fore and aft. Monty should be pleased. If there was to be a second front, we were taking enough on board to launch it.

We were homeward bound. The gang plank was pulled clear. The weather was foul and we had to make do with a few shots of

buoys and river craft passing. Manhattan was shrouded in mist and
our hopes for a dramatic pictorial departure were gone. Later, the
weather improved and we were dropping astern of the convoy.
Captain Olsen, at the Masters' Conference, had explained to the
Commodore that he had a film unit aboard, requiring a clear
horizon when the weather was fine. He had requested permission
to be able to do this. It was granted but we had to regain our
position by nightfall. We were now able to start filming essential
story material, and by the end of the day had all the shots of Griff
and Rogers threading their way aft, through the deck cargo towards
the gun platform. They were at the foot of the ladder and climbed
up it, out of shot. Tomorrow we would be shooting sync sound for
the gun duel and the death of Griff: with luck, in the can by
sundown. We should have been able to start that vital sequence
today but for the fact that the camera, the Newman Sinclair, kept
jamming and chewing up the film. This meant not only constant
reloading but canning up the unexposed or short ends of the unexposed Monopak. It was too precious for us to waste a foot.
Tomorrow we would be using 1000 foot rolls on the Vinten. We
must hope for better luck.

*

It was a fine day and by 9.00 a.m. Captain Olsen was slowing down
and allowing the convoy to get ahead. Several ships and several lines
of them would have to pass us before our horizon would be clear.
Meantime, we got set up with mike and camera in position. The
previous night, we had taken Griff and Rogers out of shot as they
climbed the ladder up to the gun platform. Our first shot this
morning would show them appearing over the rim of the platform
and crawling towards us for a tight two shot just below the breach
mechanism. There was time for a rehearsal before the horizon was
clear. Up they came and crawled exactly to their position, and now
for the lines.

GRIFF: 'Did you notice, there's a spare shell in the tray, Sir. That means
she's loaded all right.'

ROGERS: 'Great. That'll save us the trouble. Wonder what she's going to do.'

GRIFF: 'Chances are she's going to surface, Sir, or she'd have let us have another by now.'

ROGERS: 'Probably right. Anyway, nothing we can do but wait.'

GRIFF: 'Oh I'm used to that, Sir; reminds me of the Q-Ships in the last war.'

They now take time as they look at the periscope moving past. It is lowered.

GRIFF: 'Look, it's gone, Sir.'

ROGERS: 'Come on, Griff, let's see if the gun's loaded.'

GRIFF: 'Better not, Sir. Oldest trick in the world. They pop it up again and catch you napping. Got to wait.'

They wait and imagine that they see the U-Boat surfacing.

GRIFF: 'My God, here she comes, Sir.'

ROGERS: 'Come on, Griff, let's bang away at her now.'

GRIFF: 'No Sir, she can crash-dive before we get her range. We gotta get her committed, gun crew on the casing, then we've got her, Sir.'

It requires all their will power to stay put, and then Griff gives the word.

GRIFF: 'Right Sir, here we go.'

They jump up out of shot.

A wonderful rehearsal. Beautifully acted by both of them. We would make a fine climax. It was thrilling. Weather was set fair. We would complete this vital sequence before the sun got too red for Jack. I was genuine in my congratulations to them. 'Well done, fellows, couldn't be better. We go for a take right away.'

The usual routine followed. Kay was ready, Jack was happy that the sun was O.K. The horizon was clear and off we went. Speed. I put in the clapper and dashed behind the camera. Action. Griff and Rogers appeared over the rim, crawled to their exact position, got to Griff's line 'Chances are she's going to surface or she'd have let us have another' . . . and the camera jammed. Imagine the anguish. This was proof that this new batch of Monopak was faulty. It must have shrunk by the tiniest fraction of a millimetre: enough to jump the sprockets and cause a pile-up. Imagine what this meant. We put on a new magazine: time-consuming. The camera had to be cleared of chewed-up film and reloaded, now with another 1000 feet of this stock. My apologies to Griff and Basky. They were wonderful about it. This was a problem not of our making. We repeated the process after at least a twenty-minute delay ... and the same thing happened again. A camera jam. We might have advanced a line, but no more. Perhaps a quarter of the scene in both takes.

We were facing a disastrous situation. Bear with me a moment and you will realise how disastrous. We had two 1000-foot magazines. Both now had about 100 feet of exposed film carrying a line or two of the opening scene, which must be preserved. They also had 900 feet of unexposed film which, though faulty, had to be preserved, for they were the only means we had of completing the film or, at any rate, the scenes scheduled for this convoy trip. It was not a comforting prospect and the immediate consequence was devastating. It meant that Denny Densham, Jack Cardiff's wonderful assistant now had to go below with both magazines, break off the two lengths of 100 feet of exposed, seal them in cans, made safe with masking tape, rethread and reload the magazines with the remaining 900 feet, retrace his steps through the deck cargo, and reload the camera for another attempt. It took him half an hour. We waited. The sun was shining. Griff and Basky were on the boil. Denny was back. Camera reloaded. Everything ready. Action. And the same thing happened. We were cursed. This production, from the word go, had been a bloody battle, every foot of the way, and now this. It was almost too much and for the first time I thought I would have to go to the rail and be sick. Half an hour later, dear old Denny, ever smiling, returned with magazines. The only thing to do was to assume that we had 50 seconds of screen time before the jam. It was as though we had entered a hurdle race in which we fell at every fence, picked ourselves up, knowing that we would fall at the next, and so on until the course was completed. There was no other way. Once again, I was supported by the wonderful way everyone responded to this intolerable situation. We limped along in this farcical fashion until around 4.30 p.m. when the sun became too red for Jack to continue.

My diary tells me that it was 14 August 1943. That night, after dinner, in our fashion we were playing bridge. About 9.30 there was a tremendous bang. The shock waves took our bridge set to the deck. We picked up the score pads and reshuffled the pack. We all thought of one thing, quite naturally, and tried to look ridiculously unconcerned. I remember thinking was this the sound of things to come and that the next time we heard a bang the results might be very different? Funny, only yesterday, Bill Kerr had asked me whether we kept the cameras loaded, and this morning Kay Ash asked Denny the same. Jack left to help Denny divide one of the Vinten 1000-foot rolls into a 200-foot roll for the Newman Sinclair, having run out of them this afternoon. Foghorns were tooting all round like a herd of stricken sheep crying out in the night. One, particularly plaintive, became more insistent than the rest and sounded too near our stern.

Basky and I had started a game of cribbage. Just as I was counting my hand, I'd got to 15–4 and one for his knob when Basky tensed like a well-trained hunting dog and said: 'Six short blasts . . . Submarine on starboard bow.' We hurried on deck. On our port beam the sky was lit up with a nasty red glow. I chased up the camera and met Denny on the companion with the Sinclair and then Jack with the one and only loaded magazine. By now the masts, funnel and rigging were silhouetted against the glare. The stricken vessel had dropped astern, off our port quarter. We groped our way through the deck cargo. We set the camera up on the bulwark. Through the fog, we could see flames licking through a thick black smoke screen. It must have been a tanker for the flames were riding and spreading over the water. Hundreds-of-feet-high balloons of flame burst through the black cloud. There was no point in shooting any more. This was no part of our story and we had covered this tragic episode. We moved back the way we had come, the roar of the flames, sporadic gunfire and exploding ammunition a diabolic commentary on what had just happened. We hung around on deck for a while, rather lost and distracted, and fully expecting that it would be our turn, any minute. But the minutes passed by and we had time enough to think about this sudden and brutal attack.

From an oily calm to instant carnage for high octane allows of no sirens, no orderly move to a shelter or underground station. For those poor men it was life to death in the act of respiration. Gradually the minutes passed, lulling us into the belief that the attack was not being pressed home and that, once more, our concerns would be free to return to the safety, if frustrating prospect, of camera jams. How insignificant all that seemed, but how lucky we would be to be able to pick up those old threads and continue to knit them together.

Thursday, 15 August. Thick fog: no shooting.

Friday, 16 August. Thick fog: no shooting.

Saturday. Promising. We are able to get to work. In spite of more jams we could see the end of the gun duel and we completed the sequence. As I described earlier, before Griff is hit, we show an insert of bullets spraying across the gun shield towards the viewing aperture. We are now immediately behind him as he places a new shell in the loading tray. What a remarkable man he was—he had seen men killed in action—he gave the impression of almost being lifted off the ground by the impact of the bullet. He jumped almost full length back into camera. No thought of mattresses or boxes to soften the fall. He wasn't going to have waste on such niceties. He just did it, falling back on to the steel deck, miraculously none the worse for it, his head nestling between the empty shell holders, around the periphery of the platform. Basky, having fired the killing shot, comes back to Griff, just in time to tell him that the U-Boat is sinking. Griff, with his last breath, replies: 'Good . . . Tell the wife, we almost made that wedding anniversary.' His head lolls away and his eyes glaze in death. As he did it, I knew that we had captured a great cinematic moment by a non-actor and a great bit of First World War England.

22

How to round up the remnants

A week or so later we docked at Liverpool and Peter Lupino was there to meet us. What a help he had been to us and was still to be. He took me to lunch and then back to Derby House for a council of war. What a blessing it was that he knew show business. His first question: 'What have we got left, Pat?'

'Only the climax of the picture, Peter, that's all.'

'Involving what exactly?' Pencil in hand, at his desk, surrounded by pneumatic tubes, occasionally spewing messages into their wire baskets. He ignored them, a sixth sense suggesting that they were unimportant. He had more important business on hand. I started to enumerate what remained to be done. 'We have to sink the U-Boat. To do that convincingly we have to have the *Leander*'s gun barrel firing at it in foreground.'

'Any gun barrel will do?'

'Yes. The first shot goes over so we must see the splash beyond the U-Boat, the second short and the third a direct hit.'

'You've done all the action leading up to the gun firing?'

'Yes. Then there's the cat-and-mouse game. Griff and Rogers watching the periscope circling as they make for the gun aft.'

'That means a submarine and the *Patricia* again, if she'll play. Her gun'll do, one barrel's like another.'

'Sadly we couldn't get the shots of *Leander* with her lifeboats in foreground as seen by the U-Boat.'

'Oh Gawd.'

'I know; wasn't through want of trying. Both Vinten motors burnt out through constant camera jamming due to faulty stock: strain on the motors was too much.'

'Those may be more difficult to lay on than the mock battle. Means sending out a special escort to meet her. Pray God she'll still be with us. She'll have to be detached from the convoy . . . My sainted aunt, rather organise the Spithead review. Anyway, let's go for mock battle first.'

*

We had had hardly time to unpack, get our bearings and see the rushes when news came through that Peter had arranged for a submarine and the *Patricia*, which had helped us in the rescue scenes of the lifeboat survivors, would be at our disposal at Holyhead for a day on 7 September. Once more, we were on our old stamping ground. A small unit, this time: Jack and his assistant with the three-strip camera; Baskyfield and Captain Kerr and our two Pinewood special effects experts. I was relying on them to provide the splashes from the supposed shells after signal flashes had been fired from the gun barrel. I thought that it would be as well to make sure that the special effects were effective. I asked Captain MacKenzie whether he would be kind enough to lend me his powerful motor launch, once more, explaining my reasons. He was only too willing. The two Pinewood experts and myself loaded all the clobber aboard and off we went into the inner harbour. 'O.K., you two. It's all yours. Let's make sure everything works.'

'It'll work all right, Pat; you saw for yourself at Denham.'

'Yes, Dan, but a studio tank's one thing, the ocean another. Just as well to make sure.' We were now ready to pay out the charge, attached to its cable. We let a hundred yards, we'd need at least that amount to get the towing launch out of shot, and I said: 'Dan, you ready?'

'Yes, Pat.'

'I'll count to three and then press the tit. One. Two. Three. FIRE.' As I feared, nothing happened. He kept pressing the tit as though suffering from St Vitus' dance. This was par for the course. I was conditioned to it. Poor fellow, he looked at death's door, pressing the tit ever more frantically.

'Just as well we had a dummy run.'

'It worked at Denham . . . You saw for yourself, Pat.'

'It doesn't work here, does it?'

'Doesn't seem to.'

'You have only tomorrow to make it work or I shall cancel the submarine.' But it was already too late. It was entering the harbour. There was no point in lashing out at our poor expert. As it was, he was ready to throw himself over the side. I was in a similar frame of mind. He pulled in his pathetic device which spewed its powdery mess on to the deck. I had had my moments on this production. This was the worst. This was inexcusably shaming. He wanted another try with his spare set. He had it. The result was the same. As though keel hauled we returned and I walked slowly back to the hotel. Our charming manageress was in the foyer to greet me. 'Mr Jackson, Lt Meeke, the Commander of the submarine that has just berthed, is here to meet you. He is waiting for you in the lounge.' She was not the double for Groucho Marx's leading lady for nothing, and with great panache introduced me to the Lieutenant. Her duty done, the manageress withdrew. The Lieutenant's sense of humour was soon apparent. He said: 'I've just brought you my submarine. You want to sink her, I understand.'

'That's the idea, but I have a ghastly confession to make.'

'You've changed your mind? You don't want to?'

'No, that is I do want to, of course I do.' We were of the same age. He was enjoying my confusion in a very genial way. I said: 'Come and have a snort. I may find it easier to explain, though I doubt it.'

'Nothing serious, I hope.'

'Yes, very. I don't know how to sink you. Our special effects have seriously boobed. We've just had a dummy run . . . Talk about a damp squib . . . We wouldn't even blow a bubble, let alone mock up an explosion . . . Cheers and jolly nice to see you.'

'Cheers, good to be here . . . You were saying . . .'

'I've said it. We couldn't even blow a bubble and we're supposed to blow you out of the water.'

'It's these shell splashes, you're after, isn't it?'

'My God, you're on the ball, aren't you?'

Western Approaches: production stills

The Masters' Conference in New York.

Captain Pakenham, Captain (Destroyers) in Liverpool, who played the senior officer of the escort in the film, and very convincingly too.

C.P.O. Hills who played the gunner of S.S. *Leander*. One of the finest men that I have ever met and, as an actor, the equal of Bob Banner.

As he feared, Captain Kerr of the *Leander* has trouble to keep station now that the convoy has reduced speed. He is about to ask the Commodore for permission to steam ahead and rejoin the convoy in the morning. This will be the time when he picks up the S.O.S. of the lifeboat being used as a decoy by the U-Boat, leading to the ever increasingly suspenseful climax.

Chief Officer Rogers promises Griff that he will get him home in time to celebrate his wedding anniversary.

Captain Tomlinson is burdened with the prospect of meeting the west coast of Ireland in a treacherous rocky section. In the enfeebled state that they would all be in, their chances would be poor.

Making for Ireland.

The U-Boat's captain takes a look at the lifeboat and dismisses it as of passing interest only. However, when his wireless operator picks up an S.O.S. he realises that it is being sent from the lifeboat, and decides to use it as a decoy. A dramatic equation is established.

The thirteenth day.

Captain Pycraft thinks that he is hearing engine noise. It is dead of night, and his chief engineer confirms that it is so. A U-Boat has surfaced to charge its batteries.

Captain Kerr, on the bridge of *Leander*, has decided to find the lifeboat, having picked up its S.O.S., has it in sight, and with his Chief Officer is trying to decipher a message that is being sent from it.

Captain Pycraft tries to semaphore, reflecting the sun by the use of an opened flare canister.

Griff is blown up by the second torpedo.

Captain Kerr orders his radio operators to abandon ship temporarily, until
they know what the U-Boat is going to do with them.

'I wonder what she's going to do with us.'
'Chances are she's going to surface, Sir, or she'd have let us have another by now.'

'Here she comes.'

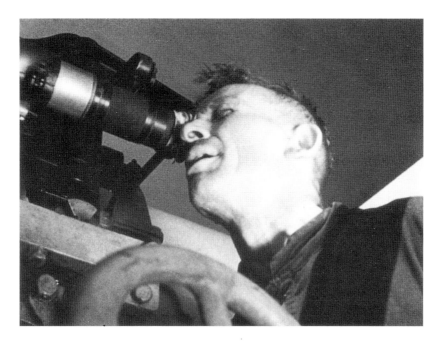

Griff lays the gun.

As he lies dying, he tells his officer to come up one hundred and he'll do it. His last words: 'Tell the wife we almost made that wedding anniversary'.

The direct hit below the waterline . . .

. . . has immediate and dramatic effect.

Inside the submarine, survivors of the explosion struggle hopelessly to escape, while the crew of the lifeboat are picked up by the *Leander*.

White Corridors (1951)

Googie Withers as Dr Sophie Dean

'Go back into the ward. Help Sister cut off those bandages and however bad his facial burns, look him in the eye and make him feel he's going to be all right. That's real nursing.' Petula Clark and James Donald.

'I've got to. It's his only chance.' Dr Sophie Dean prepares to administer Dr Marriner a dose of his own untested serum.

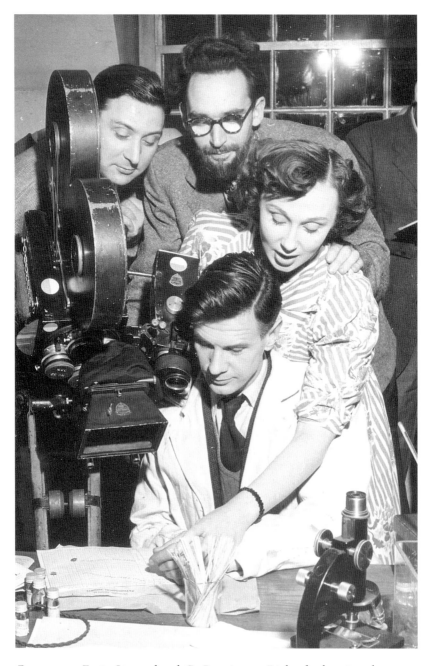

Cameramen Ernie Steward and C. Pennington Richards shooting the close-up of Dr Marriner's discovery: the formula of the drug for patients allergic to penicillin.

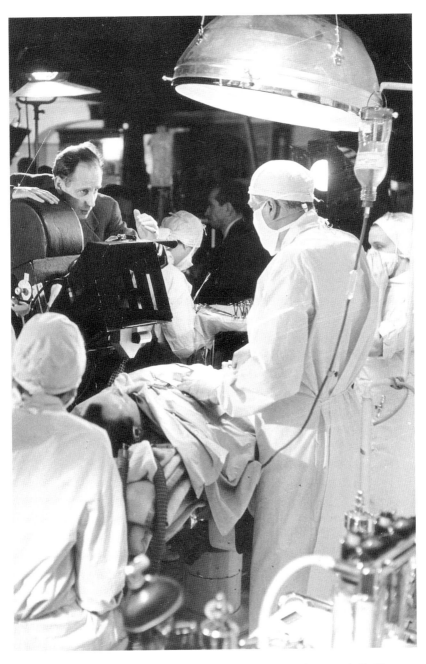

'It's no good, it's gone too far. We're too late. Sew him up.' Godfrey
Tearle, playing the consultant surgeon, was a joy to work with. What more
can a director ask when his star says 'If I HAM, I shall expect you to
tell me'.

Having saved the life of her fiancé, Dr Marriner, by administering his recently discovered antidote, Dr Dean strides down the white corridor to become a consultant at Yeoman's Hospital.

'Lupino put me in the picture. We can provide the splashes, no problem at all.' I looked at him, shocked with the relief, if that is possible: 'How?'

'We have devices, obviously, to blow up the ship, rather than let her suffer a fate worse than death. They vary in power. I have already selected, or, cast is the more apt word, the one that you need to sink me.'

'My dear Sir, you are adding years to my life. I was in quite a state, just now.'

'You hid it quite well, but I sensed that all was not quite ship-shape.'

'About these splashes', I persisted.

'A medium disposal bomb. I've brought about three hundred yards of cable. Also half a dozen red petrol cans—be as well to have a few more if you can rustle them up. We'll attach them to the cable, say every thirty yards. You got a good pair of binoculars, by the way?'

'No . . . not with us. I'm sure we haven't.'

'I'll lend you mine . . . Or *Patricia*'s bound to have a good pair. You've got Chief Officer Baskeyfield with you and Captain Kerr, Lupino tells me.'

'Yes, they still have a small scene to play.'

'Good, get one of them to follow the last petrol can and when it's in line with the gun, he orders ''FIRE'' and the *Patricia* fires her gun, with a signal flash charge—they won't know the difference and one of my chaps in the launch will count two and press the tit. Eruption, and Bob's your uncle. Q.E.D. . . . .' I looked at him, just this side of idolatry. He continued: 'I can see no reason why this can fail. We'll give it a go tomorrow. If it works, and I'm sure it will, then all we have to do is repeat the process for the shot that falls short. For the direct hit below the conning tower I'd like to give you a bigger one, but we might end up doing the job for real.'

*

The following morning, thanks to the kindness of Captain Mac-Kenzie, his launch appeared. A different team of special effects experts climbed aboard with their tackle: Lt Meeke and his boatswain. We let go two hundred yards of cable and Baskeyfield with his binoculars had no difficulty in sighting the last red petrol can. The boatswain pressed the tit and up shot a superb water spout. We were in business.

Later, *Patricia* steamed into harbour and we held our final council of war at the hotel. Shot by shot with Lt Meeke and the *Patricia*'s Captain, we went over what we hoped to film the next day. Hard to believe, but everything went according to plan. Unless the gods and Lt Meeke are with you, this was the sort of filming that can take days and days. Had I been the Monarch, I would have ordered him, there and then, on to his casing and, with my rapier, tapped him lightly on both shoulders: 'Surface, Sir William'. Nobody could have deserved it more.

Finally, Lt Meeke helped us to get the most dramatic shot in the film. When we had sunk him in long shot, we boarded him to sink him in close shot. Jack set up the camera half way along the forrard casing. I went down into the control to have a word with Lt Meeke. An idea had occurred to me. It took several seconds to climb down the conning tower, into the control room. 'Bill, would it be possible to give the impression that you were sinking by the stern? Camera being up forrard ... it would make a wonderful shot.' He looked at me as if to say: 'We've given you the earth already', which he had. But, he was an enthusiast in everything he did. He could imagine the shot, immediately.

'O.K., but xxxxxx you, Pat. We'll try.'

'Thanks, Bill.'

'Flood both, aft.' I could hear the water rushing into the tanks as I hurried up the conning tower. As I reached the top I could hear him shouting: 'BLOW AFT ... FOR CHRIST'S SAKE. BLOW.' I jumped off the conning tower and joined the other members of Lt Meeke's crew who were supposedly abandoning ship. I looked back and saw Jack still peering through the camera, its tripod almost submerged. But Jack would still have been turning if he'd gone under. Fortunately, our U-Boat popped up just in time, with only inches to spare for the camera.

We returned to Pinewood for the interior scenes of the U-Boat's flooding. Throughout, Jack had been an enormous help with visual suggestions which I gratefully accepted. Now he came up with one of his most imaginative. 'Pat', he said: 'For the flooding of the U-Boat, if we put the camera in a huge watertight crate, insert an optical glass panel, when the tank fills—and it will very quickly— all we have to do, when the water creeps up the panel, is pan down a little. This will give the impression that we're going down with it.'

'Brilliant, Jack, brilliant. We'll do that.'

Our crate was built and tested that it was watertight. It was. Part of the submarine set, which Teddy Carrick had reconstructed for Jack Lee's film *Close Quarters*, was now transferred, slightly butchered and the right piece set up in the studio tank. Our crate was in position. Jack and I climbed in and our artists, Czech and Südeten refugee volunteers to play the drowning crew, were at action stations and ready.

As though Niagara and Victoria were falling in unison, in poured the water. In a moment or two, Jack and I were afloat and bouncing about. The flood was turned off. Insufficient thought had been given by 'our riggers'. The crate should have been bolted into the tank and locked into the wall with tubular scaffolding. The show had to go on. Anything and everything that had any weight was scrounged. Like homing ants came the ballast gatherers. Still not enough.

The only way was to assemble all hands to stand on planks which were put across the crate. A silent army stood as though on 'sentry go' along their planks. There was just time for a take before lunch. In went the board. The poor little clapper boy, his waders just above the water line: slate 603, take one. Bang. The water came roaring in. The men came swimming towards us, giving a horri- fying panic-stricken performance. The water was creeping up and up the optical glass panel. Jack, imperceptibly, panned down into the water, conveying the impression to the audience that they, too, were trapped in the sinking U-Boat. It was a great shot. I cut and we knew that we had filmed all that was needed on this set. Jack took off the magazine, tucked it under his arm and climbed out of the crate. I followed. The third assistant looked at his watch. He shouted: 'Lunch. Break everybody.' Everybody did, including our anchor men. They had forgotten what they were there for and off their planks they went. Our crate shot up out of the water, like a playful dolphin. Its entry back was not so graceful. With a belching gurgle it slowly sank and took the camera with it to the bottom: still well within the three-mile limit.

Strange, that of all places to sink it, we had to choose a point in the U.K. as far away as it is possible to be from any ocean. One way and another it had been a strange production. We were very nearly at the end of it. The shooting, anyway.

*

What was left? Only shots of the *Samuel Bakke* as seen through the periscope. They were vital to build up the suspense to the point when the conning tower breaks through the surface. Without them, the climax could not reach its peak.

A special escort was provided for us to go out into the Atlantic again and meet the *Samuel Bakke*, homeward bound. It was one of those 50 American destroyers from the moth-balled fleet that Sir Winston had obtained for bases in the Azores or some such lollipop. She seemed to be a narrow affair, suggesting not much more stability than her countrywoman *Tyella*. She had an inordinate number of funnels looking as though the base section of the Albert Hall's organ had found a new home. One or two seemed to have some practical use judging by the whisps of smoke emerging.

Jack's new assistant, like an eventing horse, suddenly shied (maybe those six funnels put him off) and decided that this trip was beyond his usual call of duty. He dug his hooves in. So, we turned around and had another run at it and were soon safely aboard. All four of us: cameraman, assistant and a 17-year-old loading boy who had only been with Technicolor a few weeks, this being his first job.

We set out in a very nasty sou'-wester which was obviously going to get even nastier, and with the windage of those organ pipes aloft we were in for a rare old dusting. As we turned our stern on

Crosby and headed out across Liverpool Bay and down the Irish Channel, into wind, our narrow bows were cutting through those mounting seas like wire through cheddar. A magnificent sight.

Our skipper was a Lieutenant R.N.V.R. I asked him if his boatswain could give us a hand to get the gear up on to the bridge for a shot of the bows cleaving through the water which I had to have. He agreed. I went below to marshall my forces. There weren't any. They were prostrate and in a bad way, poor chaps. The youngster, however, was in great nick and raring to go. The boatswain and a rating appeared. The four of us shared out the spoils. Tripod, Vinten camera, magazine and battery. We were ready to make an assault on the summit.

Off we went and the deck came up to meet us with an unwelcome upper-cut. We went forward and waited for the pitch. As she started to climb we would go forward and wait again for the descent. In this haphazard fashion, we reached the bridge. We put up the tripod and the boatswain made it fast with a lifetime's knowledge of knots. Against the spray they held a tarpaulin as we mounted the camera and connected the battery. We guessed at a stop for the lens and hoped for the best. The tarpaulin was lowered and we let rip. That young lad got one of the finest shots in the film. Those needle bows of ours burst through that rearing wall of water as though puncturing a balloon. Well satisfied, we prepared for the descent. Back in the wardroom we dried off the equipment and with the aid of the boatswain's knots made sure that it was well and truly secured.

There was nothing more that we could do except anchor ourselves in chairs rivetted to the deck and sit it out. Until the sea abated somewhat it would be impossible for the stewards to serve any sort of a meal. The deck was heaving around and one was doing well to hold fast to the seat.

Two days later we made our rendez-vous and by merciful providence the sea had abated, though, as a result of the gale, there was a long oily swell. The Senior Officer of Escort was a wonderful man, Commander Bridgeman, and his frigate was a sister ship to the *Black Swan*. He did everything for us, lowered his launch to act as our camera boat, and though the ocean looked calm enough from the frigate's deck, from the launch the height of the swell was astonishing. The *Samuel Bakke* left the convoy for us and within an hour or so we had all the shots we wanted. The filming of *Western Approaches* was over.

Three days later I was back at Pinewood and the final battle began—in the cutting room. As so often happens, the editor who had been assigned to cut my material while I was away shooting was not the right man for the job. He had no feel for the subject. Every cut seemed to be wrongly timed and some of the best stuff wasn't even used. On first viewing it seemed that all I had succeeded in doing was to produce a botched inconsequential mess. Thanks to my dear old sister, Joss, who mercifully had been assisting the previous editor, now, in her best Marjorie Main manner, read me the riot act. We stripped the lot down, all eight reels, and started again. When we had our final cut, Muir Mathieson, our musical adviser, saw and felt that the ideal composer would be Clifton Parker. He came down the next day. He was finely drawn with a most enchanting smile. Having seen the film we walked round the lot and chatted. He interrupted me and said: 'I think I've got it. I wish I could play it to you.'

'You can, Cliff: a baby Broadwood is in my office.' He sat down and played one of the most beautiful melodies that I have ever heard. It came to him literally within ten minutes of having seen the film. Vaughan Williams had written a majestic melody for *Forty-Ninth Parallel*, but this one of Cliff's had something mysteriously ethereal which moved one deeply. It was to give the film a special quality that it would not have had without Clifton Parker's wonderful contribution.

Some weeks later we were ready to show the film to the powers that be—the Ministry of Information wallahs. They did not know what to make of it. Had they value for money? Had they a viable proposition? To get their money back it had to be shown on the commercial circuit as a normal feature. They didn't seem at all certain. They would ask their honorary consultant for his opinion. One day, Joss and I were informed that the film must be ready to show to Sir Alexander Korda at 10.00 a.m. the next day. Sir Alex was under contract to Metro Goldwyn Mayer.

We spent the whole day making sure that all the joins in the cutting copy were solid and well stuck. There were eight reels of picture and each reel could have anything between two to three hundred joins in it, so perhaps two thousand joins had to be inspected and, if necessary, re-cemented. It needed only one of these joins to come unstuck during tomorrow's vital showing for the initial impact and flow of the story to be ruined—a delay of ten minutes to rejoin and the impact, if any, can never be recaptured. One break, that's all. It was a nightmarish prospect, but, hopefully, the last on this production. Neither of us slept very much that night.

At 10.00 the following morning we were waiting in Theatre Two. Dear old Duggie Smith, our projectionist, who had been with us since the start of the old G.P.O. Film Unit, winked at us through the glass panel of his projection room. He gave us the thumbs up: Duggie, who had projected every cutting copy for us since the early rough cuts of *Night Mail*. What a bond there was between us all. I acknowledged his encouraging signal and turned as I heard: 'Good morning'. A rather insignificant man, in a broad-brimmed trilby hat and none-too-immaculate mackintosh, wearing horn-rimmed glasses, had walked in, unannounced and with no retinue. His arrival caught me napping. 'My name is Korda. I have come to see a film called *Western Approaches*. Is it ready, please?'

'Yes, Sir Alex.'

'Please run it when you are ready. I will sit here in the front.'

I climbed up to the back and pressed the button. Duggie slowly dimmed the lights and pulled the tabs. We were off. Up swelled Cliffie's glorious title music, and when the opening storm sequence was over we could just hear those joins going through the projector like an express train running over maladjusted points. A derailment seemed likely, any minute.

During the next hour-and-a-half I would not have liked our blood pressure or heartbeat to have been checked. They would have made alarming reading. But, the 'cutting copy' held. We were on the final shots. The two captains aboard *Leander* were meeting. Clifton Parker's music for the end title started and we were home without a break, and now for the fireworks.

The lights came up and the man in the mackintosh stood up from the front and slowly looked round. Very accusingly, I thought, he looked at me and asked: 'Who made this?'

There was nothing for it but to own up. 'I did, Sir Alex.'

'But it is magnificent . . . You will come with me. I will give you a contract.' Having expected to have every strip torn off me, I thought I must be in need of a hearing aid. Before I had time to gather my wits, Sir Alex, asked: 'Who is your agent, Jackson?'

'I haven't one, Sir Alex.'

'You will be hearing from me.' He left Theatre Two of Pinewood and we were left with a profound sense of relief. The crisis was over. The 'cutting copy' with its thousands of joins had held. The film had run through without a break. Such a deep sense of relief we had never before experienced.

23

So, this is Hollywood!

I had arrived in Mecca, the Mecca of cinema and the cage of the Roaring Lion, Metro Goldwyn Mayer Studios in Culver City, Hollywood. I was staring up at the Irving Thalberg Building, built in memory of the young executive producer and late husband of Norma Shearer.

I was on crutches, in plaster from ankle to hip, having had a skiing accident on the second day of my honeymoon. I had broken my leg in what was poetically described as a 'butterfly fracture' in 30 or more splinters a few inches above the ankle. Not the most glamorous way to arrive and launch a career as a feature film director. However, those massive steps as in front of a Greek temple had to be climbed so that I could announce my arrival.

It was now six weeks since my unfortunate fall in Stowe, Vermont. I was skiing on a hill aptly called 'Suicide Six'. No, I was not showing off, trying to 'vedell' at 70 miles an hour. I might have been doing, perhaps seven or eight, gliding just off the flat, to the hotel. Everything was in shadow and contours hard to see. I hit a rut, regained my balance, immediately hit another and spreadeagled between the skis. The upturned metal running edge of one treated my leg as though it were a piece of kindling.

Now, I must climb those steps, deeply regretting that Korda was no longer at Metro. He had, to put it crudely, been sacked after his first film for them. They considered it a disaster. Korda, free of Metro, was now independent and successfully running Shepperton, taking Ian Dalrymple with him, but I was not released from the contract that Korda had drawn up for me on behalf of Metro. Much had happened since we showed him *Western Approaches*, but the net result was that I was out here to try and do battle against the 'mighty moguls'. My poor wife of only a few weeks, Kitty Talbot of Boston, Massachusetts, slowly climbed the steps with me.

Whether by accident or design, we were met by Ben Goetz who was supposed to be running the Metro Studios at Boreham Wood, Elstree. They hadn't turned a foot since Korda's disaster but were, at least, preventing competitors from using the studio space. Ben made himself very agreeable and kindly shepherded us to the vast studio commissariat. All eyes suddenly focused on us. We were an odd trio. My wife, a tall, willowy figure with blonde 'page boy' hair to her shoulders, the portly Ben Goetz and becrutched me. Dear me, what an entrance. And there they all were, these romantic figures that over the years we had queued up to see from the two-and-fourpennies. Robert Taylor, Clark Gable, Lana Turner, Walter Pidgeon, a dazzling array of stars gawking at us. I knew, now, what it felt like to be a duck out of water. As Ben tried to lead us to some inconspicuous corner, I wondered whether I could or would ever integrate and be accepted by this extraordinary motley of talented people. The G.P.O. Film Unit's messenger boy did not feel at home at all.

The largest table running down the centre was reserved for M.G.M.'s film directors. Smoking the biggest cigar I have ever seen was Mervyn LeRoy, director of *The Wizard of Oz* and the great film, *Prisoner of a Chain Gang*—I knew that I would never sit at that table. I recognised Clarence Brown, Garbo's director, and Sidney Franklin who had made *Mrs Miniver*. The greats of the industry, all right. As for Ben, I never quite knew what he did, either in Elstree or his exact role here. He was vaguely related to L. B. Mayer which was an advantage. He had an engaging smile and was kind to everyone, and that's already something. During lunch I asked him what he had in mind for me; after all it was he who suggested that we drove out here from Boston. He looked embarrassed and clearly had nothing in mind, as he said: 'Well, Pat, we kinda thought you might like to see how we make pictures over here. We start a big picture here in a week or so, Clark Gable in *Command Decision*, with Sam Wood directing. Might pick up a few wrinkles, eh?'

'Yes, Ben, I'm sure I would, but I hope you'll soon put me to work.'

'Yeah, but you'll have to get over these, won't you?'

'As you saw, I'm pretty nimble on 'em.'

'Yeah. First thing to do is get yourselves sorted out and housed . . . and then we'll see.'

He told us that we could stay in the M.G.M. guest house until this coming Saturday, three days away, when M.G.M. was selling the place. Was this the start of an economy drive, I wondered. The hunt started as soon as we'd found the guest house, not far from the renowned Beverley Hills Hotel and our base for three days. One 'Realty' Office after another. Prices high and our spirits low as for the next two days we saw one pricey dump after another. Then on my birthday, one of the Realty Offices rang us at the guest house— luckily we had just that moment returned from another abortive hunt—to tell us that they had 'just the cutest little doll's house you ever saw, and not for nothing was it Shirley Temple's honeymoon cottage, and you just must go see it for yourselves'. The thought of being haunted by that little performing doll singing the 'Good ship lollipop' gave me the shakes. Mustn't be prejudiced, not in our parlous state. Worth a look.

We swept off Sunset Boulevard and down the king-palmed Avenue of San Vicente Boulevard, in Brentwood, well on the way to the golden beaches of Santa Monica. No. 12947, and there it was, a massive mansion, but just visible in the large back garden 'the cutest little doll's house you ever saw'. Not far from the truth, and it was embroidered with pink and purple bougainvillaeas. Quite adorable. The owner was a jolly porpoise of an old boy, a retired salesman of Ford and General Motors. He showed us round and cut a huge bouquet of sweet peas for Kitty. To the left was an orchard of avocado pears which belonged to the old villain of the silent pictures, Charles Bancroft; to the right Fred MacMurray's palatial pad. Avocados were now plumetting down on to what could be our flower beds. Very nice, too. The rent was higher than we wanted but he would rent the place by the month, and as we had discovered that nobody would consider anything less than a year's lease, this was an added bonus to the place. An hour later, with the understanding that he would discuss terms with the agent, agreeing that he would try and meet us, we left, floating on air. We were too excited to eat much and rang the Realty Office. We were told that another couple had just seen the cottage and offered a year's rent in advance at Mr Woolfe's terms. The old boy, very decently, had refused this because he said he had already given first refusal to a younger couple. If everyone is as honourable as this out here, things may turn out all right. We had found our camp from which to launch our campaign against Hollywood.

*

On my daily trip to the stage to watch the great Sam Wood directing *Command Decision*, I became a familiar figure, hobbling along on my crutches, not as the man who broke the bank at Monte Carlo but his leg on his honeymoon. Any publicity is better than none, the saying goes, and as the days passed another new face would smile or I'd get a wink or a wave from a chippie or sparks or one of the crew.

Command Decision had started shooting two weeks ago. It was an epic on the U.S. Air Force with an all male cast. It starred Clark Gable, Walter Pidgeon, Van Johnson, John Hodiak, Charles Bickford and Edward Arnold. I was there from day one and was amazed—amazed at not being spellbound by the drive and efficiency of the high-powered studio. Had it not been for the dynamism of the ace cameraman Hal Rosson, the late Jean Harlow's husband, I don't think much would have happened on that first day. It was Hal who chose the 'set-up' and worked out the action. He was the director and the lighting cameraman. Both were second nature to him. A wonderful little man, a dynamo and an artist. I sat, watched, listened and longed to take over.

There's no business like show business. That may be, but I hadn't realised how mysteriously it works. Judging from that day, it seemed a miracle that it worked at all. There was a nice working practice, though, on the floor. Behind the set there was a sort of miniature coffee shop, run by the prop department, and the property men shared the daily take. They had a constant brew of coffee, sandwiches, doughnuts and biscuits—'cookies'. This was a wonderful way of getting to know the stage hands, and all the crew as well as the cast. When they were not needed in the next shot or two they would nip backstage for a snack and a chat. This procedure went on throughout the day and prevented these annoying set tea breaks which we have in England and which tend to interrupt the surge of work when a good rhythm has been established.

As the days went by and I sat there, members of the cast would come over, introduce themselves, draw up a chair and have a chat. I was most impressed by their kindness and the professionalism of the older brigade. Charles Bickford, for example, and Clark Gable always came on scene word-perfect for the entire day's work. Charles Bickford was a fine artist and knew his business blindfold. He had a great presence both on and off the screen. Totally relaxed, confident and at ease all the time. A most charming companion, and to see him work was a joy; a real old trouper from the silent days. No wonder he had no trouble surviving the 'talkies' which so quickly and brutally put an end to many a silent picture star.

On the fourth day, Walter Pidgeon appeared for his first scene. He had been given a moustache, and his hair greyed at the temples. He looked most distinguished. He oozed charm and bonhomie. Later that week, he had a tricky seven-minute scene, with complicated camera moves, handling of props and pointers at the vast wall map of Europe. He was word-perfect, of course, and after a couple of rehearsals they went for a take. He got it first time and everyone appeared from nowhere and gave him a thundering round of applause—not lost on Walter Pidgeon, who was quite moved by this spontaneous outburst of warmth and appreciation. He was obviously as popular as Gable. Not for nothing were they revered; they helped to bring in the bacon for everyone, not only the shareholders. He was exactly as one hoped he would be, for there is nobody who could help but fall for his charm in *Mrs Miniver*. He was a Canadian, First World War, Western Front veteran and totally without 'side'. Warm and friendly to everyone.

*

Today Clark Gable sat alongside and had a chat. He couldn't have been more friendly or more simple. He talked of his love of fishing and the pleasures of simple country life pursuits. He was not happy with the state of affairs in the studio: too much bureaucratic front office control from people who have no real flair. He regretted the loss of Irving Thalberg who really knew the business, understood the medium and, when problems arose, knew how to solve them without playing the mad genius.

Clark had a biggish scene coming up. He had just sent off his best friend John Hodiak on a dangerous mission. He was waiting for news as he faced the wall map in the control room. Various people came and went, requiring quick-firing dialogue. He was alone, pacing; someone came in and he learnt that his friend had been shot down in flames. He left me to rehearse the scene. On his first line, he fluffed—his dentures had slipped. Quite unruffled, and smiling all over his face, he turned to the unit and mimed jamming his plate against his palate. Then on with the job: a perfect rehearsal; and a perfect take. He came back and joined me. I took the liberty of congratulating him and telling him how moving I found the scene. He smiled and then I said: 'May I ask you what you were thinking about?' He grinned and gave me a quizzical look. All he said was: 'Sweet F.A.'. He was a wise enough cookie to know that these situations carried him. The less he did, the more effective he would be.

As 5.00 p.m. approached, a certain tension descended on the unit, for if Clark Gable was in a scene that may have required a few takes and runs for two or three minutes, everyone knew that it must be in the 'can' by 5 o'clock, for Clark was one of only three stars in Hollywood who had the 5 o'clock 'shadow'. At 5.00, he walked off the floor. If the camera, however, rolled at one minute to five and the scene lasted three or four minutes, he would do it and give the unit that extra minute or two. If another take was required, too bad. It must wait for the morning. I saw both situations, several times. So Clark left. Another take was needed.

What would the unit do? To break the set-up and strip the lighting wasn't sensible or economical. It would take time to reset every-thing. Best leave things alone and offer to the camera, in situ, those inserts, the odd close-up that may have been forgotten. A bore. Everyone knew that time was being wasted, but that was the price you had to pay if you used 'the King'.

A charming man, who walked with his fame and had not got too big for his boots. All the ravishing beauties, often the secretaries of high executives, came to the set during the day to pay him court, just for the pleasure of talking to him. He had one or two special ones who made a point of seeing him once a day. He was still unmarried, still trying to get over the tragic death of his great love, Carole Lombard.

There is something magical about a film unit at work. Even a hanger-on like me, a rubbernecker, becomes part of the family. John Hodiak introduced himself, and what a delightful chap. He let his hair down after a bit and said: 'It doesn't help having to work with a director who is totally incoherent'. The poor man seemed to have lost all confidence and was constantly calling his producer, Sidney Franklin (director of *Mrs Miniver*) to approve certain scenes before shooting them. There must have been something astray. He could not be a hundred per cent fit. No unit could expect to work this way. It was as if the conductor had fallen off the podium and the orchestra kept playing. Not long after filming *Command Decision* Sam Wood died of a sudden heart attack. It suggests to me that all could not have been well with him when I saw him at work, for if this had been his norm, he could never have made a career. Never.

Days went by, and the end of shooting was in sight. An English sound engineer working on the picture came up to me in a strangely theatrical manner and, looking furtively round, said: 'Watch it Pat!!'

'Dear old chum, I have been and am getting heartily sick of it. I want to do it for real, for myself, now.'

'Yes, I bet. What I mean is be careful what you say, it's getting to the front office.'

'Sorry, I'm not with you.'

'All this socialist stuff.'

'Oh, you mean the National Health Service.'

'Yes, that and other stuff.'

'I don't know about the other stuff, but when I'm asked about the National Health Service, naturally I tell 'em what I know. Free health care. Bloody marvellous, boy.'

'Yes, I know, but they'll think you're a socialist.'

'But I am. I voted for them.'

'But that's being a communist over here, don't you see. They'll have you up before the Un-American Activities Committee.'

'I don't see they can do that; you have to be an American for that, don't you?'

'Not at all. You can be brought before them as an unfriendly alien and your visa confiscated.'

'That's one way of getting home, I suppose.'

'Up to you, of course, but I thought I'd just tip you the wink, anyway.'

'Jolly good of you, and thanks, I appreciate it. As I said, I did vote Labour, but that's a light year away from being a communist.'

'Not out here it isn't, Pat. Hardly dare be a democrat, these days. Anyway, be seeing you.' And off he went. It was kind of him and I began to know what he meant. There was an indefinable undercurrent of not exactly fear, but it was almost as if one could smell a sort of creeping unease; people far too ready to state their allegiance to the Republican Party. Three times I'd heard this, people stating their political loyalty for no reason at all. This was something I had never experienced before. I recalled James' reporting of Churchill's words in Rome: 'We have never known what it is to live under a reign of fear'. Was that possible over here? I hoped not. There was certainly increasing anxiety, but I had put that down to the state of the film industry.

The following day everything looked decidedly brighter. On my way towards Stage One, I saw two gorgeous looking girls, their light summer dresses clinging to two very shapely figures. I increased the swing between my crutches and was gaining fast.

As I overtook them, I cast a sideways look. I have never seen anything so beautiful. It was she, National Velvet. Elizabeth Taylor, sweet seventeen, and my word she was. She smiled as I passed and I can see the gleam in those violet eyes. There are things to remember about Hollywood. Her companion was Janet Leigh, equally easy on the eye. Two more beautiful young girls have never before or since been seen together, I do declare. Yes, Sir.

With a light heart and full of the joys of spring, I took up my vigil as the last days of *Command Decision* were fast approaching. I lunched with Walter Pidgeon, and his eyes as well as mine were darting in all directions. A musical had just started on the neighbouring stage and the most gorgeous dancers kept flitting past as we attacked the second course. They were diaphanously clad, as though about to be chosen for the beauty contest of the world. As a bird-watching exercise we were in the right neck of the woods and no binoculars were needed. A revelatory experience, that luncheon with Walter Pidgeon, and I was glad to see that the eye of that hardened old trooper flitted, like mine, from branch to branch as yet another gorgeous bird flew past.

Soon, the English sound engineer, my new-found friend, gave me the latest on the bush telegraph. Even though the high-ups had been shown *Western Approaches*—it had been nominated the previous year for an Oscar—the feeling was that I was too young and too inexperienced to be trusted with a picture. Right or wrong, this message from my informant was spur enough for me to plan a frontal attack. I was finished with rubber-necking. They were either going to use me or I would go.

Poor Kitty came, as usual, to pick me up and drive me home. I say poor Kitty deliberately for there is no business like show business to separate one unless you are both in it up to your necks, and that, very often, is no solution either—very much the reverse. All that she had been was a chauffeur, trying to get involved and understand a business which is probably more confused and confusing for all concerned: certainly for us, at this time, so anxious and perturbed was I to find a way of extricating myself from this deep professional rut of stagnation in which I was bogged. How to extricate myself? I would appeal to the all-high: to the great L. B. Mayer, himself.

I wrote him a short letter, and though I have long since mislaid my copy, it was so important to me that the gist of it is engraved on my memory. It was as follows:

Dear Mr Mayer,

Rightly or wrongly, I am under the impression that you and your executives consider that I am too young and too inexperienced to be trusted with a film, even though your own Academy of Arts and Sciences graciously nominated my work for an Oscar.

If I am not wrong, then, clearly this situation is of benefit to neither of us. You are wasting your money, and I, my time. We must put a stop to this ridiculous situation.

Accordingly, unless I hear from you shortly I shall assume that you are in accord and that our agreement no longer exists.

      With kind regards
        Yours sincerely,
          Pat Jackson.

Kitty was in full agreement and we decided to get the letter off our hands and into L. B.'s as quickly as possible. She drove the now familiar route to Culver City and deposited me, once more, below the familiar steps of Thalberg's monument.

The letter safely delivered to the secretariat, we felt invigorated that we had taken action to put an end to this soul-destroying in-activity. We drove down to Santa Monica and sat on the glorious sands and watched the Pacific rollers, appearing by magic from a flat calm, break, boom in a flurry of spray and surge up the beach to within a few feet of us. As the water receded, the sun turned the golden sands into a deep purple, hypnotising and bewitchingly beautiful. If only one could get the work front functioning satis-factorily there might be a way of life out here. The setting was lovely, a gorgeous ocean, golden sands, waving palm trees, all the visual clichés from travel agents' brochures. If only one could live happily off a view and riding a surf board. We agreed that we would give Mr Mayer a week to reply, and if no word came, then we would make tracks to return.

The following morning, having collected Charles Bancroft's generous windfalls of avocado pears and some sweet peas from Mr Wolfe's garden, the phone rang. I sauntered inside, in no great hurry, not expecting a call, and lifted the receiver. A quietly spoken, male New England accent said: 'May I speak to Mr Pat Jackson, please?'

'Speaking.'

'Mr Jackson, good morning, my name is Hanley; I am Mr Mayer's personal assistant. Mr Mayer has received your letter and would like to see you. He wondered whether 2 o'clock this afternoon would be convenient.'

'It certainly would. I will be there, and will you thank Mr Mayer on my behalf?'

'I will indeed; until 2 o'clock then. Goodbye, Mr Jackson.' Understandably, you could have knocked me over with the proverbial feather. This business takes a lot of understanding.

At a quarter to two, Kitty deposited me in the old familiar place. She would wait for me in the nearby car park. Even more nimbly, I made short work of those steps and went through the huge open temple doors, across the patterned marble floor to the elevators. First floor; to the right, towards the Mayer wing. Under an Adam's archway and I was in—Chippendale, Georgian England, his lovely chairs profusely scattered along the corridor, with a marble-topped table on a finely moulded carved gilt base with a beautifully arranged bowl of flowers. Under another archway to the right, an ante-chamber, and through what reminded me of a large serving hatch were three typist secretaries chatting like parrots with spasms of girlish giggles. A devout looking young man in an immaculately cut blue blazer and newly pressed clerical grey trousers, as though about to offer me a candle as a welcome to this holy shrine, said, scarcely above a whisper: 'Mr Jackson?'

'Yes, Mr Hanley, I'm a few minutes early.'

'Never mind. Mr Mayer is very rarely late for an appointment. I am sure he won't keep you waiting long.' He pointed to a Chippendale carver by the side of the doors which must lead to the sanctum. I sat down and waited; time to wonder whether this really was me, late of the G.P.O. Film Unit, and how on earth I could ever have got myself into this ridiculous situation. I looked at my watch. It was five minutes to two. A buzzer buzzed in the typing pool; three covers were snatched off three typewriters, which were promptly pounded.

I was staring at those beautifully pannelled doors opposite me, and by no apparent human means that I could fathom they opened with phantom-like silence. A few seconds later a small, silver-haired, tiny figure appeared, looking dead ahead through ice cold eyes as his office doors opened by magic and he disappeared inside. Mr Hanley had followed with eyes respectfully lowered. The doors closed. I waited and listened to typewriters pounding away to my right. I sat there and realised that I had been much more anxious sitting in the dentist's waiting room. Now I was calm. Dead calm. I had never felt so assured in my life. I had a mission: regain my freedom. The door opened. It was Mr Hanley. 'Mr Jackson, have you met Mr Mayer?'

'No, I'm looking forward to doing so very much indeed.'

'Mr Mayer will see you now.'

'Splendid.' I got up from 'my carver' and adjusted my crutches and launched myself into the office of the great one. I sank into several inches of piled carpet. Blinding sun had been discreetly shaded by golden satin curtains, drawn across a huge curved window. I was amazed how quickly these impressions registered; endless choice of camera set-ups trains the eye, I suppose, without one realising it. To the right an imposing wall display of his stars. Garbo caught the eye and then, of course, Mrs Miniver, Greer Garson. There was time for these instant impressions for I had some distance to cover. His office was a big, big set: almost the control room of *Command Decision*, from which I had thankfully escaped. On my left, photographs of all his race horses that he had run and was running at Santa Annita. He was sitting behind a beautiful kidney desk, genuine, I'd say, and worth a penny or two. He didn't look up, yet. He too knew his business. He was reading his letter. Heaven knows it was short enough, but his timing was perfect. When I could go no further, he looked up, smiled, pointed to a chair to his right, and when I had sat down and arranged my crutches, neatly in parallel, he put down my letter and totally disarmed me with his opening remark. 'Mr Jackson, you have made me feel very stupid.'

'Oh, I hope not, Mr Mayer; that was not my intention.'

'Stupid that we sign up your talent and I have seen your film, and then we do nothing with it. Very stupid.' I had not expected this sort of talk, and I can only say that even after nearly fifty years, almost every word of that interview is indelibly memorised: he could not have been more charming and considerate. Of course one had heard how hard and fearful he could be. I only met him once and I have never forgotten it because he was kind and avuncular. He gained my respect at once because he was so human, and when today his old stars reminisce about those golden days, in the height of Metro's fame, and refer to him with almost the affection given to a parent, I can understand that. He showed me this facet of his character and I could understand how, from nothing, this seemingly insignificant little man had built a great empire of film making, who had been responsible for producing some of the finest films ever made. He pressed a button on his desk as he continued to tell me that he was as interested in me as the day his studio had signed me. I naturally didn't mention that it was Korda whom he had subsequently sacked. Hardly tactful. I listened. As a result of having pressed the button, Hanley appeared. Mr Mayer said: 'Get on the phone to Mr Schary and tell him that I want him to arrange a meeting with Mr Jackson as soon as possible.' Hanley bowed his head and retired. Mr Mayer went on to say that thanks to the spoilt puppy Howard Hughes— quite some vituperation evident at this point—having bought R.K.O. Studios, Doré Schary had returned to Metro. He was to be the new Irving Thalberg who would help take the heavy burden of running this studio. He was becoming an old man and finding this burden almost too much. Doré would help to bring the studio back to the glory of its former years. A knock on the door and Mr Hanley reappeared. 'Mr Schary thanks Mr. Mayer for his message but regrets that for at least another three weeks, he will be unable to see anyone.'

Mr Mayer nodded, Hanley retired and Mr Mayer said: 'Having just arrived here, he has much to do, heavy executive burdens. Please be patient. You have invested already quite a lot of time with us. Invest a little more and I assure you that we are still interested in you. We don't like people to leave—though some we are pleased to see go. Be patient until you have seen Mr Schary. I am sure that you and he will get along and he will get you started happily with us.' He held out his hand. I thanked him for his kindness and courtesy and, almost unconscious of my crutches, floated over his carpet—not free, but hopeful, and, I felt certain, justifiably so.

There must be worse prospects than a three-week highly paid holiday in California, in the spring, in Santa Monica with the glorious Pacific and its wondrous surf continuously rolling ashore, and for several days we rolled on it with fishing trips from Balboa, some twenty miles down the coast.

But, the rude awakening must come soon enough. What lay ahead I could not imagine, but I was sure about one thing. Even if I were worthy of it, I was not in the least interested in fame. Surely ambition should be made of sterner stuff? Perhaps, but it is a word with many facets, and fame is but one, and it demanded a price that I was not prepared to pay. Gertrude Lawrence, I know, found it very satisfying to be instantly recognised whenever she entered a fashionable restaurant. The first taste of stardom and walking down a street instantly to be mobbed by autograph-hunters might be heady stuff until you realise that you are no longer yourself but a piece of public property. Can anything be more awful? What then? What was the ideal? Creative freedom such as we had experienced already and which enabled us to break new ground. Once tasted it is sweet, not easily forgotten and worth fighting for. This was where the battlefield would lie.

There was no denying that the early conditioning of the great Robert Flaherty and Grierson was deeply engrained and not easily eradicated. Also, from the lasting impressions of films that I had seen as a child and which had frightened me, I was aware of the power that cinema wielded. If not dynamite, it was an instrument of powerful persuasion for good or ill. I know, too, that the effect of images that we put on the screen is unquantifiable for there is no sure means of knowing what effect they will have on the viewer. We are dealing with tolerances and they, too, are unquantifiable. Give me a double scotch and I may become lethal behind the wheel. You, on the other hand, might down half a bottle and be perfectly safe. Similarly, after viewing a scene of vicious bestiality, one man might be so deranged as to commit an act of lunacy while 999 other men would remain unaffected. But that convincing statistic does not give learned committees the right to conclude that there is no evidence to support the claim that scenes of violence and degradation affect behaviour.

One disturbed man can create havoc, having been unaware of a destructive, murderous streak in his nature until it was awakened and aroused by an unnatural stimulus that caught him off guard. Once aroused he could not control it. Who knows? As cinema, and now television, allow themselves to become more violent and degrading make no mistake, they will create havoc.

However, on a happier note, after a glorious day, having caught a barracuda and with these happy thoughts in mind, we returned to Shirley Temple's nest.

As can well be imagined, in such a playground three weeks can pass in a flash, and before I knew it the time to take up the cudgels again had arrived. I phoned Mr Schary's office. A charming voice answered and I asked to speak to Mr Schary's secretary. 'You are', replied the charming voice.

'Oh, splendid; my name is Pat Jackson . . . Just over three weeks ago I had a most friendly interview with Mr Mayer, who promised me that he would arrange for me to meet Mr Schary. I was in his office when he phoned Mr Schary and was told that this would not be possible for three weeks. Well, they're up, and past by several days.'

'I understand, Mr Jackson, and I'm sorry to tell you that Mr Schary is so snowed under that he is seeing nobody.'

'I see. Isn't there a chance that I could dig him out for a few moments?'

'I'm afraid not, Mr Jackson.'

'May I talk to him?'

'I'm afraid not.'

'How long is this extraordinary state of affairs to continue?'

'I have no idea, Mr Jackson.'

'It doesn't seem very hopeful, does it?'

'For what, Mr Jackson?'

'My seeing him.'

'Oh that. No, not at the moment.'

'Moment? I've waited over three weeks already. What does it mean now? Are we talking of days, weeks, years, or what?'

'I wish I could tell you.'

'So do I, and you won't put me through?'

'Those are my orders, Mr Jackson. I'm sorry.'

'Nice of you, and it's not your fault, I know that. Oh well, it was nice talking to a pretty voice, anyhow.'

'Why, thank you, Mr Jackson.'

'Not at all. Goodbye.' I was beyond caring. All I knew was that this lunacy must stop. Immediately I wrote exactly the same letter that I had written to Mr Mayer, except for the name change. And just as my letter, word for word, repeated itself, so did the re-action to it.

The following day, almost to the minute, the phone rang. Mr Schary would be pleased to see me that afternoon. This time I turned left from the elevator on the first floor. No more Adams and Merrie Georgian England. This was Wild West territory as I proceeded down the corridor. Past three sets of chest-sized swing latticed doors through which Billy the Kid would bounce and size up the joint. A waggon wheel and pots of ferns. No stetsons or lassos, which surprised me. Perhaps round the next corner. But no, I was into the ante-room of the deputy all high. A charming looking girl, and it was she with the pretty voice, who greeted me: 'Mr Jackson?'

'Ah, we've met before, over the phone.'

'That's right.' She pressed a button on the intercom. 'Mr

Jackson is here, Mr Schary.' Voice off said: 'Show him in.' She did. I looked across the room and was immediately conscious of the thickest pair of horn-rimmed glasses staring at me. I hadn't time to get much impression of the face that was looking at me for it immediately spluttered: 'Well, what's your beef?'

It was cryptic, and that is why I have had no problem in recalling those few words of greeting. No great strain on the memory, after all, and my reply was also hardly a soliloquy: 'I have no beef. Only a simple request. Use me or let me go.'

He took a moment or two to digest and then said: 'Hm . . . Seems reasonable.' He pointed to a chair and it was clear that my opening broadside, if not exactly blowing him out of the water, had mollified him, disarmed him a little—just as L.B.'s had those weeks ago. By now the ball was passing to and fro in a friendly rally. Then he served me a nasty one. 'What makes you think, Jackson, you can come over here and make films about our way of life?'

As I said, I was beyond caring and had no hesitation in saying: 'Mr Schary, you might have asked yourself that before signing an Englishman when you were making no films in his country. But that didn't stop you making *Mrs Miniver* in America about England under the Blitz.' He nodded, said nothing. 'But to answer your question, I shall have no problem. I don't have to tell you that since classical times, drama is an international language, and if the story is honest and the situations valid, it doesn't matter what language you use.' He liked that and thoroughly agreed. It clearly puzzled him, as it had L.B., that here was someone who had no axe to grind, where the money seemed to be no attraction unless he could earn it; to be gone if they wouldn't use him. It intrigued them, and in a curious sort of way made them wonder whether there might be something worth keeping, in this curious creature. We chatted on pleasantly for a few more moments, and then he said: 'Look here, you see all that lot', pointing to piles of scripts.

'Yes, Mr Schary.'

'Studio properties. I have to wade through them and decide on the studio's programme, to keep it ticking over, and profitably. Give me another three weeks and I'll find you a story I know will be up your street. That's a promise. I can't say fairer than that, can I?'

'No, Mr Schary, in the circumstances you can't. Three weeks, then?'

'Three weeks.' He held out his hand and I thanked him for seeing me. The trouble was and is that once you broke the ice, everyone was so agreeable. Ah well, another three weeks in the Garden of Eden. Couldn't be bad.

*

Metro had a craft grade that we do not have in English film studios. He is the 'Dialogue Director'. This sounds very grand and suggests that he not only writes it but supervises its interpretation. Nothing so responsible. His job is to make sure that the artists are word-perfect before they come on the floor. He will sit with the stars in their caravans—dressing rooms which are mobile and wheeled on to the stage. The bigger the star, the more impressive the dressing room. There he will be closeted until the artist is likely to be called for a first rehearsal. But, no matter how word-perfect in rehearsal and how hard 'Dialogue Director' and artist have worked, there is no guarantee that the nightmare of all artists will not occur: the blockage; the log jam, and not even the most powerful spate will release that stumbling word, that phrase, that final thought, or whatever. It is a kind of torture that at any time may attack the bit player with one line and the star. Nobody is immune.

Half-way through *Command Decision*, one of Hollywood's most renowned character actors, Edward Arnold, was suddenly attacked by 'the blockage'. He had a difficult scene with moves and variations of mood. He was the trouble-making senator who had come to question Clark Gable about the high rate of casualties being suffered by his group; whether these missions which had taken such losses were justified. It was a three- to four-minute scene and the first take was going beautifully, and I thought 'Sam Wood's going to be in luck, he's going to have it in the can in one take'. And then, like your horse in the Grand National, in the lead, it comes to the last fence and, for seemingly no reason, trips and falls. Edward Arnold, with a negligent toss of the head, smiled at Sam and laughingly apologised. At exactly the same word, a few seconds before the end of the scene, he dried again. Still no sign of worry. By the tenth take, twenty minutes or so later, the smiles had gone. Tension. The poor man was starting to fry. We had now reached take 15—forty-five to fifty minutes of film wasted—not that that mattered in the overall budget; what did matter was what was happening to the actor. The stress was becoming apparent and I marvelled at the professionalism of a great actor. He was carrying his cross, and what a burden it was becoming, and yet, as the camera started to turn again for the sixteenth take, no one would have suspected that there was inner turmoil raging within him.

And Sam just sat there. It didn't occur to him to unnail the man from his cross. By take 5 he could have realised that there was something in the line that didn't connect with the artist. All he had to do was tell him to use his own words to express the same thought. Edward would have been released at once. But no. I suppose Sam was frightened that the writer might complain that 'he'd altered his text, changed the dialogue—who does he think he is?', and so on. No, the script was the gospel and to change it was tampering with the faith. Excommunication. If not the Inquisition. What a ludicrous system. Dear Edward Arnold. What a wonderful actor. He got it in the end, of course, but at the cost of quite unnecessary suffering and stress. The poor old Dialogue Director had not enjoyed watching the ordeal and I believe he suffered as much. He was a wonderful chap—Bill Anderson, he was a Mormon, but he only had one wife, a delightful ingénue commedienne Jeff Donell. Bill became a great friend and I am indebted to him not only for that but for the fact that he introduced me to the wonders of fly fishing, though his manner of introducing me to that noble art was a travesty—not his fault, though. The second three-week enforced holiday was up. It was a Saturday. Perhaps on Monday, I'd hear from Doré.

Bill suggested that we saw an exhibition of 'Grandma Moses' type of primitive paintings. There would be free drinks and, who knows, Jeff Donell, his pretty wife, might get spotted for a part as there were bound to be 'all sorts of producers'. Anything to further the careers of others, even though ours were still stuck in the rut. Off we went. Along the highway, under the tunnel into what was known as the St Burdoo 'Valley', past Disney's studio and on into the desert, as it was called. Beginnings of wild land and full of spring flowers, and here was this settlement with the art gallery. In we went. Soon got the message, always seemed to miss the drink tray and the canapés, and on the point of bitter disillusionment I looked through the window of the gallery and saw a cricket pavilion. It certainly was rustic enough. Surely, Aubrey Smith would soon be leading out his team. Men started to emerge, certainly not dressed for cricket. Instead of bats, it was fishing rods they were carrying. Logical, because instead of a cricket field was a lake. 'Bill, they've got fishing rods.'

'Sure, they're going trout fishing.'

'Something I've always longed to do.'

'Now's your chance, son. Come on.'

We walked through the tropical gardens towards this lake and 'pavvy'. By now, I was hobbling well, with a walking stick. I said: 'Bill, you must try and teach me how to cast. I gather it's not mastered in a second or two.'

'Cast? Shucks, we don't cast. We dangle.'

'You what?'

'Dangle.'

'I see.' I didn't, but time would reveal all, no doubt. For five dollars we were handed our rods and our flies, or their equivalents. The equivalents were two dollops of liver paste wrapped up in grease-proof paper. Armed with these deadly weapons, we stalked our foe, marching like 'The Brigade' to the water's edge—concreted water's edge, which I saw could be floodlit when the time was ripe. Copying my mentor, I sculpted a perfect spheroid of liver paste and with fiendish ingenuity worked it on to my hook. As you can imagine, the barb could just be felt below. Brilliant. We were ready now to dangle. There I stood like a park statue and waited with no great expectation. I raised my sights and looked into the three-foot depths some ten yards away. Why it should have, to this day I can't imagine, but a pasty-faced, washed-out looking trout came towards me, and on it came as though on a predestined mission, and took my pill. I struck and he was on and I was hooked for life, for that little electric shock that went up and down my spine is with me for ever. It has cost me a fortune, but as a result of Bill's introduction to 'fly fishing' what memories have been stored in the log book: what wondrous miracles of nature I have been lucky enough to have seen from the banks of rivers. Thank you Bill and Grandma Moses.

Monday, third week in May. Perhaps he'll call. He didn't.

Tuesday. Perhaps he'll call. He didn't.

Wednesday. Ditto.

Thursday. Ditto.

Friday. Ditto.

Saturday. ENOUGH. I must repeat this, by now, well-worn act of mine. The letter of resignation was even shorter than the first. I handed it over to the secretary with the friendly voice, laid it on her desk and with an exchanged smile was gone without a word. It was as though I had become a puppeteer, so automatic were the responses to this strange stimulus of mine. Letters of resignation.

24

An assignment, at last!

Early on Monday morning, Doré was on the phone. 'Pat, you won't believe me, but the day I received your letter I found an assignment for you.' He was right, I didn't believe him, though I showed great interest, of course.

'How splendid, Mr Schary. What is it?'

'I want you to come over, meet the producer, and we'll take it from there.'

'Wonderful. Shall I come right away?'

'You do that.'

'Say half an hour, that's about what it takes.'

'That'll do fine. Till then.'

'Till then, Mr Schary, and thanks.' Blimey oh Riley, we were on our way. We'd an assignment at last. Kitty did her chauffeuring act and I was up those steps, bursting through those Billy the Kid saloon doors and into the secretary's ante-room. She was on to the intercom and I was into Mr Schary's Office. He said to her: 'Tell Mr Sisk to call in right away'. He gestured for me to sit down and with a broad smile—they were all genuinely warm-hearted people—held up my letter and said, 'We shan't need that any more' . . . and tore it up.

'I'm thrilled, Mr Schary, I really am. Do tell me about it.'

'I'm going to let you read it cold. Don't want to risk prejudicing you in any way. All I will say is that you'll have two of our finest actors—from your country, too. Edmund Gwenn and Donald Crisp.'

'Donald Crisp. Played National Velvet's father.'

'That's right.'

'And I knew the real one and the real Velvet from Rottingdean. Hilder was his name and he was the local butcher, wonderful old boy, and his daughter was Whin, and she had won a horse in a raffle.'

'I didn't know that.'

'God, she was pretty, too, like your Elizabeth. I passed her the other day on my crutches and took a sideways look: just as well I had them. Knock out, isn't she?' He laughed. We were totally at ease and I liked him enormously. He had heart, there was no doubt, and so had L.B. No doubt. And in came my producer-to-be . . . a bit like, in manner, the March Hare entering court. Undercurrent of fear was all too clear.

'Ah Bob, I'd like you to meet Pat, here, Pat Jackson. He's going to direct your next picture, *Owd Bob*. Now I want you two to get acquainted and show him your last picture with the team he'll be playing with. Do that will you, Bob.'

'Of course, Mr Schary, with the greatest pleasure.'

'O.K. you two, off you go, and the best of luck, Pat, and here's your story.' He handed over a script. I thanked him, we shook hands and we were on our way . . . I to do my first picture without an idea in the world what it was about.

Bob Sisk took me down to his office. His secretary brewed some coffee whilst we endeavoured to get acquainted. It wasn't difficult. He was a kind and friendly man. He had been Eugene O'Neil's right hand man, assistant and amanuensis. He had met the great script writer Dalton Trumbo and, to my delight, told me that he had produced one of his finest scripts, *Our Vines have Tender Grapes*, which featured that adorable freckled little boy star in *National Velvet*, Butch Jenkins. In every way, it was a memorable film, starring Edward G. Robinson, and I was thrilled to think that I would be associated with someone who had produced one of my favourite films. I looked at the cover of the script that Doré had given me and read out the title. '*Owd Bob*: obviously you've read this, Bob?'

'Yes.'

'Any good?'

'You read it: see what you think.'

'Is it a thriller, a love story or what?' He wanted to hedge just as Doré had, but it would have been too obvious if he had persisted. 'No, it's about a dog and the love he has for his master, Edmund Gwenn, who will be wonderful in it.'

'Yes, he's a fine actor. I remember him in Priestley's *The Good Companions*.'

'And Mr Bennett in *Pride and Prejudice*.'

'Who plays the dog, Bob?'

'Lassie.' I went numb and vaguely heard Bob as he continued talking, telling me that poor Edmund Gwenn was home-sick for dear old London Town, but that since his flat in the Adelphi had been bombed in the Blitz he hadn't the heart to go back and must face the fact that his life must be made over here from now on, and all the while I was saying to myself: 'Don't be prejudiced, a collie dog's a collie dog. If it's a good story it couldn't matter less if it's about a pig's ear or a camel, if it's a good story.' But oh dear, it's a Lassie picture, and like it or not there was no escaping the derision and the sentimental treacly twaddle that was inevitably associated with that poor animal. I had already learnt that 'the Lassie' consisted of three different collies, each with a different trick up its snout. One collie looks very like another with the expert art of the hairdresser and make-up. So what? So what? So what? Don't be a snob, Jackson. Give the story a chance.

After lunch, Bob Sisk showed me the last Lassie film that he had produced. It did not fire me with enthusiasm. On the contrary, it cast me into a deeper gloom, and my battle not to be prejudiced against the wretched animal took a serious turn for the worse.

At last, with *Owd Bob* tucked under my arm, I got home and determined to be impartial, detached and to let the story have every chance, and pray heaven I could fall for it, hook, line and sinker. My prayer was not answered. The story stank and I spewed out the hook, line and stinker. It was as bad as that. An awkward situation, to say the least. Here I was, having received their pay for almost two years, 'creating' to get an assignment, and when given one I cock a snook at it. Really, it was a bit much. Who was I to take this top lofty attitude? Who did I think I was, for goodness sake? I didn't know who I thought I was; all I knew was that I wasn't going to make tripe: Lassie tripe or any other tripe. It wasn't pride, it was respect for cinema. At the best of times it's a hard enough medium when you love the subject and will fight for every foot to get things right. But when you despise the subject and know that there is not one foot worth processing, absolute hell, and nothing is worth that sort of torture. There was only one thing to do and that was to be perfectly frank.

Next day, first thing, I went to see Bob Sisk. He was brewing coffee in his Cona machine. 'Well Pat, what do you think?'

'I'm in a hell of a hole, Bob, but I have to be honest and tell you that I hated it. Feeling as I do, it would be wrong of me to undertake it, just to get a film under my belt.'

Clearly, turning down an assignment from the all high was not standard practice. From Bob's demeanour in front of Doré yesterday, it was clear that the norm was to do what you're told: carry out orders or else. But these chaps had staked their future in the company, had pension rights; like it or not, they had to toe the line. It was not so easy for them to play the rebel. It was easy for me. I had no record in the company to preserve. All I wanted was my freedom to work, and work that I could wholeheartedly endorse. It was easy for me to take this top lofty attitude. But, it was also not lost on me that it took them by surprise and earned me a grudging respect that my respect for their values was not very high. Bob had taken time to reply. 'Thanks for being so frank. I don't quite know what the next move should be.'

'I shall have to write another letter of resignation to Doré Schary. He'll be getting used to them by now. He's had two already.'

'Has he . . . I think the best thing is for me to tell him and that I appreciate your having been so frank. I don't want a director who hates the subject. Thank you for letting me know. Leave it to me, will you?'

'Very good of you, Bob. Thanks . . . Appreciate it.'

The next day I saw Doré Schary, and though my behaviour was

unusual, the fact that the ice had once been broken meant we were on cordial terms.

'I gather you don't want to do the Lassie picture.'

'No, I'm terribly sorry, I don't.'

'Why not?'

'To be brutally frank, I found the story nauseatingly sentimental. I hated it and I'm sure you agree that this is not the proper frame of mind for a director to have about the story he is asked to direct.'

'So you think your judgement is better than mine?'

'I can only express my honest opinion. Right or wrong . . . I can only, once again, tender you my resignation.' He didn't reply. He sat there for an eternity and then with an expressionless face said: 'I tell you what you do. You go down to Robert Sisk's office and you tell him to give you a copy of *Death in a Doll's House*. As soon as you've read it, let me know what you think.'

'Thanks, Mr Schary. I'll read it as soon as possible.' He held out his hand. Nobody could have been more friendly or fairer than he was. Bob looked up and smiled as if to say 'I know the form'.

'I believe this is all your doing. Thank you for your help', I said and was genuinely grateful to him.

'I've done nothing. All I said was that I appreciated your frankness. We discussed *Owd Bob*'s new director. Richard Thorpe's going to make it.'

'Richard Thorpe. He's got credits a mile long.'

'That's right. A film's a film, not a crusade. If it's to be made, it's to be made. That's what a director's job is. He's given a script and turns it into a moving picture. Just like any other job. A postman delivers letters and a surgeon rips out your appendix.'

'No matter what you think about it?'

'A luxury not everyone can afford.'

'But Bob, *Our Vines have Tender Grapes*: it must have been great to have been associated with a wonderful film like that.'

'They don't grow on every vine, that's the trouble. If you're lucky they crop up once in a while. Now how did you get on?'

'He couldn't have been nicer or more understanding. He wanted you to give me a copy of *Death in a Doll's House*.'

'Good. Let's hope it goes down better than *Owd Bob*.'

'And you say you had nothing to do with this?'

'I might have mentioned it, I can't remember.' He took the script from a drawer and gave it to me.

It took only a few pages of *Owd Bob* to know that I would not do it. Conversely, it took only a few pages of *Death in a Doll's House* to know that I would make it. My 'snooty' top lofty act had, after all, produced something out of the conjuror's hat. Maybe the story was only in the 'penny-dreadful' melodrama category, but melodrama indicates suspense, and without that vital ingredient cinema would be mighty dull. So, Eureka! Hooray! Oh, the joy of knowing that I had a story I could genuinely undertake was like seeing an oasis when on the point of dropping from thirst, and I am being unfair to the story when I said it was a 'penny-dreadful'. It was a notch above that. The following premise has possibilities: a girl of eight is asleep in her comfortable and seemingly happy home. Her father has just returned from a long business trip and everything seems perfect. She is awakened by angry voices from her parents' bedroom. She opens their door and sees her mother shot dead. The child goes into immediate shock and becomes hospitalised. On circumstantial evidence the father is found guilty and sentenced to death. The audience knows that he is innocent and that his wife was shot by her sister for reasons that can be skipped. However, in order to pose as a concerned and caring relative, the guilty aunt visits her niece in the psychiatric hospital and is alarmed to learn from the woman psychiatrist that from what she has been able to glean, so far, if she is interpreting the confused images from the child correctly, there must have been a third person in the room at the time of the shooting. The more the treatment advances and, hopefully, the progress of the patient, a clearer picture will emerge and, finally, the truth of what happened. The aunt now knows that she is threatened and from now on the child's life is threatened. Well, I have heard worse and been held by worse in many a film. It was up to me to try and lift it a notch or two above its present level. A fair and thrilling challenge, and certainly more stimulating than Lassie's sentimental drivel and dripping dewlaps.

The next day, it was with joy that I was able to visit Doré and enthuse about the story. He smiled, gave me a searching look: 'Pat . . . Do you think you can do it?'

'Mr Schary, I know I can.'

'Good enough: it's yours. I told you we'd find you something and I'm glad you're so keen on the story.'

'I jotted down a few notes, if I may show you.'

He read them. They were short—my first reactions and where I thought we might improve the story. 'Interesting. You make valid points.'

'There's quite a lot more I'd like to suggest; if nobody's any objection I'd like to work them out in more detail.'

'Go ahead, I'd like you to do that.'

'Great . . . and thanks, Mr Schary. I'm thrilled, I really am.'

'Fine . . . You get at it.' Out I trundled, and now I honestly felt that we were in the 'Trade Winds' and on our way.

*

I had discarded every inch of plaster cast and was now walking normally, but it had taken nine months. How dangerous a semi-stationary fall can be. A nine-month gestation period, too, to bring forth an assignment. It was going well. My suggestions and alterations in the story outline had been accepted by the writer, Bill Ludwig and, of course, our producer Robert Sisk. We were now facing a final 'story conference' with Doré Schary. This went well and all the alterations were agreed. I had a most pleasant surprise for both Bob Sisk and Bill Ludwig told Schary that I had been a great help and they were glad to be working with me. This is so unusual, at least in my experience, that I was lost for words. Much as I loved the old Crown Film Unit, I don't remember that sort of generous gesture happening very often. Everyone is so friendly and genuinely kind, and were it not for this undercurrent of fear about MacCarthy and the crisis in the industry—Paramount sacking more than half its staff—everything would be rosy. For many it was not going to be a very happy Christmas.

We were hoping to get on the floor in early February. There was very little rewriting and I would have plenty of time to get out a detailed shooting script and look for the little girl and test her thoroughly. If she didn't come up to scratch, we were sunk. They were toying with the idea of Myrna Loy to play the psychiatrist and Ida Lupino to play the murderess. Marvellous, of course, but I couldn't see either of them accepting. The film wasn't big enough for them, and these two were bright burners in the constellation. I was going to make a strong plug for a wonderful actor whom I met on *Command Decision*. He had only played a small part but I saw at once the talent of the man. John MacIntire—a strong, fine face, a deep resonant voice with timbre. He had repose and presence. He hadn't done a lot, as yet, but he would go far. His wife was a ball of fire as well as a fine actress—Jeanette Nolan. She played Lady Macbeth in the Orson Welles production. They were the nicest people we had met so far. They farmsteaded a ranch way up in Montana. John built their log cabin and here, miles from anywhere, Jeanette gave birth to her two children: Holly, now 12, and Tim, eight or nine. A wonderful family with far-ranging interests so they were not eaten alive by the complexities and intricacies of 'show biz'.

I was getting down to a detailed shooting script: laborious and tedious work, trying to plan every move for every shot of every scene. How many shots would each scene require? Useless to go on the floor without some sort of plan of action. Without it, floundering about starts and things can get out of control very quickly.

*

Danger ahead. 'Red light' flashing. Not for a 'take' but a rewrite of my contract. L. K. Sidney, a high powered executive, called me into his office and wanted me to move with the times and consider a cut in salary. My option was coming up on 7 March—three months. He was suggesting another seven years, yearly options in their favour, and it would take me two years to earn the equivalent I should have been getting the following March under the Korda contract. L. K. Sidney was very charming about all this and asked me to consider things very carefully in view of the current climate.

Studios were not renewing contracts and Paramount was almost at a standstill. I told him I would consider what he had said. I left on cordial relations.

They had me over a barrel. We were due to start shooting around the date that my option was to be considered to be renewed or dropped—a form of blackmail. Meantime, back to the shooting script. I was planning to create a visual flow for the first fifteen minutes. Everything would move left to right across the screen—traffic, actors, everything—until the murder weapon was fired. The audience would not be aware of it but it would create a persuasive rhythm, as though watching a Pacific roller approaching the beach before breaking explosively—the revolver shot of Aunt Dell. Intriguing involvement: days went by and L. K. Sidney called me to his office. He was not best pleased. 'I had hoped to hear from you before now.'

'My apologies, Mr Sidney. I am heavily involved in the shooting script of *Death in a Doll's House*.'

'Maybe . . . Have you considered my proposition?'

'Mr Sidney, am I right in thinking that I would have to work two years to earn what my original contract gives me next March?'

'That's right.'

'Well thank you. No.' He was astonished and asked me what I had in mind, and I replied that the original contract should stand. The fact that they had not used me during its first two years was not my fault. He then told me that as a private messenger from the company, on that basis they would not be renewing their option. I said that that would be a pity as neither of us would have gained anything from a mutually unfortunate deal, and I was sorry that they had not accepted my original offer to resign way back in February. He shrugged his shoulders and we then wished each other a merry Christmas, and that was that. We were back to square one. Back to a game of snakes and ladders: 'go back to the beginning'.

I reported immediately to Robert Sisk and told him that he had better start looking for another director as I would be 'dropped' in March. He went to see Doré, who was out, so he left him a message, explaining the problem that had arisen.

Doré called me that night and we arranged to meet the following morning. We had a long talk. He was very friendly and couldn't have been more fair. He then made a most generous compromise offer, meeting me more than half way. We shook hands on it there and then. We had established a rapport and I think that I had proved to his satisfaction that I knew what I was about. I left the details to be worked out by my agent, who at that time was William Morris. Two days later they informed me that through the grape-vine they had heard that, so far as the company was concerned, Doré had over-reached himself, and would we consider a cut? The Morris office said they wouldn't consider it. Oh dear, oh dear; what a medium this was. How happy we all were making films almost for the love of it. Those days will never return. I thought that we were making a mistake and that we should meet Doré, for he had behaved very fairly with me. But having consulted with the Morris Agency further, they seemed very happy and advised me to leave well alone. They knew what was right for their clients. I supposed that's what agents were for, and this type of film making was so totally alien and, anyway, I was so involved in getting my shooting script plotted to the last detail that these contractual complications were a bore and a tiresome distraction.

The great Cedric Gibbons, head of the Art Department and responsible for all the magnificent sets that have, over the years, given such great production value to Metro wanted to discuss his early sketches for the sets of *Doll's House*. Happily I had almost finished the shooting script and knew the action and moves to be contained in each set. I asked for an addition to one of them. Perfectly correctly, he asked me why. It was a long corridor in a hospital with the usual doors right and left opening to the wards. At the end of the corridor it was established that there was a therapeutic bathroom in which disturbed patients were sedated and left to sleep in a hammock-like arrangement suspended in a bath of constantly flowing warm water. The murderous aunt learns of this treatment and has to have a hidey hole to time her entrance into that bathroom when the supervising staff have left it, and also to hide when she exits. The corridor as designed gave me no way in which this could happen. Cedric Gibbons saw the point and at once sketched in a door, leading to a little balcony for patients to take the air. He smiled and said: 'Just as well you'd thought of that. I should have spotted it. I'm glad you did; well done.'

This was what was fascinating about the place: the craftsmanship and the professionalism. Once the machine got going there was nothing it couldn't do. But to get 'on the floor'? Still some way to go. I had shown Cedric Gibbons the shooting plan for all the scenes which were involved in this set. He was interested and made the comment that it was a pity that such a layout was not prepared for all productions—might save a lot of time and trouble. It astonished me that no shooting scripts were prepared as we were taught from the old days of the G.P.O. and Crown Film Units. They had given us a better training than we had realised.

My shooting script was handed in to the production office for budgeting and the scheduling of the production. Later they expressed a wish that from then on all scripts should be prepared in a like manner. They felt that their scheduling and costing had a far better chance of being more accurate. Interesting that from Grierson's humble unit the major studio in Hollywood found something that could be adopted to their advantage.

Now the hunt was well and truly on to find our eight-year-old girl. Was I going to have the same luck as I had when hunting for the cast of *Western Approaches*, and as Nora Lee had, who found for me the Captain of the *Leander* and its Chief Officer? Two wonderful discoveries who contributed so much to the success of the film. I had my doubts, soon to be confirmed.

Thanks to eager agents and over-fond mums, like ants to honey came a long line of pathetic little hopefuls, painted and prinked, smiling inanely at me and assured by their mums that they would be the next Shirley Temple. A poor little mechanised doll of a child with pig tails stood to attention, prompted by mum to 'tell the gentleman the big part you played in *Miracle on 49th Street*'—this was poor little Natalie Wood, who was to play Maria in *Westside Story*, and already robbed of a natural childhood. What chance had any of them, let alone me, to establish any sort of rapport, under such artificial circumstances? This process went on for a few days, and from the hundreds of poor hopefuls I chose perhaps twenty who might have a spark and who were worth a little effort on our part. So we organised a sort of sports day-cum-glorified picnic from which mums and agents were barred. I wanted to see what would happen if they started to have some fun and insisted on a bonfire so that we could cook our sausages, pop corn and roast marsh-mallows—a delicacy in this part of the world. We had egg-and-spoon races and a vague imitation of a sports day.

Giggles started and the children became children. They forgot that they were 'up for a part'. At least the object of the experiment was working; they were enjoying themselves and they were be-having naturally. I watched with an eager eye, my ear straining to hear their comments and the music of their voices. As a dowser, I was not getting much response from my hazel-forked twig. I was straining and forcing myself to believe that possibly four would be worth a test. But I wasn't convinced that we had found the child who was to carry our film, who would pull at our heart strings and make us keenly concerned for her safety. Unless we had such a child, all our efforts would be wasted.

More casting problems. Anne Baxter, Ida Lupino, Susan Hayword, Teresa Wright all turned down the part of Aunt Dell. None would consider playing a role in which they had to murder a child—sensitive days, back in the early 1950s. Trying to get a film started out here seemed as difficult as pushing a steam roller uphill.

Doré Schary saw the tests of the little girls and fell for a pretty little five-and-a-half-year-old. He was all for casting her there and then, but I told him that it had been blood, sweat and tears to get the few moments of apparent spontaneity out of her. She was not a natural and she had no ear. Her voice was always in the minor and I felt that we would want to kill the child long before her Aunt Dell was given the chance. True enough, she had a pretty little face but, sadly, there was nothing behind it. He thought that I might be right and clinched a deal with Sam Goldwyn to borrow his child star, Gigi Perrau. In some ways I was sorry that we couldn't find our own, but the hunt could go on and on, not only time-consuming but very exhausting, too. At least we had a hardened trouper who knew what is camera left and right and could hit her marks without looking for them—at least I hoped she could. It would make my job much easier, and as it was my first out here I should be thankful. I was.

Doré also agreed that John MacIntire should have the part of the attorney. I was thrilled about this. It was an important part for John, also, at this stage in his film career, and I was to have the pleasure of working with someone whom I admired both as a man and as an actor.

Zachary Scott, who was so good in Jean Renoir's *The Southerner*, had agreed to play Gigi Perrau's father, and a day or two previously Ann Sothern had asked me to meet her. Happily she didn't seem to have been discouraged at the thought of working with this unknown 'limey' director and had agreed to play Gigi's Aunt Dell, which was very brave of her, especially as so many had already refused the part. She was such a fine actress that she would find all sorts of subtleties which could be brought out of the character. Dell was not just a paste-board killer; far from it. She just was not brave enough to face the consequences of admitting that she killed her sister—by accident, as it happens. Therefore, lacking the moral courage to face a trial, she took what she thought was her only escape.

Her sister, the murdered girl, Zachary Scott's wife, was to be played by a stately blonde, also a new talent, Christine Miller. Bags of sex appeal. A slightly watered-down version of Grace Kelly, but with that essential air of distinction; without it Zachary Scott, one feels, would have been even more of a fool to have married her and would thereby lose the sympathy of the audience.

Finally, the vital role of the woman psychiatrist, and this was to be played by a newcomer to Hollywood, an actress from Broadway and recently put under contract to Metro—Nancy Davis, later to become the First Lady, Mrs Reagan. This was to be her first film and so we were both for the 'high dive'.

We now had a starting date, 11 April. It was almost a year since I first limped up those Irving Thalberg steps and met Ben Goetz, who had arranged my contract with Korda. A year is what it had taken to push that steam roller up the hill. But it was there and now it was up to me. God willing, on 11 April, once again, I would say 'Action' and, presumably, 'Cut'.

*

It was 5.00 a.m. on 'the day', 11 April. I was lucky to have had a few hours' sleep as butterflies were definitely in the tummy. It must feel like this when you're next man in, sitting on the players' balcony at Lords, playing in a Test Match against the Aussies. Ten runs were needed to win the ashes and I was the last man in. Oh my God, he's bowled. Up I get, down the main staircase, through the Long Room; all the members staring at me—the last hope for England. Poor old England. Out I stride to face Lindwall one end and Miller the other.

Miraculously, I survived. At the end of the first day we had three minutes of screen time in the can—par for the course, I was told. Our schedule was thirty days over a six-day week. Five weeks and the film would be in the can. At Holyhead in those first five weeks tackling the lifeboat sequences on *Western Approaches* we might have had ten or twelve minutes of screen time. And here I was behind the wheel of a Silver Cloud Rolls Royce, with everything purring sweetly; the finest technicians in the world; the kindest camera-man, Ray June, who so discreetly took me under his wing and put me right when I was going to do the unpardonable trick of Harry Watt's and cross the line. Before we knew it we were a close-knit family. By the fifth day we were nearly two days ahead, and then Nancy Davis had to get measles. That didn't help at all and we then had to switch to scenes for which the sets were not properly completed. Our hard-won lead against a very tight schedule was lost almost immediately. As the days went by we slowly fought back, and by the eighteenth day we were half a day behind, but now every working day was a joy.

Coming out of the commissariat Hal Rosson linked arms with me and whispered a little message of encouragement. 'Hear great things . . . carry on, kid, you're doing O.K.'. He was off, but what a kind thing to do, and it notched up another happy memory. All the frustration of those early months was worth it to experience the friendship and loyalty of that unit of mine.

Then Robert Sisk appeared on the floor like an undertaker ready to lead us to the graveside. 'What's up, Bob?'

'Doré wants to recast.'

'Recast? Who?'

'Christine Miller.'

'Christine! But she's splendid, doing a wonderful job.'

'Doré doesn't think so.'

'And what do you think?' He shrugged his shoulders. Oh dear, a boss's man. Wouldn't express an opinion. Might have to commit himself. 'Will you arrange for me to see Doré after rushes. I am not agreeing to this.'

Happily it was a storm in a tea-cup. Doré had objected to a gesture which he felt was an over-reaction and proved that she was an insensitive and poor artist. I explained that if that was all he had against her he must blame me as I had asked her to make it. He had his get-out clause: 'Oh, that's very generous of you to take the blame, but make sure she doesn't go over the top again'. And that was that. The crisis was over. The pettiness of the incident seems hardly credible. But, I suppose authority was exerted, and a reminder to all that there was such a person as the overall Executive Producer and that his watchful eye was ever-present. But, for no reason at all that girl could have been sacked and her chances of future work seriously threatened. Such a set-back so early on in her career could have been catastrophic. It was an eye-opener, though. Certainly one could never know what was going on behind these smiling faces.

One friendly face, though, I could never have doubted was that of Ted, our head prop man. Half-way through the production he shoved a pencil and note pad under my nose and for no reason that I could fathom asked: 'How do you sign your name, Pat?'

'I've no idea, Ted; why?'

'Oh . . . I'm interested in handwriting.'

'Aha, a calligraphist, eh? Want to know all my bad characteristics. You won't need my signature for that.'

'No, no . . . But someone I know would like your autograph.'

'I'm very flattered, Ted. Who shall I sign it for?'

'Just your usual signature'll do fine.' I scrawled it for him and thought no more about it. A week or two later this mysterious ploy of Ted's became clear, and I have appreciated it ever since.

*

When the shooting of a film comes to an end, joy and sadness are present in equal measure. A unit that has become welded into a happy team breaks up and those various strands will never again be put on the loom in the same way and may never be together again, and so it was with very mixed feelings that I saw the last shot safely in the can. But the end-of-film party soon took over. Ted and his department suddenly produced a magnificent cake in the form of a doll's house and then the drinks started to flow. Someone in the art department produced an all-too-lifelike framed caricature of me, with every member of the unit and cast's autograph. Ray June then made a charming speech and presented me with a gift from the unit, and there was Ted's ploy, my signature embossed and tooled in the leather which bound a spring-clip script cover. Inside was mounted a little plaque with a message from the unit. That present is one of my treasured possessions and has covered many a script since that moving moment when Ray June gave it me. It is my Oscar and I value it more than if I had earned the other thing.

But, I was not allowed the luxury of feeling the golden-haired boy for very long. Already, the tide was beginning to turn and the undertow had just begun to work, though I was not to be aware of it for a little while. Pleasant days were now spent in the cutting room with my editor, an ex-All American Footballer, Cotton. I was to meet him again, many years later, when working at the Disney Studios. He was great, good company, and I revelled in being back in the cutting room.

I sensed old Harry Watt looking over my shoulder as we tried to make those rushes of his on *Night Mail* look something. Here in Metro, the director was given what is known as the director's cut: in other words, how he would like his roast presented before the butchers get at it. I gathered from Cotton that the director rarely got the last word. High-power executive committees sat and made the final decisions. Ludicrous.

Then, great news. I heard that Bill Tilden, the great Bill Tilden, champion of Wimbledon—where had he not been champion at some time of his life?—was giving tennis lessons and you didn't have to be very good, which was a blessing, for him to take you on. But the right contact would help. I served that one to Zach Scott, who kindly phoned Charlie Chaplin, who was lending his court to Bill Tilden. Charlie Chaplin said there would be no difficulty at all and that if I would like to present myself to the great man—Tilden, that is—say next Wednesday at ten o'clock, he would tell Bill to expect me.

Eager beaver, therefore, with a new Dunlop Maxply, I drove into Charlie Chaplin's palatial driveway, parked my car in the car port and walked down through the garden. I could already hear a tennis ball being pounded against the practice board. As I passed the house, I peeked through the open French windows. There was Charlie Chaplin, at his desk at work on what was to become *Limelight*. I could hardly believe that I was within speaking distance of the greatest comic genius of cinema. I was on hallowed ground. My earliest childhood memories of fun and laughter, shared roars of it from full houses at the Palace Eltham, the Savoy Lee Green and other flea pits were all thanks to this little man with white hair, intent on making more laughter for everybody. I could still see him in *Easy Street*, turning up the gas in the street lamp when he had the villain's head caught in it. *The Pawnbroker*; *The Gold Rush*; *The Skating Rink*—the joy that this man had given to countless millions of every race and creed. He had found the universal language, this man; this comic genius who had weaved a belt of merriment around the world. What king, president, or leader could compete with such an achievement?

But, I must not keep another great man waiting. I followed my ear to the sound of that bouncing ball, and there he was, an effortless forehand driving the ball to almost the same spot, just above the white line painted along the practice board. He heard me coming and, as I walked down the winding path, opened the wire netted door of the court, his outstretched hand there to greet his new pupil. 'Hi Pat, call me Bill will you. Have you played this game at all?'

'Not very well, Bill, I'm afraid; just garden tennis at home, nothing very grand.'

'Sure, sure. I'll tell you something, Pat. I've travelled pretty much everywhere, played everywhere, and England is my favourite country, but I've never seen such God awful tennis played anywhere as I have in England. Now just you get over there and let's see what you can do.'

'O.K., Bill.' Like a little prep school boy again, going into the nets for the first time, I took myself to the opposite end and, with racket held correctly, I crouched like a panther ready to pounce. I waited. Bill, six foot six of him, wheeled his basket, loaded to the brim with ammunition, and slowly loped off to the opposite base-line.

He sent me a gentlemanly one to my forehand. I pounced, got it on the wood and sent it skying way over the netting; maybe it ended up on Sunset Boulevard. He took not the slightest notice of this *faux pas*. Another was on its way, and another and another and another. Perhaps ten of them in rapid succession. None returned with much distinction. He stopped the fusillade and with his long index finger indicated that I should meet him at the net. I ran forward and waited for him to take his measured tread. With a quizzical smile, he looked down at me. 'How old are you Pat?'

'Thirty-two, Bill, just.'

'Thirty-two; eh . . . I guess you're just young enough to forget everything you thought you knew and start all over. How do you hold your racket?' I showed him.

'Wrong. Hold it like this. Like a chopper. Perpendicularly. Same for the backhand. Now bounce the ball and let's see you hit it as deep into the far court as you can.' I found the new grip awkward, and when I did get the ball decently over the net it didn't go much beyond the service-line, half way. Bill smiled. 'No depth, is there?'

'Not near enough the base-line?'

'And if that's your forehand, you're passed next shot. You must keep your opponent back on his base-line, away from you. Try again.' The same thing happened. My so-called forehand drive wasn't going much further than the service-line, half way again. 'Until you English learn how to drive the ball without this turn-over top spin, you'll never have another champion now that Fred's no longer with you. This is what you're doing.' He emphasised the effect of turning his wrist over as he hit the ball. As soon as it was over the net it dropped within the service court as mine had. 'See, no depth. Now watch.' He didn't hit the ball any harder, but it looked as though it were going out and then it suddenly dipped and fell a few inches within the base-line. 'Any idea why that happened?', he asked me with a quizzical smile.

'None at all, Bill.'

'I did two things that you didn't do and it's vital that you understand because they're the secret of getting depth into drives, backhand and forehand. I take my racket back and make sure that it is lower than the oncoming ball. I come up, therefore, when I hit it and keep the blade perpendicular as I come through the ball. Watch.' He did the movement in slow motion. The racket went down as it went back and slowly came up through the ball and remained perpendicular to the end of the swing. No suspicion of a wrist turn over. He bounced the ball again and repeated the demonstration. Again, this astonishing dive for the line. 'Coming up from below the ball puts on this delayed top spin and that keeps your opponent in his place, on the base-line. Get that grooved and you'll win most of your matches.' He made me try it, and though it looked so easy, alas I didn't find it so. 'Don't imagine you'll get it right away; you won't after all these years of that European grip. Don't worry. It'll come.'

He let me bang away for a while and then, before I got too discouraged, switched instruction on how to meet the ball, the correct positioning of the body, the footwork—dancing to it, for that is what tennis is, a kind of ballet to a bouncing ball, as he described it. The hour's lesson was over in a flash and happily I have kept careful notes of every lesson I had with him—how greatly our children in our schools, armed with their tennis rackets, are in need of his instructions. There seem to be far too few in our state-run schools to give them even an inkling of what the game demands. I thanked him for the wonderful morning that he had given me. I left the court, my tail up, convinced that when I returned to England I would be Wimbledon material.

*

Cotton and I had our final cut and we were to show it to Schary at his house. Naturally it had all the equipment necessary. I wasn't hopeful because on several occasions he had avoided seeing me when he so easily could have. We ran it, and when it was over he said: 'Yes, not as exciting as *The Boy with Green Hair*. We'll have to see what we can do with it.' Curtains for Jackson; no doubt about it. This was said in front of Bill Ludwig, the writer, and, of course, Sisk, the producer. My number was up but, so far as I was concerned . . . Ah well, I had met a wonderful bunch of people, tip-top technicians, and we all had a memorable happy time together—I was told that the unit was still talking about it. So, we had produced a 'turkey', had we? I doubted it. Certainly we had not produced a classic, only a professional bit of work, a frame or two better than the run-of-the-mill. I was proud of several sequences and still am but, at that moment, I knew what time of day it was. Never mind, there's always tomorrow, and tomorrow I was going to have another lesson with the Maestro Tilden. Why didn't I have the sense and foresight to persuade Metro to film Bill Tilden and record his teaching methods? My time in Hollywood would have been well spent. What a help he would have been to students of the game. Those sessions I had with him are very special memories. He was a fine and generous man.

*

Death in a Doll's House was to be retitled. It would be released as *Shadow on the Wall*. Someone in the story department reminded the executive that a playwright, Ibsen, had written a piece called *Doll's House*.

Zachary Scott telephoned to tell me that he had written to Doré to tell him how much he had enjoyed filming *Doll's House*. He wanted me to direct him in his next picture to be done in New York with a cast only of New York Theatre people. It was to be done in a documentary style. He didn't get very far with it so far as I was concerned because the studio wouldn't release me. But I thanked him warmly for his kindness in having written to Doré and that I was most flattered and encouraged that he should have wanted to work with me again.

Why the studio refused to release me I shall never understand because they gave me the sack two months later. I only heard of these glad tidings when I had come to England for a three-week break, and now had to go all the way back again to collect all our belongings. It would have been thoughtful, perhaps, for them to have told me that they were going to get rid of me. It would have saved so much hassle. But they didn't, so back I came and, being on the pay-roll until the end of August, three months after we came off the floor, I arrived, as usual, at the studio.

Robert Sisk was all smiles and even showed me the letter of congratulation he had received from Schary.

August 6th. Dear Bob.

What a wonderful surprise this is. So many congratulations. At the time of writing The Cleveland Indians are still top of the league, but don't worry it's still early in the season.

I had already sensed when we ran it that he disliked the picture intensely. He had to as he was determined to get rid of me. Then nothing was too bad about it. Everyone was led to believe that the studio had a first-class 'turkey' on its hands. Cotton, my cutter, told me that Bob had almost to be dragged to the 'sneak preview' of the film. To everyone's surprise, it went down very well. Cards, with a printed questionnaire, were handed to the audience as they left. Three hundred and fifty members of that audience bothered to fill them in and post them back to the studio.

Cotton took the trouble to get this dope for me. Eighty-five per cent were very much for the picture. Ten per cent marked their cards as 'outstanding', forty per cent as excellent, and so on from very good to good, and fifteen per cent didn't like it at all. My agents, still William Morris who had supervised the deal with Doré Schary, had learnt that the executives admitted their decision was wrong but would not reverse it. At the end of August I would be free—unemployed—a film industry in decline here and none too bright in England.

No doubt about it, it's a dicey game, this film business. How does one play it? Just when you think you've made your mark, in rugger, at least, they give you a free kick. Out here, it seems, they kick you out. True, I'd wanted to be free of the place, but that was because they weren't using me. Now that they had and then wanted to get rid of me, I found it insulting and degrading.

I had made many good friends, though perhaps no powerful contacts, but the word had got around that I knew what I was about and could get a team to work happily with me. Anne Sothern, bless her heart, had introduced me to her agents, Famous Artists, and they were willing to take me on, but I had just signed with Artur Lyons who handled Lewis Milestone of *All Quiet on the Western Front* fame.

We decided, therefore not to return home, tail between our legs, cap in hand and no work in prospect. I settled down to rewrite a script *Broken Barriers* based on my experiences and researches of three months in the British Zone of Germany. We still had a healthy bank balance and, interspersed with work, took the golden opportunity of soaking up the beauties of California—not difficult to find.

Time drifted by all too agreeably and we were still waiting to see how the cat would jump. It didn't. No living can be made out of dangling carrots, and things were beginning to look bleak. Then, out of the blue, a letter arrived from England.

25

John Sullivan and Pinewood to the rescue

A most welcome letter, from someone unknown to me, a John Sullivan. He wondered whether I would be interested in directing a film based on a novel by Helen Ashton, *Yeoman's Hospital*. The first draft script arrived a day later. It had more substance than a straw to a drowning man. It was good and with work could be very good. I accepted at once and a week or two later was back in my old stamping ground, Pinewood Studios, meeting Jan Read, the script writer, and a sturdy Texan, Earl St John, who was, I gathered, the right-hand man of someone called John Davis who, judging by everyone's reaction when his name was mentioned, was even more fearsome than anything that Hollywood could produce from its executive ranks. Earl St John had a mane of leonine grey hair which he forked back off his brow with both hands, a mannerism he was fond of in his eloquent moments. He had been a cinema manager which automatically made him highly qualified, but with no means of proving it, to wield considerable authority in the Rank Organisation which had really slipped into films by mistake; however, that's another story.

Having sold my studio in Bradbrook House, Kinnerton Street, to Arthur Pann, the artist who had painted the famous portrait of Winston Churchill sitting with his hands resting on the arms of a leather-backed chair, I had no base in London so Jan Read very kindly put me up. He had a flat in Dilke Street, Chelsea, and here we worked and had a most happy collaboration as we added new ingredients in reshaping the script of what was to become *White Corridors*. Amongst other strands we introduced a running gag in which poor Basil Radford, a returning colonial, finds it hard to adapt to post-war socialist Britain, and even harder to find the right procedures to take advantage of the N.H.S. He is always baulked by the hospital porter, a nice enough old boy, who with patience and sympathy tries to explain what must be done. Who better to play the part of the porter than my dear old friend, the gunner in *Western Approaches*. What a wonderful contribution he had made to that film, and he was to make just as good a one in *White Corridors*. Ex-Chief Petty Officer Hills, R.N., Chief Instructor aboard H.M.S. *President*, London Embankment. Soon he was to prove that his performance as the gunner was no fluke. He would be competing with seasoned troupers Godfrey Tearle, Googie Withers, James Donald, as well as Basil Radford. He competed and was never dominated or diminished by any of them. The sheer integrity and sincerity of the man shone through too brightly.

Soon we had a master scene script and we were both happy with it. Who finally approved it I haven't the faintest idea. Poor John Sullivan, to whom I am forever grateful for my being able to return to England with an assignment, suddenly disappeared from the scene. He had been unable to raise the money to complete the purchase of the story rights. A funny little Italian suddenly appeared on the scene, a Joseph Janni. Few of us had ever heard of him. He had made one film *Glass Mountain* with Dulcie Gray and Michael Dennison. They would keep on calling each other 'darling', which became very wearisome on the ear. However, Janni, backed by the Bowden Cable Family finance, now mercifully stepped into the breach and the project proceeded. He appointed John Croydon to be his associate producer and we three got down to the problem of casting.

Having seen that lovely and gracious actress Mary Hinton playing the mother in Somerset Maugham's *Sacred Flame*, I was determined to offer her a part. We were in luck. She consented to take quite a small part of the matron, and though throughout the film she appeared on the screen for no more than a minute or two, every second registered a commanding presence. Henry Edwards, the Flag Lieutenant and the English heart-throb of the silent days, was to play a part. Trevor Howard dithered and we could wait no longer and happily settled for James Donald. Fabia Drake, one of the great Beatrices of her time, was to play a fearsome battle-axe and the menace of the hospital committee, Jack Watling, Moira Lister and Googie Withers were happily hooked, and finally Petula Clark almost completed the cast list. However, there were two important roles still to be filled. The little nine-year-old boy who had now, with our rewrite, a very big part, a major role in the film. He still had to be found and I thought I was in for another awful dose of interviewing would-be Jackie Coogans as opposed to Shirley Temples. The prospect was nauseating. However, Jan Read had the answer. Neighbours had the wonder boy, and wonder boy he turned out to be: Brand Inglis, a nine-year-old. He had not acted before, never thought about it, but the performance he gave was outstanding. The scene he plays with Petula Clark when he comes into the ward and is told that he has to get into bed and is abnormally shy, or so it seems. Petula, who in this scene proves what a fine artist she really is, mothers him and asks him what the trouble is. He tells her that there isn't any, only he's worried about his rabbit. She assures him that his parents will look after it for him. 'They can't because I've got it.'

'How do you mean, you've got it?'

'I've got it, here.' He produces a tiny new-born rabbit from his school blazer. She looks goggle-eyed at it. It's adorable. 'Could you look after it, do you think?'

'Yes, of course I will.' She takes it and stuffs it under her apron. I can still see the ears of that little bunny sticking above the top of her apron as she runs out of the ward and up to the path lab, where Jimmy Donald promises faithfully that he will look after it and report its progress to her boy patient. Petula played this simple scene with a magical quality of concern and innocence. Lovely moments of cinema.

Googie thought that it might be a good idea if we were to see a real live operation together. I agreed and admired her professionalism. I, having seen Sir Harold at it, thought I'd come along for the ride and to prove to Googie that I was on her side. Hey ho, off we went to St Albans, I think it was. We drove in the surgeon's

Rolls. His name was Hemmings, an affable chap who chatted us up most amusingly as we drove to the hospital. 'I like to see my patients before I operate on them. Do join me.' We really were being given a privileged peep into the life of a surgeon on an average Monday morning. He was to perform a caesarian section. I had not a very clear idea of what that might entail. I was soon to find out. He was charming with the mother-to-be. He told her that there was nothing to worry about: all routine and that she would have her baby in her arms in no time. She was most comforted by his visit. But 'no time' was being stretched somewhat. The anaesthetist had not arrived. Tension was now evident. A thin line of sweat appeared on Hemmings' upper lip. The actor has nerves waiting to make his entrance. But he knows when he is going to make it. He could control his tension. Hemmings didn't know when he was going on stage. The anaesthetist wasn't there. He looked at his watch. He started pacing. He forgot about Googie, whom he was anxious to impress. The cool, calm and debonair were all very much in retreat. And how understandably. A woman's life and a new life were soon to be in his hands. He wanted to get on with the job and here he was held up by this idiot of an anaesthetist. It was intolerable. Maddening. Where is the little . . . Then he arrived, like a bookmaker's runner, holding a ridiculous little Gladstone bag.

'Get changed and washed up. Smart about it or you'll never work for me again.' Off they went. The patient was wheeled into the 'prep' room. The Sister, who was ready to give her the knock-out injection, chatted with her, waiting for Hemmings who soon reappeared and gave her a nod. She smiled at the patient and said: 'Start counting and I bet you won't get much beyond five or six'. She jabbed the needle home and, true enough, the patient didn't get beyond five. She was wheeled into the theatre; Googie and I followed, suitably gowned. When the anaesthetist was satisfied that all was ready, Hemmings picked up the scalpel and, with a deft, firm movement, sliced open a stomach. Hardened to operations, was I? My foot! I felt very queasy indeed. I hung on for a bit, pretending to be soaking up the atmosphere for future realistic effects, and then beat a hasty retreat before I passed out. I went out and put my head quickly between my knees and came back to see Hemmings holding up this baby form, covered in blood and gesturing over it the sign of the cross. Googie hadn't turned a hair. Good for her. In her memoirs I am told that she said I, of course, passed out. Not having read them I don't know whether this is so. If it is, no matter, except to remind her that there is a difference between going out and passing out.

There was one more part to be filled: the senior ward sister whose patients included our Brand Inglis and a severely burnt patient whose head is totally swathed in bandages. Only his voice links him with the outside world. I asked Bernard Lee to play the part. He had a fine voice with timbre and resonance. Even though he is never seen, Bernard agreed to do it.

Petula looks after him and chats, taken by his voice and good humour. The time comes when his dressings must be changed and Petula, the 18-year-old trainee nurse, is assigned to help the Ward Sister. As she starts to unravel the bandages, fearful of what awful sight is to be revealed, she panics and rushes from the ward into the nearest wash room. Here James Donald finds her and persuades her to go back, not for her sake but the patient's, to help restore his morale. She does, with the help of the Ward Sister, whose sympathy supports the trainee nurse through her ordeal.

We still had to find someone to play this very important part. I took a chance and cast an amateur, a woman who had never acted before and had never thought of acting. But neither had Bob Banner, who was the undoubted star of *Western Approaches*. I found him in a pub and I found my Ward Sister in a pub, The Hinds Head, at Bray. We got talking and I loved the lilt of her lovely Scot's accent, her humanity and her outgoing nature. She was a loving, lovely person and there she is, for all time, the Ward Sister in *White Corridors*.

The cast was now set. We were ready to go. Joe Janni and his wife Stella gave a pre-production party in their flat in Chelsea. Here, I met Godfrey Tearle for the first time. I had seen his Mark Anthony when I was 14 and had never forgotten his performance. I was thrilled to have such a fine actor to help us. I remember his generous opening remark: 'Ah, Jackson, I'm told I ham a bit on the screen. I shall expect you to tell me when I do.'

I laughed and said: 'I'm quite sure it's untrue, but if ever there were the slightest danger of its ever happening, I promise I'll let you know in plenty of time.' Only twice did I indicate there might be a danger and did this by slowly starting to squeeze my thumb and index finger together. 'I get it. Hamming.' Then, he would give a little less and be perfect.

I don't ever remember seeing Janni during the filming, though he was now officially the producer. He appointed John Croydon as his associate and he did all the admin, booking the studio space and crew, though I insisted on Pennington Richards as my cameraman: Penny, who had saved the day at Holyhead by finding the mini generator. Jan Read made a further great contribution in knowing the right person to be our technical adviser. In his undergraduate days at St Andrews he had met Daphne Scott, at this time just appointed an F.R.C.S., and to take a break from that onerous examination she agreed to act as our adviser, and what a contribution she made. She made sure that every detail of ward and theatre procedure was accurately portrayed: the correct way to put on surgical gloves, laying out of instruments and how to handle them. Therefore every detail was correct—an enormous help to a director.

We were ready to go, and as though pulling into a garage for a full tank, oil check and cleaning of windscreen, we pulled into Pinewood Studios for its facilities. Nobody bothered us. Nobody acted the genius and tried to impress. We were just a good unit and knew what we were about. We shot the film in five weeks (the average at Pinewood at that time was 12). Admittedly, it was not a complicated film to shoot: no chariot races, no crashes and no corpses being hurled about. Scenes, nonetheless, of considerable emotional force and delicate human values. I insisted that there should be no music. This was treason, but I argued that natural sounds would be far more effective in capturing the atmosphere of life in hospital than overlaying the frequent knife-edged scenes with sacchariny strings sawing away. This would have killed the illusion of reality that we all struggled so hard to achieve.

After *Western Approaches* my favourite film is *White Corridors* for, by intermingling the amateur and professional actor without the audience being aware of any difference, I got as near as possible to applying the documentary method and melding it into commercial cinema and, moreover, without making any compromise or concession towards commercialism. It came from everyone's heart and made a mint for Rank and Joe Janni, whom I have to admit I never once saw during the making of the film and who created not a comma on the script. But, of course, without his financial contacts the film would not have been made, and it is the man with the money who makes the money. Poor John Sullivan who had the nous and the discrimination, originally, to see the potential in the book did not have that vital contact and he lost his subject and his chance. It broke him and his health. He died within a year so it's a dicey game and can be very cruel to its most ardent acolytes.

White Corridors cost £110,000—a hundred and ten thousand pounds. Unbelievable! Today that sum would not cover a thirty-second commercial. It was beaten by one vote for the British Film Academy award, pipped by my old friend Charlie Chrichton's *Lavender Hill Mob*. That did not stop our fishing the Usk together on many happy occasions.

Those five weeks of filming at Pinewood, back in the early 1950s, were perhaps the beginning of the end of unfettered film making before the 'éminence grise' started to raise his ugly head: this accountant fellow who was soon to imagine that he was Diaghilev and Nijinsky homogenised into a single being, whose knowledge of cinema was nil, who had had no experience, had never joined two pieces of film, let alone made one, had no knowledge of the craft and was therefore ideally endowed to have the power of life or death over the most promising story proposition and talent. For some reason, and it does not speak highly for J. Arthur Rank's acumen, he was given this power by one of the most successful businessmen in England. It is, clearly, one thing to be a miller and quite another to be a great impressario who knows and recognises talent when he sees it. We had to leave that, it seems, to the Hungarians, the Kordas, the Pascals and the Italians,

Del Dudices, but the home grown article, no. Maybe the soil is wrong. Wrong it certainly was to give this accountant—if he ever were—so much unmerited power, and power without taste, to run an industry which can claim, if nothing more, to be on the fringes of the arts was to prove lethal for the British film industry. It doesn't take too many overpriced, appalling flops for an industry to feel the pinch, and if this process is allowed to continue, it just withers away, and that, sadly, is what was 'allowed' to happen.

When we showed *White Corridors* to 'their eminences' in Theatre Two, Pinewood, there was a deadly silence. All waited for J.A. to comment. I have already mentioned this but will repeat it in its proper context. The film's basic story was based on a research scientist who realised that a tiny percentage of the population could be penicillin-resistant. He was trying to find a suitable vaccine to treat this rare incidence. In inoculating our boy hero, who is penicillin-resistant and dies, the boy, in his fever, jerks convulsively so that the needle just withdrawn from him pricks the scientist. He becomes infected. The drama depends on whether the new antidote will save the life of this newly infected person. A simple enough equation, one might have thought. Now their eminences await England's equivalent of L. B. Mayer, Sam Goldwyn, whom you will. And what does he say!! 'Yes, Mr Jackson ... A very nice little film. I congratulate you. But I don't think the little boy ought to die. That's sad and I don't want sad pictures. I want hope. I think you ought to retake that.'

'Mr Rank, if the little boy doesn't die, you haven't got a film.' We were aboard the *Titanic*, our craft run by filmic illiterates. As though leaving the graveside, they left the theatre. As the publicity man passed, he whispered encouragingly: 'Don't know how we're going to sell it.'

They sneak previewed it at 'The Angel', Islington. To their surprise, the audience devoured it. They laughed when they should have and they were silent when we hoped they would be. What more can one ask? The press show followed soon after, mercifully with rave reviews.

'The "guvnor" would like to offer you a contract.' I thanked

Earl St John and explained my reasons for refusing John Davis' offer, but that I would be delighted to freelance. 'What do you know about this Janni fellow?', Earl asked, and I was baldly frank in my reply: 'I hardly know the man. He never appeared and, so far as I know, made no comment about the script either to Jan or me. But, without his financial contact, we wouldn't have made the film, so naturally I am very grateful to him. That's all I can tell you about him.'

I left as a freelance and Janni was put under contract. The rest is history. Joe's contribution to British cinema was considerable and we eventually became firm friends. I introduced him to the delights of fly fishing and he introduced me to the delights of Sam Brabner's wonderful fishing hotel Gliffaes, on the Usk. So it was quits.

This is now the time for me to 'pull the tabs' at the moment when I like to think I merged drama documentary with the commercial cinema and made a happy marriage. Nobody would deny that this wonderful cinema is a dicey game if you hope to live something approaching a normal life in being her servant. She tempts you in every possible way. She offers you fame and in-calculable riches. Gradually, it dawns on you that you give in return, in a way that you may not have considered. You may have to bend the knee a little, and very soon bend all round, more and more. Work brings work; never mind the content, not your business. Keep up with the pack. Don't shy at a fence. Don't say 'No'. You may never be asked again. Very soon it becomes an indiscriminate 'Yes, yes, of course I'll do it . . . Oh dear . . . Well, if I absolutely have to . . . so long as it's discreetly done, but is it really necessary do you think? . . . With whom? . . . Ah, that does make a difference . . . O.K., then, yes of course.' You daren't say no, and on that basis the greatest talents will not hesitate. They'll bend, all right. They'll say yes.

To our Michael Grades and his ilk they can no longer shelter behind their belief that their programmes merely reflect their times. Nothing that they do could ever possibly adversely affect human behaviour. 'If I believed that, I couldn't sleep at night', Michael Grade is on record as saying in his interview with John

Humphrys on the *Today* programme way back in mid-June. Sooner or later he will wake up to the obvious and become an insomniac.

At the turn of the century, on Brighton pier, all the piers around our coasts, the birth of cinema dawned with a penny in the slot machine to see what the butler saw. Now we put in considerably more to see goodness knows what.

Dicey game it may be, but I'd like a retake.